Peace River Boundary

By

Douglas W. Houck

A Story of War and Peace in Southwestern Florida

A LEGACY Imprint Book
Historical Publishing Network
A division of Lammert Inc.
San Antonio, Texas

About the Story:

Southwest Florida has a unique history characterized by conspiracy, uncertainty, and conflict during the thirty year period extending from the 1830's to the 1860's. Many of the decisions impacting the region were made by government officials and others in far off Tallahassee, Richmond, and Washington. Men and women living in Tampa, Key West, Fort Meade, Fort Myers, Charlotte Harbor, and other settlements scattered on the Florida frontier endured and managed to survive wars, difficulties, and disturbances.

Peace River Boundary is a historical novel derived from the era and a portrayal of people who participated in events occurring during the Seminole Wars, the Filibuster Era, and the American Civil War.

About the Author:

Douglas Houck and his wife Nancy live in the Historic District of Punta Gorda. Dr. Houck teaches English and writing at Edison State College and is a member of the Peace River Center for Writers, the Florida Writer's Association, and the Charlotte County Historical Center Society.

Cover Photo: *Peace River Mangroves* by Paul Holmes

First Edition
Copyright 2011 Historical Publishing Network
All inquiries should be addressed to
Historical Publishing Network, 11535 Galm Rd., Suite 101, San Antonio, Texas 78254.
Phone (210) 688-9006 • www.hpnbooks.com

ISBN: 9781935377375
Library of Congress Card Catalog Number: 2011921894

PEACE RIVER BOUNDARY
By Douglas W. Houck

HISTORICAL PUBLISHING NETWORK
president: Ron Lammert
graphic production: Colin Hart

CHAPTER ONE

Florida

Washington City
March 1839

Two gentlemen, one wearing the cutaway coat and top hat of a federal official and the other clad in a military costume of his own making, emerged from the basement entrance to the War Department Building. They trudged up the worn pathway leading through the poplar thicket to the Executive Mansion. Major General Alexander Macomb grumbled, "Never figured out why Tom Jefferson ever planted these things."

Secretary of War Louis Poinsett said, "Probably wanted something fast growing. Lombardy poplar was a poor choice though. It doesn't last, doesn't hold up."

"Suits me fine," General Macomb grunted as he pushed a drooping bough aside to step over and around branches littering the path. "Sooner they're gone, the better."

The gentlemen took their time climbing the wooden steps leading to the back door of the mansion. Secretary Poinsett rapped on the door with his cane. A uniformed guard opened the door.

President Martin Van Buren had recently departed from the long standing traditions of the republic by hiring guards and stationing them at the front and back doors of the Executive Mansion. He even outfitted them in European style uniforms with brass buttons and gold braid. The president claimed he was setting a proper tone to the office, but his adversaries were clamoring that this was yet another example of the president's aristocratic pretensions.

Rumors circulated that the president had installed a copper bathing tub in his living quarters. Some were even accusing the president of taking up the decadent Roman custom of daily bathing. It was becoming a matter of concern. The guard said, "His Excellency will see you in his upstairs study."

Secretary Poinsett said, "We'll go up."

General Macomb followed Secretary Poinsett down the hall and up the staircase. The general wasn't a frequent guest at the Executive Mansion, but the secretary seemed to know his way around.

The door to the president's study was open. President Martin Van Buren was seated on an imported French sofa behind the old oak library table, the one he brought over from the State Department. A relatively young woman sat beside him. Her form-fitting tea dress did little to obscure or diminish her charms. Lip rouge adorned her lips. They were reading a dispatch. Other dispatches were scattered on the table.

"Sorry," Secretary Poinsett blurted, "Didn't mean to intrude."

"Don't stand there," President Van Buren growled. "Get in here and sit down."

The gentleman scrambled into the room. Sitting on chairs across the table from the president and his companion, they noticed a little man on a stool behind the door. Secretary Poinsett said, "Hello, Caleb."

Caleb nodded. President Van Buren swept the dispatches aside. "Mary Ann brought these over. There's an interesting one from Buffalo."

"Juliet sent it." Mary Ann picked up a dispatch. "MacKenzie's holding public rallies in broad daylight in the middle of the afternoon on Niagara Square."

"Got some gall," President Van Buren grumbled. "Trying to start a war, claims he's got a thousand men."

"Doubt it," Caleb suggested. "My sources tell me he's only got eighty-seven disaffected Irishmen signed up at this point."

"Fifty or a hundred and fifty," President Van Buren replied. "The British are burying us with protests. I can't go

4

into this election with this business hanging over my head." The president glared at Secretary Poinsett. "Do something."

Secretary Poinsett twisted in his chair. "What?"

"Send up Scott." President Van Buren shook his finger. "The Brits will listen to him. He kicked their butts at Chippawa."

"I'll get on it," Secretary Poinsett assured the president.

"Gotta do something," President Van Buren continued. "We've only got a couple of hundred thousand left in our whole treasury and your Florida fiasco's chewing that up. What's going on down there?"

Secretary Poinsett deferred to General Macomb. The general hesitated. "We're making progress. General Taylor's built forty-seven bridges, opened thirty more miles of wagon road, and put up eleven stockades. He's getting a lot done."

"Doing what?" President Van Buren frowned. "That's not killing Injuns. What does he think we're doing?"

"Don't think he knows," Mary Ann snapped, telling General Macomb, "Your people better get their act together."

General Macomb gasped. Secretary Poinsett said, "Perhaps you can be more specific."

Mary Ann answered, "Our Buffalo border fracas and your Florida fiasco are two sides of the same coin. It's the British. They're stirring up the Indians down there because they're upset about their unpaid loans. The Brits do their dirty work with Indians."

Caleb said, "None of my sources have verified such a linkage."

"Come on," Mary Ann pleaded. "Juliet already told us that the British Foreign Office has moved Lord Gordon Renfrew, their special branch agent, from Fort Erie to Nassau. The British are getting ready to make a move."

"Possible," Secretary Poinsett conceded. "What do you want me to do, start another war with Great Britain?"

"No way," President Van Buren sputtered, "we can't afford another war. We can't even afford to keep dumping what precious little money we've got into your Florida fracas. Go down there and stop it! That's what I want you to do."

"Talking to me," Secretary Poinsett stammered.

"Not you, Macomb. Scott screwed it up when I sent him down. Taylor's not doing anything. Macomb's the commanding general. He's got the clout. He's got to go down there and stop it."

"Or at least lower the intensity of the discourse," Caleb suggested. "That would help."

General Macomb asked, "How do I do that?"

"You're the commanding general," President Van Buren yelled. "Figure it out. Those Injuns want something. Find out what they want and give it to them."

"Probably want to stay in Florida," General Macomb suggested.

"Then give them some land that nobody wants," President Van Buren insisted. "Cut a deal. End it!"

Caleb said, "So long as we maintain the integrity of the public perception of our long standing commitment to President Jackson's avowed Indian Removal policy."

"Remove them to somewhere that nobody wants," President Van Buren insisted. "That's policy. We're running out of money and I'm not about to beg congress for a bond issue to keep this place afloat. I've got an election coming up. We have to quiet this thing down and keep it under wraps until after the election."

Caleb muttered, "Noble aspiration."

Secretary Poinsett said, "The Florida territorial government has its own policy. They want to be rid of the Indians."

"When all is said and done," President Van Buren replied, "those people work for me. Go down there and cut a deal."

Secretary Poinsett asked, "Should I recall General Taylor?"

"What for," President Van Buren demanded. "Someone's got to work out the deal after Macomb puts it together. I'm keeping this job for another four years."

"Provided you keep this place afloat," Mary Ann cautioned, "secure the nomination, and win the election."

"I'm not going down as another Adams, a one term president."

"Could happen," Mary Ann replied. "But I don't know that much about politics."

"Really," President Van Buren sputtered. He reached over, grabbed a folded newspaper off the table, and shook it at Secretary Poinsett. "And do something about this while you're at it."

Secretary Poinsett mumbled, "What you got?"

"*Albany Evening Journal*," President Van Buren stormed. "Thurlow Weed's whipped himself into a tizzy and printing a bunch of garbage about your Florida fiasco. He had a field day when Gaines got stuck in Camp Izard. He made us look like fools when Gaines lost fifty men and ate his horses. How is Weed getting this information?"

Secretary Poinsett shrugged his shoulders. "Don't know."

"Thurlow has a way of doing things," Mary Ann suggested. "He's probably planted a man down there. Sorry! I can't help. I don't have any assets in that part of the world."

The president nodded, tossing the paper aside, he said, "Get somebody down there. That's it! That's all. Go! Get out of here. Do what you've gotta do."

As the meeting appeared to be over, Secretary Poinsett got up, saying "Right away, Mr. President. We'll get right on it."

General Macomb followed Secretary Poinsett out the door. The gentlemen sauntered down the hall and stairs without speaking, nodded at the guard, left the mansion, and plodded back over the path to the War Department building.

As they made their way through the poplar thicket, General Macomb asked, "About the woman, what does she know?"

"More than you might think. The president set her up in a fancy club on Maryland Avenue when he was secretary of state. She has her sources."

7

"The fellow behind the door, what do you know about him?"

"Not much," Secretary Poinsett admitted. "He was with Van Buren at the State Department. Van Buren had seven men when he got the job. Now, there's at least twenty."

"All the departments are getting bigger."

"And trees are dying," Secretary Poinsett lamented.

"Not soon enough," General Macomb insisted as he shoved a branch aside. "Guess I gotta go to Florida."

"Guess so. Take Cotesworth and his cavalry with you. You'll need to impress a few people on the way down."

"Probably," General Macomb deferred to his superior. Captain Haines Cotesworth had become an item of controversy. He came to the department upon graduation from the academy, was immediately promoted to captain, and put in command of the Fort McNair Ceremonial Cavalry Unit. The House Military Affairs Committee was threatening an investigation of the rapid promotion and appointment as it was being rumored that Cotesworth was related to Poinsett.

Having efficiently disposed of his most pressing problem, Secretary Poinsett said, "Take Lieutenant Sprague. He's a writer and historian of sorts. He'll make the mission look good."

"Is there anyone else?"

Secretary Poinsett hesitated. "Take Cambreleng's clerk."

"Why do I need a clerk?"

"The kid's a snitch," Secretary Poinsett explained. "Congressman Cambreleng sent him over to spy on the department when he chaired Ways and Means."

"Cambreleng got defeated in the midterm. He's not here anymore."

"But his clerk's still here. Take Henry with you. Drop him off along the way. Don't bring him back."

CHAPTER TWO

Garey's Ferry

Florida Territory
April through May 1839

Major General Macomb and Lieutenant Sprague left Washington City riding in a gilded Abbot-Downing coach pulled by four white horses. Captain Cotesworth and the Ceremonial Cavalry Unit followed the coach. Henry, the clerk, grabbed a perch on the transport wagon.

It was a long trip. The Peace Mission took a week to get to Richmond and spent a week in Richmond after they got there. Then it was on to Charleston and a week in Charleston. A week in Savannah slipped by with a round of parties and festivities. Henry wasn't included. Then it was on to the Florida Territory and Garey's Ferry, a supply depot located at the north end of the long demarcation road that ran across the Florida peninsula.

Garey's Ferry was hard to find and easy to miss. The coach bumped and jolted along to the junction of two slow moving streams. The road ended but there didn't seem to be anything or anyone around. The coach halted and Captain Cotesworth rode up to the coach. General Macomb stuck out his head. "This oughta be the place."

"Don't see anything," Captain Cotesworth replied. "We must have missed a turn or something."

"Go look."

"I'll do that." Captain Cotesworth spun his horse around and rode back up the trail to see what he could find.

Henry Lane decided to look around. He slid off the wagon and sauntered by the coach to look at the streams. Henry couldn't tell which way the dark water was flowing or if it was flowing. If these things were rivers or creeks, they were different than the creeks back home. Creeks in Cayuga County sparkled with sunlight as they splashed and plunged over rocks on their way to Owasco Lake.

These things had to be something else. General Macomb got out of the coach, looked around, and spotted Henry, calling out, "Hey, you the clerk! What's your name?"

Henry said, "Henry."

"That's a prissy sounding name." General Macomb strolled over. "I'm not making myself look like a fool by yelling Henry." General Macomb took another look at the clerk. "You're a Harry. That's what I'm calling you. That's a man's name."

"Harry it is," Henry replied. But then Henry, now Harry, was startled by the unexpected appearance of the biggest, ugliest, and meanest looking snake he had ever seen. The fat serpent slid off the bank and dropped into the water. Harry watched the snake swim away. General Macomb took a quick look before scurrying back to the relative safety of the coach.

Captain Cotesworth came back. "This is it. We're here."

"Gathered as much," General Macomb insisted. "Where is everybody?"

"There's a work detail over yonder." Captain Cotesworth motioned toward a building partially obscured by the dense foliage. "We went by the turn-off."

"Where's the guard," General Macomb sputtered. "There oughta be a stockade!"

"Didn't see any stockade or guards," Cotesworth answered. "There's a parade ground. The command center's probably on the other side."

"What are you talking about," General Macomb demanded. "I can't see anything, there's too much brush. Why don't they cut it?"

"Follow me," Captain Cotesworth insisted. "I'll take you there."

They backed the carriage around, went back up the road a short distance, and turned onto a narrow pathway between large pines. They rode past a tumble-down, moss covered shack, crossed a partially cleared field, and stopped in front of a white washed, squared timber, dog-trot cabin. Captain Cotesworth halted his horse and dismounted. "This is it."

General Macomb crawled out of the carriage, straightened up, and looked around. Dense foliage obscured his view. An elderly sergeant stuck his head out the cabin door, took a look, and pulled his head back. A few minutes later an ashen faced, partially dressed officer limped out. Shielding his eyes against the glare of the sun, the officer mumbled, "You gotta be Macomb. Heard you were coming but didn't know when you'd get here."

The man was General Zachary Taylor. General Taylor was never known for pomp or circumstance under the best of conditions and given to wearing old straw hats and cast-off clothing. Today was not one of the best occasions. He was recovering from a bout of malaria, fed up with Florida, and hoping to be relieved.

General Macomb took in the sickness and squalor without speaking. General Taylor offered excuses, "If I'd have known when you were coming, I'd have cleaned up the place a little and scheduled a change of command ceremony."

"No need for that," General Macomb replied. "You're not going anywhere. You're staying here and handling the details after I end this thing."

Being disappointed, General Taylor sat on the edge of the porch, catching his breath. "How are you going to do that?"

"Do what?"

"End this thing."

"Telling the Injuns its over," General Macomb snapped. "They can't have a war if we aint fighting. That's pretty simple."

Taylor didn't say anything. He sat on the porch and glanced around. "Nobody's tried that. It might work."

"It'll work," General Macomb insisted, "then I'm going home."

General Taylor struggled to his feet, adjusting to the situation as best he could. "I've gotta give you a proper welcome so I'll roust out the band."

General Macomb and the peace mission waited while General Taylor sent his sergeant off to gather up the band and assemble his officers. The dozen members of the brass band brought out their instruments and gathered in a ragged formation off to the side of the cleared space that served as a parade ground. The officers lined up and waited for the ceremony to begin.

Once the sergeant got the group organized, the band tuned up their instruments and played a sprightly rendition of *Hail to the Chief*. Fourteen commissioned officers formed a receiving line and shook General Macomb's hand as General Taylor led General Macomb and Captain Cotesworth down the line.

Harry and Lieutenant Sprague watched from a distance. Once the festivities were finished, General Taylor invited Major General Macomb into his cabin for a drink. Captain Cotesworth and Lieutenant Sprague followed General Macomb and General Taylor up the path to the cabin. Henry, having nothing else to do, followed along and sat on the porch.

An hour or so went by before General Macomb stuck his head out the door. "Harry, get in here!" Henry looked up but didn't say anything. General Macomb blustered, "Damn it Harry, I'm talking to you."

Remembering who he was, Henry said, "Oh!" Being Harry, he stood up to ask, "What do you want?"

"Get in here," General Macomb insisted.

Harry followed General Macomb into the cabin. The cabin didn't offer much in the way of amenities but probably kept off most of the rain. General Taylor was seated on a cot. The sergeant was pouring whiskey into tin cups for Captain Cotesworth and Lieutenant Sprague. General Macomb brushed a fly off his forehead. He said, "Get some Injuns."

"What do you mean," Harry sputtered.

"You're the clerk," General Macomb replied. "You know how to do these things. Get some Injuns. I gotta cut a deal with them."

"Where do I look?"

General Taylor said, "I'd start with the Injun agent."

The sergeant said, "That's Old Bill, the sutler. He's filling in as our subagent these days. He might help if he's not drunk."

"Where do I find him?"

"Sutler's shack," the sergeant answered. "You passed it on the way in."

That being decided, Harry left the cabin and retraced his steps back to the sutler's shack. The plank door was closed and bolted, so Harry waited on the wooden bench outside the door. Harry waited for a good hour for the subagent to stagger back from wherever he had been.

Old Bill straightened up a bit when he spotted Harry. He took a good look at Harry before saying, "And what can I do fer you, my good fellow?"

"Gotta find some Indians," Harry replied. "How do I do that?"

"Damned if I know." Bill fumbled around trying to find the latch string. "No Injuns around here. At least I aint seen any. Guess you gotta wait to see if any show up."

"Do they come here?"

Old Bill opened the door. "Not likely but some might," He cautioned, "Might not be a good thing if they did."

Harry said, "We can't wait."

"Then you gotta go find 'em. If they don't come here, and I sure hope they don't; you gotta go where they are."

"Where's that?"

"I'd try Fort King," Bill suggested. He staggered inside and shut the door. As the meeting appeared to be over, Harry walked back to tell Lieutenant Sprague, "We gotta go find them. They're at Fort King."

Lieutenant Sprague told Captain Cotesworth and Captain Cotesworth told General Macomb. Major General Macomb

13

received the news with a frown. He asked General Taylor, "Where's this place?"

"Down the road a ways," General Taylor replied. "It'll take awhile to get there."

"Let me think on it," General Macomb answered. "Some might show up." When none did, General Macomb decided to go to Fort King. He gathered up his staff, rousted out the ceremonial cavalry unit, and commandeered the brass band. That being done, Harry transferred items and supplies from the transport wagon to a string of pack mules.

"Careful about the uniform," General Macomb grumbled. "I'll need that." That being said, they were on their way. The demarcation road was a wagon path delineated by wheel ruts meandering through wiregrass, over pine-barrens, and around sand-hills. The terrain was intersected with streams swarming with water moccasins, turtles, and alligators. Each day started hot and every day got hotter.

.They didn't see any Indians. Huge black birds circled overhead and big white birds waded in the streams, bogs, and ponds along the way. The sorry procession of officers, cavalry, and forlorn brass band camped out in the evenings where they endured massive swarms of hungry mosquitoes. Wolves howled in the distance and the blood curdling screams of catamounts spooked the horses. Sentinels were set but nobody did much sleeping.

The weather changed for the worse on the fourth day. Low clouds tumbled in from the west. The wind picked up. Thunder was heard in the distance. The entourage continued on its way, plodding down the dusty, dreary, everlasting demarcation road.

Drops splattered the dust. Torrents started falling as they happened upon a pine grove. A sudden gust launched a deluge. Water pummeled the ground. A brutal concussion slammed them as lightning shattered a nearby pine. They caught their breath, but another blast splintered another tree.

"Move it," General Macomb yelled, "Let's get out of here."

They dashed to an open area. Lightning crashed. Thunder crashed, rumbled, and roared. Falling, twisting, blowing water tumbled around them, over them, and on them. Gasping at the intensity, they struggled to hold their horses, waiting in the turmoil for the storm to end.

None had ever seen or experienced such a thing. But then the storm abated as the blazing sun came back to burn through the overcast. Three drenched officers, one subdued clerk, a disconcerted cavalry unit, and disgruntled brass band continued on their way down the everlasting, unending, muddy path through the wilderness. Insects swarmed around them and crawled into their drenched clothing. There was no way to avoid the insects, escape the heat, or endure the humidity.

Later that afternoon, the desperate band of dispirited travelers finally crunched through yet another thicket to stumble upon a partially cleared fire zone surrounding a dilapidated stockade. A ripped, soiled, sodden American flag drooped from the solitary pole standing next to an open, yawning gate.

CHAPTER THREE

Swan Feathers and a Proclamation

Florida Territory
May 1839

Fort King wasn't much of a fort. It was a ramshackle stockade made by driving twelve foot lengths of split cypress into marshy soil. Mud and wattle patched the gaping cracks. An old fieldpiece was perched on a precarious platform stuck on the top of a log blockhouse. The rickety walls enclosed a refuse strewn area maybe a hundred yards long and about fifty yards wide.

Two officers, an Indian agent, and eighty or so enlisted men survived at the fort and managed to live in a couple of slab covered log huts. The dozen or so slaves made do with a thatched lean-to. Twelve sickly horses and a mule were sheltered under a shed leaning against a far wall.

A slovenly sentinel greeted them. "Spects you wanta see Captain Cobb."

The salutation being uttered, the sentinel took them inside to an open shelter where they found two army officers and an Indian agent seated at a hand hewn table. Slaves were ladling out a pork, bean, and rice stew. Captain Cobb pushed his bowl aside and jumped up. "I heard you were coming."

"How'd you hear that?" General Macomb demanded. "I didn't know I was coming."

"News travels in these parts," Captain Cobb replied. "Couple of Injuns told us you were coming. They shadowed you on the trail."

"No way," General Macomb sputtered. "We didn't see any Injuns."

"Saw you," Captain Cobb insisted, "and described your outfit right down to the last musician."

16

Lieutenant Sprague said, "Sounds like you got Injuns."

"Sure do," the Indian agent replied. "They walk in when they get hungry and walk out after they get fed."

"Speaking of hungry," Harry asserted, "any chance of getting some stew?"

"Sure," Captain Cobb answered. "Help yourself."

Harry grabbed a bowl, but General Macomb held back, scrutinizing the officers and men waiting to be served before saying, "The absence of military decorum and lack of propriety prevailing in this place can only be described as appalling."

Captain Cobb asked, "What's the problem?"

"You're taking your meals with enlisted men. You're not properly attired. Where are your uniforms?"

Regulations required a sky-blue woolen jacket with white cross belts worn over starched, white trousers. Polished, black leather boots and the tall shako hat completed the uniform. Epaulettes, badges, and chevrons were worn to indicate rank. Nobody was wearing anything that even resembled a uniform.

The officers and men looked alike. All of them were wearing ripped, soiled shirts over battered trousers of various lengths, hues, and descriptions. Some were wearing mismatched boots but most were wearing moccasins.

Captain Cobb said, "Regulation uniforms don't work down here and we're not much on formality."

"It shows," General Macomb snapped. "I'm hereby putting you on notice that you and your officers need to be properly and formally attired throughout my stay."

"How long you going to be here?"

"No longer then I have to."

"Then Lieutenant Perry and I'll do what we can. I can't do anything about my men. They're wearing what they got."

"That'll do," General Macomb conceded as he took a last look at the ragamuffins lined up to get their stew. Then he acquiesced to forces he couldn't control. He sat down at the table and waited for someone to bring him a bowl of stew. Rank still had privileges, even at Fort King.

The meal wasn't much but it was better than the boiled coffee and cold biscuit that sustained them on the trail. The defenders of Fort King were a sorry lot, but then, the better class of men didn't come to Florida.

General Macomb finished his meal before announcing, "I gotta have a place to stay."

"Aint got much," Captain Cobb replied.

"You've made that clear. I'll take what you got."

Lieutenant Perry said, "I'd go with the blockhouse if I were you. The roof's about as good as we've got. It'll keep you dry if it doesn't rain."

"It'll do," General Macomb conceded.

Supper wasn't much better. A trooper hauled a wild pig in from the bushes. Then the slaves dressed it out and roasted it over an open fire. Otherwise, they made do with rice and biscuits. A couple of black boys brought in a bucket of water from the creek, strained it through a piece of woolen cloth, and mixed in a dab of molasses so they could drink it.

General Macomb grumbled but got through the night. Breakfast consisted of leftover pork and hardtack. That was the best they could offer.

General Macomb gathered his staff for an impromptu meeting. The two captains, two lieutenants, Indian agent, and clerk sat around the hand-hewn table under the mess shelter. General Macomb looked around. "We're in the middle of a mess."

This was acknowledged with nods and grunts. Captain Cobb said, "It's about as good as I got."

"Not what I'm talking about," General Macomb insisted. "We've got to end the war and do it quickly. Anybody got any suggestions?"

Nobody said anything. Captain Cobb took out a corn cob pipe, tamped in a wad of tobacco, and lit it before suggesting, "You're gonna have to give the Injuns something if ya want them to back off."

Agent Casey argued, "I've given them about all we got. I've been handing out trade goods, cloth, and tobacco but it aint getting us nowhere. They grab what we got, complain about it, and leave."

General Macomb said, "We've got to go for them where they live, get their attention, that sort of thing. Probably living in wigwams somewhere out in the swamps."

"Don't know," Agent Casey confessed. "They were a pretty civilized bunch before the war, had houses, farms, cattle, that sort of thing."

"Even had slaves," Captain Cobb added. "That makes them about as civilized as you can get. We've burned their houses, taken their farms, run off their cattle, and stole their slaves, but they're still here."

Agent Casey said, "They'd be starving if we didn't feed them."

"Doesn't make sense," General Macomb grumbled. "You're burning their houses, driving off their cattle, and stealing their slaves so they'll turn themselves in and go west at the same time as you're giving them rations and trade goods so they don't have to turn themselves in and go west. What's going on?"

"Pretty simple," Agent Casey replied. "They've got to come in here to get their rations and trade goods."

"Not what I meant," General Macomb growled.

"Let me explain," Captain Cobb insisted. "We've got two policies. The army's telling us to burn them out and Bureau of Indian Affairs is telling us to feed them. So we're starving them while we're feeding them."

"Feeding is the policy," Agent Casey argued. "It brings them in so we can send them west."

"But they're not going west," General Macomb grumbled. "They walk in and out like they own the place."

"That's policy," Captain Cobb insisted. "We follow policy."

General Macomb pulled himself up to his full six foot height. "But you don't wear proper uniforms. Forget those policies! I'm giving you a new one. If the Injuns won't go west and we can't make them go west, then we'll find a way to leave them where they are."

Lieutenant Sprague said, "Might work."

"So long as we don't give in to their demands," Agent Casey insisted. "There's an important principle at stake."

"The war's at stake," General Macomb insisted. "We're cooling this thing down until after the election. We've gotta work out a temporary solution and buy time. We'll finish it later."

Captain Cobb said, "Then you've got to give them some land and get them to go along with the deal."

Agent Casey said, "You could put them on a reservation for awhile but you've got to let them know that you mean business. These are primitive people and primitive people aren't given to subtlety."

Captain Cotesworth cautioned, "Giving them land might set a bad precedent."

General Macomb said, "I've got my orders. The president wants me to end this war and I'm ending it. Do any of you have any objections?

Nobody objected. Captain Cobb said, "I'd give them the land south of Pea Creek. It's pretty worthless. Nobody wants it."

General Macomb asked, "Where's Pea Creek?"

"South of here," Captain Cobb explained. "It's an alligator infested backwater that empties into Charlotte Harbor. I took a trip up that creek with some Louisiana boys a couple of years ago. We were trying to round up Injuns but didn't find any. Nobody lives there."

"Sounds like a decent idea," General Macomb conceded. "But we gotta have a better name. I can't tell the Injuns they gotta go live on the other side of piss crick. They'd never go for that. We've got to have a better name."

"Whatever you want," Captain Cobb suggested. "You're calling the shots."

"You got that right, mister," General Macomb insisted. "I'm calling the shots. I'm telling the Injuns they've gotta go live on the other side of the Peace River. That sounds better and maybe the Injuns will get the message. They'll stay on their side and we'll stay on our side. That'll work. Get a map and we'll lay out the boundaries."

Captain Cob hustled off to his quarters and came back with a map of the Florida peninsula. They rolled the map out on the table and General Macomb sketched out a reservation on the south side of the Peace River. Then General Macomb said, "Now, get the Injuns in here and I'll tell them our offer. They'll go for it."

"They might," Captain Cobb agreed. "Do you need anything else?"

"An interpreter," General Macomb insisted. "I can't talk Injun."

"We've got Lloyd," Lieutenant Perry suggested. "He's a slave we rescued from the Injuns. He can talk their lingo."

"What did you call him?"

"Lloyd," Lieutenant Perry replied. "He was going by a pagan name when we picked him up so we gave him a Christian name. We call him Lloyd. It means black in Welsh."

"Who's talking Welsh?" General Macomb snapped. "I'm not talking Welsh. I'm calling him Floyd."

They brought Floyd in and he didn't seem to have a problem with his new name. Then they waited for the Indians. A small group came in a few days later to collect their usual assortment of rations and gifts. One claimed he was a chief.

General Macomb needed to confirm the chief's status so asked John Casey, the Indian agent. John said, "Might be."

The chief's status being confirmed, General Macomb proceeded with the peace conference. This auspicious occasion required a proper setting and interpreter. The troops spent a couple of days erecting a formal council pavilion a short distance outside the fort. The Indians settled down to watch.

A huge council fire blazed away to clear the insects from the area. Then a half dozen or so Indians moved into the

21

council house, formed a circle, and waited for the council to begin. When everything was ready, the brass band marched out of the fort playing a special rendition of *Hail to the Chief.* Major General Macomb strutted behind the band wearing his dress uniform.

The ceremonial cavalry followed along behind General Macomb as he led the way into the pavilion. The troops marched in step keeping time to the rumble and blare of the band. The gold epaulets and brass buttons on General Macomb's blue tunic sparkled in the sunlight.

A gold medallion commemorating his victory at Plattsburgh hung from a gold chain around his neck. His sword belt held an elaborate scabbard containing his ornamental sword. Glistening knee length boots and silver spurs set off the white trousers. A magnificent plume of bright yellow swan feathers drooped from his gold encrusted hat. General Macomb was a sight to be seen.

The Indians had never seen anything like it. The honor guard presented arms as General Macomb stepped forward. General Macomb started to speak. Floyd stood off to the side as he waited to interpret the general's speech.

General Macomb proclaimed, "The great father in Washington City has sent me on this mission to express his concern for your safety, well-being, and prosperity. He will allow you to live out your life in your homeland provided you live in harmony with your neighbors and withdraw to those lands south of the Peace River that are being reserved for you."

That being said, the general waited for Floyd to make the translation. Floyd labored away and appeared to make a couple of false starts before getting into the rhythm of the language. He finished his oration with a flourish.

The chief nodded, shook his head, and replied, "Not bad. You got most right."

General Macomb blurted, "You understand English?"

"Some," the chief replied. "What you got to offer?"

General Macomb proceeded, "I am empowered to offer you the land south of the Peace River, from the mouth of the river up its left bank to the fork and along the north branch to the head of Lake Istokpoga; thence down the eastern margin of that lake to the stream which empties from it into the Kissimmee; than down the left ban of the river to Lake Okeechobee; then south through the lake and the Everglades to the Shark River, and along the right bank of that river to the Gulf of Mexico. The Peace River will be a fitting and lasting boundary between our people."

The chief nodded. "You've changed some names but sounds like you want to give us land south of Pea Creek."

General Macomb nodded and smiled as he asked "Any questions?"

The chief said, "About the feathers on your hat. I assume you must have shot some kind of bird but I don't recognize the feathers. What kind was it?"

The conference went downhill after that. Two days went by while the Indians discussed the offer, haggled over gifts, and collected bribes. Then the chief said, "We're going but we'll consider your offer providing you open a store and trading post down there. It takes too long to get here and the trip's a bother!"

That being said, General Macomb determined that peace was at hand. He called his troops together and issued a general order proclaiming an end to the war. Once that was done, General Macomb told Captain Cotesworth, "Take half the cavalry unit, Lieutenant Sprague, Harry, and Floyd down the road to Fort Brooke and effectuate the terms of the agreement."

"How do I do that," Captain Cotesworth sputtered.

"Your problem," General Macomb grumbled. "You're the academy graduate. You figure it out." Then General Macomb took half the cavalry unit and the brass band back to Garey's Ferry.

The Tallahassee *Florida Observer* reacted to the news of the agreement by proclaiming: "This arrangement can only be viewed as an act of insanity promulgated by an idiot."

A public meeting held in Tallahassee passed several resolutions disavowing the agreement, but most Florida residents didn't seem to care. They continued drawing government rations while they lived in little shanty towns clustered around the forts.

Thirty Indians being held at Fort Brooke jumped the fence and ran into the woods. This was followed by reports of marauders attacking a homestead near Cedar Key and rumors of atrocities at Fort Lauderdale. General Taylor asked to be relieved of his command but General Macomb denied the request.

Then General Macomb went back to Washington City and left the task of effectuating the terms of the peace agreement to an underage captain, an overage lieutenant, and a despondent clerk.

CHAPTER FOUR

Fort Brooke Pilgrimage

Tampa Bay
May through early June 1839

Captain Cotesworth lined up his men and led the way out of Fort King. Lieutenant Sprague, Harry, and Floyd, the slave, followed. The road to Fort Brooke was almost impassable but got worse as the dispirited group plodded through the semi-tropical terrain of south central Florida.

They came upon the site of the Dade massacre a couple of days out. Shallow graves had been disturbed and sun-bleached bones were scattered about. Floyd said, "This aint no place to be!"

Lieutenant Sprague scratched a note in his journal and Captain Cotesworth kept them moving. They suffered under the blazing sun and endured the bothersome storms that came their way almost every afternoon. Mosquitoes, sand-flies, and deer-flies attacked and harassed them. Raccoons raided their camp at night. Squirrels, wild turkeys, pelicans, vultures, and deer were seen during the day. Alligators lay in wait.

Men complained about the heat and started taking sick. When it seemed the dreadful journey would never end, they came upon a river and a few palm-thatched huts. Indian children dashed out to watch as they passed. Women and old men were clustered around the huts. Young men were probably in the woods avoiding capture and doing their best to prolong the war.

The Indian encampment gave way to a collection of shacks and cabins inhabited by white refugees who fled to the fort when the war started. The number and quality of cabins improved as they approached the twenty foot high cypress walls of Fort Brooke. A deep dry moat, filled with pointed sticks, was dug in front of the wall and blockhouses located at every corner sprouted cannon.

"This is it," Captain Cotesworth shouted. "We're here. Look alive. We'll be greeted with acclaim."

Lieutenant Sprague said, "Perhaps." Harry didn't say anything. Captain Cotesworth lined up his entourage and marched them to the gate. The two private soldiers standing guard didn't seem to pay much attention. They stood there in the mid-day heat, leaning on their muskets.

One glanced up, rousted the other, and called out to a duty sergeant sheltered in the shade of a sentry box. When the sergeant noticed a commissioned officer leading the procession, he sauntered out of his shelter and touched the rim of his cap. "Top of the day to you, sir," he called out, "surely a hot one aint it? What can I do fer ya?"

Captain Cotesworth returned the salute with a flourish. "We're on a special mission to bring news of the peace accord to Colonel Davers, your commanding officer. The war's over. General Macomb cut a deal with the Injuns."

"Aint heard nothing about it," the sergeant replied. "If you wanta tell the colonel, you gotta go to headquarters. It's on the left past the hospital, got a big cupola, and a porch out front. They white-washed it so ya can't miss it. If ya get to the big cypress, ya went too far."

Captain Cotesworth nodded, spurred his horse forward, and led his procession through the gate, turned to the left alongside a parade ground, and followed a crushed shell roadway leading past a commissary building, hospital, several horse sheds, and through an oak grove. They rode up to the whitewashed building with a cupola and front porch. It had to be the place.

Captain Cotesworth and Lieutenant Sprague dismounted. They stomped up the steps and strolled into the front room, a lobby of sorts, where they found a staff sergeant. The sergeant said, "Yes, gentlemen. What can I do for you?"

"Here to see Colonel Davers," Captain Cotesworth insisted. "We've come to effectuate the terms of the peace accord."

"Don't know anything about that," the sergeant replied. "Colonel might know something. I'll check."

The sergeant scurried off. He came back to say, "The colonel says he don't know what you're talking about, but he'll see you."

Captain Cotesworth nodded and strolled down the hall. He entered the colonel's office to find Colonel Davers at his desk. The colonel looked up. "How may I help you?"

Captain Cotesworth snapped off an academy style salute. "I'm bearing news of the peace accord. I've been sent to effectuate the terms of the agreement."

"I see," Colonel Davers replied. "Perhaps you can tell me what you're talking about."

"I'm part of the peace mission sent down to conclude the Seminole War. That's been accomplished. General Macomb, having achieved his objective, has gone back to Washington City leaving me with task of concluding the mission."

"Heard something about Macomb being here," Colonel Davers replied, "but haven't heard anything about a treaty."

"It was in the form of a proclamation."

"Be that as it may," the colonel concluded. "I'll need verification of your assignment and confirmation of the agreement before I can do much about it. In the meantime, you fellows better check in here while I check it out."

Captain Cotesworth said, "I'll need accommodations for my men and stables for my horses. I've got twenty-four men, a clerk, and a slave."

"That'll be provided," Colonel Davers replied. "I can use a few more troops and another slave, but who's the clerk?"

Captain Cotesworth said, "Don't know much about him."

"He's a printer," Lieutenant Sprague insisted. "Being a clerk's an afterthought."

"Printers do much with afterthoughts." Colonel Davers chuckled to himself before saying, "Maybe I can use him. The war department sent down an old flatbed press, some ink, and a bunch of type a while back, but nobody can figure out how to run it. Perhaps your printer can figure it out."

"Expect so," Lieutenant Sprague replied. "And I'm a special mission."

"That figures, what's your mission?"

"Writing the definitive history of the war," Lieutenant Sprague answered. "I'll need a place to write."

Colonel Davers said, "I'll put you with the clerk in the print shop. There's a bunch of paper over there and your printer can print your history after you write it."

"That'll work."

Captain Cotesworth took lodging in the bachelor officer's quarters and his cavalrymen moved into the barracks. Floyd, the slave, was put to work at the saw mill and the horses were added to the herd at Fort Brooke.

Once lodging was secured, the group settled down in relative comfort. Dispatches were sent up the trail to General Taylor, but otherwise, not much happened. Lieutenant Sprague started writing his definitive history of the war and Harry scurried around the print shop setting up the press and unpacking the type. He printed a few bulletins for Colonel Davers.

As he didn't have much to do, Harry decided to take a look at the town. He left the fort one afternoon and sauntered down the road toward the harbor. There wasn't much to see. Wooden coffins were stacked in an open shed next to a rundown store. A hand lettered sign on the shed proclaimed:

Undertaking and Mail Taking
Services performed by
Diggory Dunigan
Postmaster and Undertaker

There was a log building housing a fish market and slaughter house. A wide-eyed group of children were jostling each other in front of the building. They were all trying to get a better view of a somewhat inebriated fellow getting ready to slaughter a hog. Harry walked by, continuing on his way to the harbor.

Four fishing smacks were tied up along one side of the pier. Spanish fishermen and their wives were unloading the daily catch. The *USS ERIE,* a three-masted sloop-of-war was moored on the other side. Marine guards and sailors stood around the gangway.

Two black men were taking barrels off a high wheeled ox cart and rolling them to the warship. A cracker fellow wielding a bullwhip seemed to be in charge. He steadied his oxen, but otherwise, wasn't doing much.

Harry sauntered over. "How's it going?"

"As expected," the man replied. "What can I do fer ya?"

"Wondering if there's a place to get a drink?"

The man pointed his whip toward a rambling log structure sheltered under an oak tree at the shore end of the pier. "The Groggery," the man insisted. "You walked by it. They got what ya want."

"Didn't see it," Harry explained. "I'm Harry. I'm new here."

"Been here awhile," the man replied. "I'm Carey Hayes, Tampa Town cart man. I've got carts, bulls, and bullwhackers. I haul trash and treasure. Look me up if you've ever got anything to haul."

"I'll do that," Harry promised. "But I gotta get a drink first." Harry walked back to the Groggery.

Sailors from the *Erie* and a few fishermen were clustered around a couple of painted ladies. Harry ducked through a low doorway and stepped into the gloom of the taproom. Off-duty soldiers, sailors, and townspeople were rolling dice, playing cards, and drinking.

A slick fellow clad in a yellow waist coat and boiled shirt was chatting up a painted lady at the first table. The fellow looked up as Harry approached. The lady took a look before deciding Harry didn't warrant her attention.

The slick fellow had a different reaction. He jumped up and pulled out a chair for Harry. "Hello, my good fellow. Sit down and make yourself comfortable. I'll get drinks."

As Harry hadn't seen a payday since leaving Washington, he accepted the offer. The painted lady left. The fellow beckoned to the barkeep and the barkeep hustled over. The fellow asked Harry, "What'll you have?"

"What you got?"

The barkeep said, "Grog or tonic, take your pick."

"What's the difference?"

"Grog is Cuban rum, cut with boiling water, and flavored with cinnamon. It'll get your blood flowing and warm you up."

"I'm warm enough," Harry replied. "What's the other?"

"Tonic, it's the same rum but cut with spring water, flavored with lime, cane sugar, and some quinine, to keep the fevers away."

Harry said, "I'll try the tonic."

"Good choice," the slick fellow concurred. "We'll take two tonics."

"Coming up," the barkeep bellowed as he hustled off.

The slick fellow introduced himself. "I'm Sid. Mother named me Sidney but my friends call me Sid. It's a good name. Tell me, how did you get here? I hear you were part of a mission."

"Peace mission," Harry boasted. "How'd you hear about us?"

"Small town," Sid replied. "I picked up a few rumblings. Heard you fellows had a big meeting with a bunch of Indians at Fort King. What do you know about it?"

The barkeep brought the tonics. Harry picked up the mug and looked at it. "So this is tonic."

"Go ahead," Sid insisted. "Try it. You'll like it."

Harry took a sip. The momentary flash of sugar was followed by the burning sensation of raw rum. The second sip went down easier."

Sid persisted, "About Fort King?"

"I was there," Harry replied. He took another sip.

Sid probed, "A bunch of you."

"Three," Harry replied as he finished the tonic. "Captain Cotesworth, Lieutenant Sprague, and I were there. We came down with Macomb."

Sid motioned for a second round. "Are you by any chance making reference to Major General Macomb, the hero of Plattsburg, and commanding general of the United States Army?"

"Yeah, that's him," Harry agreed as he started on his second drink. "I came down with Macomb. We even had a band."

"So I heard," Sid agreed. "You must have met all the principal chiefs when you were at Fort King."

"Naw," Harry grunted. He took a sip. "Just one and he wasn't much of anything. He grabbed what he could get and went home. He didn't agree to nothing."

"But I heard all the chiefs were there."

"Naw, just one," Harry insisted as he took another drink. "Maybe he wasn't even a chief. He spoke a little English but didn't know a hell of a lot about anything. He showed up to get a handout but got a conference."

"So it wasn't a real conference," Sid suggested.

"Don't think so," Harry mumbled as he examined his empty mug. "Macomb went through the motions, dumped us, and hustled his happy ass back to Washington."

Sid bought the third round and Harry continued talking. Harry told Sidney about being in the War Department, the mid-term election, Indians, and swan feathers. Sidney bought the fourth and final round.

Harry tried to push back from the table but couldn't find his feet. He tried to stand but couldn't catch his balance. Standing was difficult, but Harry managed. Sid said, "We gotta do this again."

"Oh, sure," Harry mumbled as he stumbled. He caught his balance and managed to get to the door. Getting through the doorway was difficult, but he made his way across the porch, up the slope to Fort Brooke, and back to the print shop.

CHAPTER FIVE

McRae and the Mission

Tampa Town
June 1839

It took a couple of weeks to get a dispatch to Garey's Ferry and a few more to get a response. When Colonel Davers received confirmation of the agreement, he summoned Captain Cotesworth, Lieutenant Sprague, and Harry to his office. A somewhat overweight major was waiting for them. Colonel Davers said, "This is Major Garland, our supply officer. We've checked your story and got a job for you."

Captain Cotesworth nodded. "Doing what?"

"General Taylor believes you boys cut a deal with the Injuns at Fort King. He says you told the Injuns you were giving them a store and the Injuns are saying they aint settling anything until they get their store. Is that about right?"

Captain Cotesworth said, "There was talk of a store."

"What for," Major Garland grumbled. "I'm already giving those Injuns just about everything they could possibly want. It gets them in here so that we can pack them up and ship them west."

"Transportation by deception," Harry suggested, "a hell of a deal."

Colonel Davers glowered. "You have some rather pronounced opinions for a clerk."

Captain Cotesworth said, "The Injuns don't have to go west."

Major Garland said, "That's the policy."

"Not any more," Captain Cotesworth argued. "General Macomb changed the policy. He gave them the land south of the Peace River."

Major Garland blurted, "What's that?"

"Pea Creek, I believe,' Lieutenant Sprague explained. "Macomb changed the name."

"Nothing down there," Colonel Davers argued. "It's a swamp!"

"That's why they got the store," Captain Cotesworth explained. "General Macomb had to give them something to sweeten the deal."

"Damn fool notion," Colonel Davers grumbled. "Now, I've got Taylor on my back about setting up a store. Why didn't you tell me about the agreement and store when you came waltzing in here?"

"Never asked," Captain Cotesworth argued. "It's not my fault. I didn't make the deal. I just came with the cavalry."

"Gotta do something," Major Garland insisted. He brightened a little as he said, "The clerk can run the store."

"Not me," Harry protested. "I'm a printer not a storekeeper."

Colonel Davers said, "You fellows brought this on and you're gonna clean it up. So get off your butt and set up your store. Garland can send down a commissary man to help with the storekeeping. He'll sell the stuff and you keep the books. That'll work."

"But I'm civilian," Harry argued. "I'm not in the army."

"Not a problem," Colonel Davers replied. "You're a War Department employee who happens to be in a war zone. I'm putting you in uniform for your own protection."

Harry said, "Not as a private."

"Perhaps sergeant," Major Garland suggested, "I can use a supply sergeant."

Harry turned to Captain Cotesworth for assistance, but Captain Cotesworth went along with the idea. "That'll work."

The matter being resolved, Major Garland told Harry, "Run down to the harbor and make arrangements with McRea for merchandise."

"What merchandise," Harry sputtered. "Who's McRae?"

"We're doing you a big favor," Colonel Davers growled. "Make yourself useful."

"Didn't mean anything," Harry pleaded. "I'm just asking a question."

Major Garland told Harry, "I'm talking about the merchandise you'll need for your store. You gotta sell something, and you gotta see McRae to get it."

"Who's McRae?"

"The Scotsman who owns the brig at the pier," Major Garland replied. He's buying cows from the cow catchers. He'll take the cows to Havana and bring back merchandise. That's how we get our merchandise. You've gotta see McRae."

"I don't know what to order."

"Tell him to double my order," Major Garland suggested. "He'll want half the money up front but you've got to make the arrangements before I can get you the money."

"When do I do this?"

"Now," Colonel Davers insisted. "Get at it."

Major Garland said, "Run along."

"But I'm not in the army yet," Harry protested. "Don't you have to swear me in or something?"

"Don't worry about it," Colonel Davers insisted. "We'll take care of it."

Captain Cotesworth asked, "How do I fit into this?"

"You're expediting the policy," Colonel Davers replied, "so I'm putting you in charge of the mission."

"What mission?"

"Caloosahatche store mission."

Captain Cotesworth asked, "What's Caloosahatche?"

"You boys sure got a lot of questions!" Colonel Davers grumbled. He explained, "The Caloosahatchee is a river on the far side of Pea Creek. It's far enough away to keep the Injuns on their side of your boundary. Got anymore questions?"

Captain Cotesworth said, "No, sir."

Colonel Davers glared at Harry. "Are you still here?"

"Going," Harry answered as he turned, walked out the door, and made his way down to the harbor. The *Erie* was gone and the *Highland Princess,* a two-masted cattle boat, was tied up on its place.

A cow-catcher on a squatty, big-eared horse had fifteen or twenty cows bunched at the far end of the pier. Harry asked the cow-catcher, "Where do I find McRae?"

"On the boat," the cow-catcher answered. "You'd better hustle if you wanta see him. We're getting ready to load cows."

Harry dashed up the gangway. A bearded man was stomping about shouting orders at his mate and crewmen. The man stopped. "And who might ye be?"

"Looking for McRea," Harry answered.

"You got him. What do ya want?"

Harry mumbled, "Order merchandise."

"Speak up if you're talking to me," McRae ordered. "What do you want?"

"I need to order merchandise for my store," Harry shouted.

"What store you talking about?"

"Caloosahatche store," Harry answered.

"What store," Captain McRae demanded. "Who are you anyway?

"I'm with the army."

"Don't look army to me," Captain McRae blustered. "I figure you to be a newspaperman. They're crawling all over this place like flies on a dead skunk."

"Not me," Harry replied. "I'm with the army. I just joined. I don't have a uniform yet, but I'm getting it. Major Garland asked me to tell you to double his order. That's it. That's all."

"I can do that," Captain McRae agreed. "I'll need twenty gold eagles up front and got to have another twenty when I get back or I keep my deposit and your merchandise. That's how it works."

"I'll get the money," Harry promised. "How long is it going to take?"

"For what," Captain McRae replied.

"To get back with the merchandise," Harry insisted.

"How do I know," Captain McRae grumbled, "depends on the wind and weather. You got anything else?"

"I'll need to make arrangements to get us to the Caloosahatchee. I guess that's down the coast a ways."

"A good day's haul," Captain McRae replied. "I can drop ya off at the Caloosahatchee on my way to Key West. Ye'll be sharing my boat with my cows and paying me for the privilege."

"How much," Harry asked.

"A dollar a head oughta cover it."

"Eagles," Harry suggested.

"Gold eagles," Captain McRae insisted. "I'll haul ten of you fer each eagle and twenty for a double. I can't take more than forty. You figure it out."

"I will."

"Got a deal," Captain McRae announced. "Now, I can't stand around gabbing fer the rest of the day. I got to be loading my cows and get underway. Bring me my money."

Harry nodded and left. He walked back to the fort, looked up Major Garland "McRae wants twenty gold eagles."

"How come he didn't take silver?"

"He wants gold."

"Should have taken care of this myself," Major Garland grumbled. "I don't keep that much gold around. I'll have to get it from the bursar."

Major Garland walked off leaving Harry waiting. The major came back to say, "The bursar's coming up with the eagles but you people are going to have to sign a chit and reimburse us after you sell your merchandise. Come back this afternoon and I'll have the money."

Harry left and went over to the base tailor's shop to make arrangements for his uniforms. The tailor took his measurements and promised the uniforms would be ready in a couple of days. Then Harry hustled back to the commissary, checked with Major Garland, and picked up a satchel of coins.

He took the satchel down to the *Highland Princess*, made his way around the cows, and found the captain at the stern. He was getting ready to get underway.

Captain McRae said, "Wondered if you were coming back."

"Here it is." Harry handed the captain the satchel. Captain McRae, took the satchel, opened it, and counted the coins.

That being done, Captain McRea concluded "Guess it's here. I'll get your merchandise, but you fellows are gonna owe me the rest when I get back." Harry nodded his agreement. The captain continued, "I gotta be going so ye'd better get moving. Otherwise, ye'll be coming along as my passenger and that'll cost ya a gold eagle."

"For the trip," Harry suggested.

"The day," Captain McRea grumbled. "I gotta go."

"Guess I'll pass up the opportunity." Harry walked off the deck and down the gangway. Harry watched from the pier as the crew took in the lines and the brig departed.

Harry picked up his uniforms a couple of days later and tried one on. He felt a bit uncomfortable in the uniform, but it fit. He liked the chevrons. Deciding to show off a bit, he sauntered down to the Groggery.

Private soldiers standing around the door stepped back to make way for Harry's stripes. Harry liked being a sergeant. Sidney, his drinking companion, was standing at the bar with a couple of cow catchers.

Sidney stepped aside to make room for Harry. A cow-catcher said, "See you got your soldier suit."

Harry didn't recognize the man at first, but then realized it was the cow-catcher he met on the pier. Harry said, "Didn't catch your name."

"Jake," the cow-catcher answered. "Jake Sutherlin and this fellow's Rube Rigby. He's my foreman. We're shagging cows most of the time. It's a poor way to make a living but a good way to stir up a powerful thirst."

"Sure is," Rube agreed. He drained his tonic in a gulp and brushed his hand across his mouth. Rube looked at Harry's stripes before asking, "How'd you get those things?"

Harry ignored the question. Jake said, "Hear you're taking a boat ride to the Caloosahatche. I'd find something else to do if I was you. There's a passel of hostile Injuns down that way."

Harry said, "Probably so."

Sid asked, "What boat ride?"

Harry said, "We're opening an Indian store on the Caloosahatche. It's part of the peace plan."

"I'll get drinks," Sidney offered. "Tell me about the plan."

The tonic was good. Harry talked about the plan and the store. The second tonic was better and Harry talked about Colonel Davers. Everyone listened. The third tonic was best and Harry lost track after the third.

Captain McRea came back a few weeks later. Harry, eighteen surviving members of the ceremonial cavalry unit, a squad of veterans, Captain Cotesworth, and Major Garland came down to the pier. They boarded the *Highland Princess*. Private Dallam, a former storekeeper from Connecticut, came with them. He brought his Irish setter and Floyd, the slave who spoke Seminole.

Dallam figured he might need an interpreter.

CHAPTER SIX

Dallam's Store Massacre

The Caloosahatchee River
July and August 1839

Captain McRea viewed the matter with some concern as the thirty-five soldiers, dog, and slave boarded his brig. About half the troops appeared to be rank amateurs. The other half were wearing the combat gear of veterans, battered axes and skinning knives in their belts. They seemed to know what they were doing.

Harry appeared in a new uniform sporting sergeant's stripes. Most important, he was lugging a heavy satchel. Captain McRae asked, "Got my eagles?"

"In the bag," Harry replied. "Where do you want them?"

"Follow me," Captain McRae insisted. He led the way, down a companionway, and into the master's cabin at the stern. The place was cleaner than most of the ship. Cow hauling wasn't compatible with cleanliness.

Harry said, "Nice place."

"Keep it up," Captain McRea explained. "Let's see the eagles." Harry dumped the coins on the table and waited while Captain McRea counted the coins before scooping them up, putting them in a box, and locking the box in a locker.

"Takes care of that," Captain McRae muttered. "Now, are you sure you want me to drop you off on the Caloosahatchee?"

"Certainly," Harry insisted, with a measure of trepidation.

"Then let's go. One thing though, you got to fit your boys around my cows."

"What about the dog?"

"Keep him tied. I don't want him spooking the cows."

"Will do," Harry replied.

They went on deck and waited for Major Garland. Major Garland came aboard a few minutes later and Captain McRae shouted the orders to get underway. Crewmen scurried around, tossed off mooring lines, and yanked up the sails as the brig eased from the pier and drifted into the bay. It took the rest of that day, that night, and part of the next day to reach the Caloosahatchee. Then the crewmen spent several hours shuttling the passengers and supplies ashore. The *Highland Princess* departed as the sun settled over the Gulf of Mexico.

The amateurs and veterans settled around a campfire on the shore. It was another uncomfortable evening complete with the usual mosquitoes and other life forms swarming around. Captain Cotesworth posted guards around the camp while Dallam and Major Garland carried on a lengthy conversation regarding the proper site for the store. Harry didn't say anything.

Major Garland selected the site the next morning. It was a short distance back from the river but close enough to be able to haul the merchandise to the store. The veterans went to work. They chopped down trees and started putting up a log building for the store. The dispirited members of the old ceremonial guard spent most of the day lugging heavy crates of trade goods to the store.

Major Garland ordered Captain Cotesworth to have his troops clear an encampment about halfway between the store and the river so that they could keep their eyes on both locations. The men spent the next few days clearing land, stacking logs, building the store, and roofing the building with slabs of cypress. Then Major Garland, Private Dallam, and Harry set up the store. This required making an inventory, pricing items, and stocking the shelves.

Major Garland said, "Remember, you've gotta cover your costs. Trade your merchandise for products of intrinsic value. Get gold or silver if you can. Otherwise, fur, alligator skins, and produce will do."

Dallam said, "Will do."

"And keep your eyes on the Injuns," Major Garland cautioned. "I've dealt with them before. They're a conniving, scheming, walking, talking bunch of thieves. They'll steal you blind if given half a chance."

A welcome visitor sailed up the river that week. Lieutenant Franklin Farley, United States Navy, brought his sloop-of-war *Erie* up the river to check on the progress being made at the store. He anchored the warship in the deep water and his marine detachment rowed him ashore. The naval officer stalked up the river bank, checked out the camp, and looked at the store.

Lieutenant Farley cautioned Major Garland, "You've put your camp in an exposed position. There's a bunch of renegades in the area. They could come down that river or through the woods and be on you before you know it."

Major Garland said, "It's a matter of good faith on our part. The Indians know we're here to help them, so they'll respect us."

"Perhaps," Lieutenant Farley replied. "I'll stop by from time to time to see how you're making out."

Major Garland asked, "Any chance of catching a ride back to Fort Brooke? We've about finished and Cotesworth's taking over."

Lieutenant Farley shrugged his shoulders. "I'm going that way. Guess I can put up with you for a day or two. But don't get the idea that I'm running a ferry service for you people."

Major Garland said. "You're supposed to be assisting us."

"Assisting is one thing! Carting you around is another," Lieutenant Farley grumbled. "Get your stuff together. Let's go."

Major Garland gathered up his belongings and Captain Cotesworth followed along behind the major and naval officer while they walked to the river. As the officers boarded the small boat, Lieutenant Farley told Captain Cotesworth, "Keep your eyes open. Faith only goes so far."

"Will do," Captain Cotesworth assured Lieutenant Farley.

Lieutenant Farley said, "I'll stop on my way back and see how you're doing."

"Appreciate that," Captain Cotesworth replied.

The *Erie* sailed away. The men finished building the store and Dallam scurried around unpacking crates and stocking shelves. Harry didn't really know what he was supposed to be doing. He went outside, stood around, and waited while Floyd came trudging up the path lugging a heavy crate of merchandise.

Harry asked the slave, "What you got there?"

"Stuff" the slave replied. "Making do with what I got to do."

"I've been wondering, what's your real name?"

"Floyd!"

"But you had a different name."

"I did, but that don't count fer nothin' no more. I'm Floyd now. I make do with what I got."

"Doesn't it bother you?"

"Make do with what I got," Floyd repeated.

"What do you mean?"

"I was a slave in Georgia. I ran off to be free. The Seminole took me in and made me a slave. Then you folks came along, took me away, and made me a slave again. I make do with what I got."

Dallam appeared in the doorway of the store. "Hey Floyd, get in here. I'm waiting for you."

Floyd lifted the crate, balanced it on his shoulder, and carried it into the store. Harry followed, moved into the back room, and waited around for customers to start arriving. An older Indian man and two Indian women wandered in that afternoon, looked around, gathered up a few items, and started to walk out.

"Hold it," Dallam shouted. He dashed around the Indians and slammed the door shut locking them in the store. The Indians looked perplexed. Dallam shouted, "Get Floyd. He's got to talk to these people."

Harry dashed out of the back room, took a look at the situation, made his way around the Indians and Dallam guarding the door, dashed outside, and came upon Floyd. Floyd was trying to talk with some warriors who had become alarmed by the shouting and commotion coming from inside the building. Harry shouted, "Dallam wants you inside."

Floyd gave up trying to talk Seminole and turned to Harry to explain, "You're getting them upset! What's going on in there?"

"I don't know. Take a look."

Harry tried to push the door open, but Dallam wasn't budging. Dallam shouted, "They're trying to get out without paying."

Harry yelled, "Let us in."

Dallam released the door, and Harry pushed his way in. The Indians tried to push by Harry. Floyd was trying to talk to the Indians. Dallam screamed, "Catch them. They're getting away."

The Indians got by Floyd and rushed off carrying their merchandise. They other Indians were getting upset. Dallam yelled, "Damn it! They got out without paying."

Floyd asked, "What's going on?"

Dallam shouted, "Tell them to get back in here and pay for the merchandise. They can't steal it."

Floyd tried to explain this to the Indians. There was confusion, sign language, and distress. Floyd said, "They don't understand. They never had to pay for anything before."

That's when Harry remembered the free rations at the fort and the free gifts given to the Indians at the council. The Indians assumed everything was free. Dallam shouted, "Tell them to get back in here and pay for those things or I'll sic my dog on them."

Floyd conferred with the Indians. Floyd said, "They don't like the idea."

The Indians spit on the ground and walked away. Dallam turned in a huff and stomped back into the store. Harry stood outside with Floyd. Harry asked Floyd, "What happens now?"

"Don't rightly know," Floyd replied. Dallam stuck his head out the door, shouting, "Floyd, get in here."

Harry followed Floyd into the store, walked by Dallam and Floyd, and went back to his room at the rear of the store. Major Garland insisted that accurate records be kept of all the sales and missing merchandise. He needed to record their first theft. Otherwise, not much happened.

Dallam closed the store at dusk and barricaded the door. Captain Cotesworth took a careful look at the situation and decided there was little need to post a guard. Nothing had happened during the two weeks that they had been at the site.

Besides, they were at peace with the Indians and the Seminoles appeared to be honoring the Peace River boundary. They were on a goodwill mission and Dallam had a large Irish setter. The dog would sound the alarm if any intruder threatened the store. That being the case, Captain Cotesworth went back to the camp and got ready for another evening of sweat and mosquitoes.

The Indians waited for darkness. These Indians were not part of the Seminole community. They were a surviving remnant of an ancient people who had dominated southwestern Florida for hundreds of years. As they traded with Spanish merchants from Cuba, some called them Spanish Indians. These people had their own way of doing things and were not pleased with this encroachment on their domain.

The Indians descended on the store and unguarded camp in the early hours of the morning. One group battered down the front door of the store, shot the dog, and killed Dallam. Then they scalped Dallam and helped themselves to his merchandise. The other group attacked the camp. They killed eleven men in the initial onslaught and wounded several others.

Harry heard the dog bark and banging on the front door. He plunged out the back window as the door gave way. He dashed through the brush and weeds and managed to avoid the warriors. Hearing shouts, screams, and shots coming from the camp, Harry headed in the opposite direction stumbling over roots and other obstacles as he made his way to the river. He pushed on by another man who stumbled in the darkness, got around him, pushed through the brush, and jumped in the river.

The man followed Harry as he splashed through the water toward a small boat moored against the bank. The man got by Harry, crawled into the boat, and released the boat. Then the man reached out, caught Harry's hand, and pulled him into the boat.

The current caught the boat and carried it slowly away from the bank out into the river. Shouts, screams, and gunshots were coming from the camp. The store burst into flames as the sun came up. Dark smoke billowed out of the forest as they drifted away.

Harry recognized his companion in the dim light of the early morning. It was Captain Cotesworth. The Indians made off with all the trade goods, took the rifles and other weapons from the defenders, cooked the dog, and spent most of the rest of the day torturing their captives until they tired of the activity and burned them at the stake.

Harry and Captain Cotesworth continued drifting down the river toward the Gulf of Mexico. They came upon the sloop-of-war later that afternoon as they approached the Gulf. Lieutenant Farley had spotted a smudge of smoke on the horizon and was coming up the river to check out the store. Lieutenant Farley fished them out of the water and took them aboard the *Erie*.

Lieutenant Farley greeted them by saying, "So much for good faith! We'll wait for the tide and make a run up the river. There might be survivors."

It took until morning to get the *Erie* up the river and anchored off the site of the camp. Lieutenant Farley sent out a shore party to reconnoiter the area. The marines found three shell-shocked survivors, buried the dead, and departed. Then they lifted anchor, drifted down the river, and sailed up the coast to Tampa Bay.

Stories of the massacre spread through the little community. Refugees rushed into town and business picked up at the Groggery. Colonel Davers sent a company of veterans down to check out the area and rescue possible survivors. A few other men were found over the course of the next two weeks but twenty-eight men were lost in the massacre. War came back with a vengeance.

Word of the massacre spread across the state and then reports of other Indian attacks started coming in from elsewhere across the state. A brisk action was reported near Orange Lake and another was reported at Fort Andrews where seventeen men held off forty Indians.

Harry went back to running his printing press, put out an official report on the action, and wandered down to the Groggery during his time off to forget the unpleasant experience. Sidney Benson greeted him upon his return and lavished him with concern, food, and drink while Harry recounted the dreadful horrors of the massacre.

A few weeks later a series of articles appeared in the *Albany Evening Journal* telling about the administration's most recent series of blunders in prosecuting the Indian War. The lurid tales of failure and incompetence made their way to President Van Buren's desk but none of these papers were delivered to Fort Brooke. Urgent dispatches were sent to General Taylor.

General Taylor had to do something about the problem so he fired off a dispatch to Colonel Davers. Colonel Davers read the dispatch and offered his resignation. General Taylor refused the resignation. Then General Taylor sent a messenger down to Fort Brooke to tell Colonel Davers that he had to stay at Fort Brooke until he got the job done.

Colonel Davers didn't know what to do. Then he remembered the dogs.

CHAPTER SEVEN

Diego and the Bloodhounds

Tallahassee
January 1840

It was General Jessup's idea. He was getting tired of chasing Indians who simply vanished into the wilderness. Perhaps bloodhounds could be used track them down. Dogs had been used with considerable success on Jamaica. He asked his aide, who happened to be Colonel Davers, to draw up a request for dogs and send the request to Washington. General Jessup was waiting for the answer to the request when he was wounded at the battle at Lockahatche and relieved of command.

General Taylor took command of the Florida operation, but nobody told General Taylor about Jessup's request. Even so, military requests frequently take on a life of their own and this request continued up the chain of command until it appeared on Secretary Poinsett's desk. Secretary Poinsett glanced at the request late one afternoon, didn't think much about it, and signed it. The authorization had been in effect for a couple of years but nobody had acted on it.

Colonel Davers remembered the request. He talked with Colonel Fitzpatrick, his Florida Militia counterpart, about the dog idea. Colonel Fitzpatrick took the idea to Governor Call, the new territorial governor. Governor Call went along with the idea and sent Colonel Bemrose, a local businessman, to Cuba to buy some bloodhounds. Colonel Bemrose went to Cuba where he bought thirty-three. He paid $151.72 for each dog.

Colonel Bemrose brought the dogs and four Cuban dog handlers back to Florida but the voyage home was rather unpleasant. The boat encountered severe storms on the way and landed at Port Leon with thirty seasick hounds. Colonel Bemrose finally managed to get his dogs and handlers to Tallahassee where he parked the dogs out behind his auction house.

When Colonel Davers got word that the dogs were available, he called Captain Cotesworth, now a battle hardened veteran, and Sergeant Lane, a once upon a time clerk, back to his office. The sergeant greeted the gentlemen upon their arrival and ushered them into the colonel's office. They approached the colonel's desk and waited to be addressed. Colonel Davers smiled. "So what have you boys been up to?"

Captain Cotesworth snapped an academy style reply, "Preparing for our next assignment, sir!"

"Well, I've got just the job for you," Colonel Davers explained. "We're going to round up the Injuns and put them on your reservation."

"How are you going to do that?"

"Dogs," Colonel Davers replied.

"Dogs," Harry blurted.

"Bloodhounds, to be specific," Colonel Davers replied. "We're putting a combined operation together with the militia. We'll use the hounds to track down the Injuns and put them on your reservation on the far side of Pea Creek."

"Peace River," Captain Cotesworth insisted. "General Macomb changed the name."

"So I heard," Colonel Davers conceded. "It's still the same place. I want you boys to run up to Tallahassee. Check with a Colonel Bemrose when you get there, familiarize yourself with his operation, and get ready to implement the mission."

Captain Cotesworth asked, "How do we do that?"

"I told you. We're using bloodhounds!" Colonel Davers insisted. "Go to Tallahassee and see if you can work a joint operation with the militia. If not, buy a few dogs and bring them back."

"Don't know anything about bloodhounds," Harry muttered.

"You're gonna learn," Colonel Davers grumbled. "Get the show on the road."

Harry asked, "How much do we pay for the dogs?"

"No more then you have to. Try to cut a deal for a joint operation if you can. If that doesn't work, then bring back a half-dozen or so but get a good price. What am I telling you this for? You're the clerk. Do what you got to do. Now, do it!"

Captain Cotesworth and Harry managed to catch a ride with Lieutenant Farley on the *Erie* a couple of days later. It took a good week to get to Port Leon on St. Marks Bay, the harbor for Tallahassee. There wasn't much happening at St. Marks. A few local boys sat on the front porch of the town's only tavern. They didn't seem to be much given to radical thoughts or impulsive activity. They didn't nod or pay attention as the army captain and his sergeant trudged up the dusty road to catch the tramway to Tallahassee.

The tramway was a mule powered carriage that ran on a twenty-two mile iron track from St. Marks to Tallahassee. Captain Cotesworth and Harry boarded the conveyance for the four hour ride. Tallahassee wasn't much to look at when they got there. A few houses and shops were crowded around a town square, a squat capitol building, and the City Hotel. They tried the capitol but it was empty. The legislature wasn't meeting and the governor wasn't in.

An elderly fellow perched on a bench outside the capitol told them, "If you wanta find the dogs, you gotta go see Bemrose. He's probably at his establishment. The dogs are out back."

The establishment was an old plantation style house that had seen better days. A big sign hanging over the front door proclaimed:

Bemrose and Foster
Bondsmen and Domestic Servants

They walked in the front door of the auction house and found a hefty fellow seated on a broken captain's chair behind a makeshift plank table. The man appeared to be a colonel of some kind as he wore gold eagles pinned to the drooping collars of his partially unbuttoned, faded blue tunic.

The hefty colonel rocked back in his chair to take a good look at his visitors as he grumbled, "Sumabitch, boys! What you got in mind?"

Captain Cotesworth said, "We're looking for Colonel Bemrose."

"That's me," the colonel blustered. "What can I do fer you?"

"We came to see about the dogs."

Colonel Bemrose said, "You came to the right place. Ever do any hunting? Do ya know anything about running hounds?"

"Nothing and nope," Harry replied. "I never got into fooling around with dogs if that's what you mean."

Colonel Bemrose glared at Harry. "Sumabitch boy, you gotta mouth on you. You gotta be one of those Yankees I been hearing about."

"Yorker," Harry insisted. "That's different."

"Not a helluva lot," Colonel Bemrose insisted. "And I'll just bet you're an abolitionist! Hear they got a lot up that way."

"Nope," Harry asserted. "Not me. I'm no abolitionist. I've got enough trouble taking care of my own business."

Colonel Bemrose growled, "Just so's you people keep your nose out of my business, that's about all that counts. I could tell right off you weren't local. I could see that as soon as you walked in that door and opened your mouth."

Captain Cotesworth asked, "What about you? You're not from around here. Where'd you come from?"

"Carolina," Bemrose boasted, "hills of Carolina. I brought down a bunch of negra field hands couple of years back and set up my own auction house. Been doin' some government work since I got here, but I do miss the hills. They got mighty fine country back home."

"Tell me about it," Captain Cotesworth asserted, "I'm from the low country."

"Sumabitch," Bemrose exclaimed. "You must have done some hunting and run a few dogs."

"No, not really," Captain Cotesworth admitted.

"Gotta be a city boy," Bemrose suggested, "you from Charleston?"

"Thereabouts, but what has that got to do with dogs?"

"You've got to know how to manage a hunting dog if you're going to do anything with these bloodhounds," Colonel Bemrose insisted. "They're highly trained animals. We got them honed to perfection and I'd be a real shame to waste that training on you boys if you don't know what you're doing."

Captain Cotesworth asked, "How are you doing this training?"

"Negras, "Colonel Bemrose explained. "We aint got no Injuns so we're usin' the next best thing. We give the negra a good head start and turn the dogs loose. The dogs run the old negra up a tree and that's when we toss out the possum. You gotta be there and see it."

Harry asked, "Who gets the possum?"

"What are ya talking about, boy? The dogs get the possum. The negra gets treed!" The colonel laughed. "Guess I gotta take you out behind the barn and show you my dogs."

The hefty colonel took his time crawling out from behind his makeshift desk. He selected a cold cigar from a tray, stuck it in his mouth, and chewed on it as he led them behind the auction house. The dogs were sprawled in the shade under the oak trees and appeared to be resting. A couple of dogs roused themselves from their slumber to stand. Most ignored their presence.

They were massive. The dogs stood over three feet tall at the shoulder, had long droopy ears, big brown eyes, and hanging jowls. A half dozen or so were spotted but the rest were a solid color. The dogs looked the part but didn't seem to be very alert.

Captain Cotesworth examined the pack. "So what do they do?"

51

Colonel Bemrose chewed on his cigar. "I told ya, we been training them. They're getting damn good at runnin' down negras."

"But we're hunting Indians," Captain Cotesworth protested.

"About the same," Colonel Bemrose insisted. "Besides, a lot of Injuns are negras."

"That's true," Captain Cotesworth admitted.

Colonel Bemrose asked, "Are you fellows taking some of the dogs? We got a bunch of good money invested in them, but I'll give you a halfway decent price for a dozen or so."

"Thought we're running a joint mission," Captain Cotesworth protested.

"Not what I heard," Colonel Bemrose insisted. "I aint got no plans to go hightailing it through any swamps chasing Injuns. I got it pretty damn good right here. Besides, the boss told me you boys were going to pick up a bunch of dogs and somebody's getting the rest. I'll give you a deal."

Captain Cotesworth asked, "How much?"

Colonel Bemrose said, "Couple of hundred a head."

Captain Cotesworth kicked the dirt a little. "That's a pretty hefty price but we'll take ten, seeing as we came all the way up here."

"Gonna need a handler," Colonel Bemrose insisted. "You boys don't know how to handle these beasts."

Captain Cotesworth said, "Figured you'd throw in a handler fer that price."

"Gotta cut your own deal with the handlers," Colonel Bemrose claimed. "They're independent contractors."

"Got any suggestions?"

"I'd go with Diego, the dog man, if I was you," Bemrose suggested. "He's about as good as it gets."

Captain Cotesworth asked, "This dog man, where do I find him?"

"Taproom at the City Hotel," Colonel Bemrose replied. "Generally hangs out at the bar over there."

Harry and Captain Cotesworth found Diego, the dog man, seated on a stool at the far end of the bar in the taproom at the City Hotel. Diego was the only man in the place wearing a brightly patterned Latin shirt. He was finishing off a tankard of Cuban rum while puffing a Cuban cigar.

Captain Cotesworth asked, "You the dog man?"

"That's me! I'm the dog man," Diego insisted as he put down his cigar and shoved the tankard to the side. "What do ya want?"

"We just bought some of your dogs."

Diego shifted around. "And who is this, we?"

Captain Cotesworth said, "United States Army at Fort Brooke."

"Those dogs are wild beasts! You're going to need someone to manage them."

"You want the job?"

"Depends on how much you're paying?"

"How much you want?"

"Dollar a day," Diego insisted, "silver."

"Got it," Captain Cotesworth replied.

Diego demanded, "And expenses."

"Got that too," Captain Cotesworth added.

Diego tossed his cigar aside and slid off the stool. "What are we standing around here for? Come on. Let's go."

They went back to the field behind the auction house and Diego selected ten dogs. "These are the best," he claimed. "I'll need supplies."

"What supplies?" Captain Cotesworth asked.

"Training materials, grooming items, personal stuff," Diego insisted. "There's a lot to the job."

"Get what you need," Captain Cotesworth agreed. "We've got to move this along."

Harry paid Colonel Bemrose the asking price for the dogs and threw in another ten dollars for expenses. Bemrose was happy to get the money. The conductor on the tramway wasn't too happy about Diego, the bloodhounds, or the crates and barrels of personal items that Diego brought along, but a substantial cash gift improved his attitude. Lieutenant Farley was less happy when they boarded the *Erie* with ten dogs, the dog man, and his cargo.

Lieutenant Farley growled, "You people are getting to be a real pain. The navy sent me here to interdict the supplies to the Seminole. Now you got me running a dog detail."

They found space for the freight and the dogs. Diego checked out the ship, set up a raffle with the ship's crew, and ended up with a sizeable share of the proceeds by the time they reached Tampa Bay. They went ashore at Tampa Town. Carey, the cart man, and his bullwhackers unloaded the freight from the sloop-of-war. Then they loaded the freight on their ox carts, cracked their whips over the backs of their oxen, and slowly hauled Diego's freight to the fort. Captain Cotesworth found space for the dogs out behind the horse sheds at Fort Brooke.

Colonel Davers sent the bloodhounds, Diego, and Captain Cotesworth out on a few missions but everyone soon discovered that the bloodhounds had absolutely no interest in pursuing Indians.

Even so, Colonel Davers tried to put a good face on the exploit. He asked Lieutenant Sprague to do a story, and Harry printed up a bulletin about using dogs to keep the Indians at bay. The bulletin was distributed and Harry took Diego down to the Groggery for rest and relaxation.

Diego was fun. He told wild yarns about Matanzas, tall tales about the Spanish authorities, and his amorous exploits in Matanzas and Havana. Sidney Benson took an active interest in Diego, joined them at the bar, and asked Diego about his dogs.

"Wild beasts, those dogs," Diego boasted. "But I manage them."

"Tell me about them," Sidney urged.

"They're ferocious."

"Then you use them to round up Indians?"

"Naw, we use them to kill Indians!"

"What about women and children?"

"Rip them to shreds," Diego boasted. "Tear them apart! Blood, guts, and gore all over the place."

Diego put on a good show. Sidney listened with horror and amazement. Sidney didn't know that the dogs spent most of the time sprawled in the shade. They had to be dragged, cajoled, and pulled to get them out of the fort and into the bush. They never found any Indians and only perked up when Diego dished out their daily rations. They devoured the rations quickly and without fuss. Then they sprawled out to rest in the shade.

Harry considered the dogs and Diego's ranting as just another meaningless episode in a meaningless war until the *Albany Evening Journal* told the world that the Van Buren administration was using vicious bloodhounds to maim, kill, and torture Indian women and children in Florida. Other Whig newspapers jumped on the story and the story spread. Editorials appeared condemning the administration for violating the accepted principles of civilized warfare.

The United States Senate intervened when Senator Hart Benton from Missouri stood in the chamber to denounce the administration's use of dogs to dismember non-combatant human beings in the Florida Indian Wars. Representative Isaac Pennybacker from Virginia called for a congressional investigation. Senator Daniel Webster of Massachusetts demanded the name of the army officer who had authorized the use of these dogs. Senator James Buchanan from Pennsylvania presented a lengthy petition from the Society of Friends protesting the massacre of innocents.

President Van Buren shouted at Secretary Poinsett. Secretary Poinsett growled at General Macomb for not heading off the matter before it got to his desk. General Macomb responded by ordering Taylor to produce the scoundrels responsible for the transgression. He wanted them sent to Washington.

General Taylor, of course, contacted Colonel Davers and Colonel Davers was happy to order Captain Cotesworth and

Harry to Washington City on the first means available. They caught a ride on Captain McRea's old brig as far as Key West.

Key West seemed to be a pretty interesting place, but they didn't get to see much of it. The Army's dispatch boat, the *Pegasus*, was heading for Washington and they scrambled to get on board before she departed.

CHAPTER EIGHT

Amanda and the Gentlemen's Club

Washington City
April 1840

The *Pegasus* was a schooner rigged vessel, but she relied more on her steam engine than the wind. A week after departing Key West, the boat chugged up the Potomac River. Captain Cotesworth figured they would be greeted by some sort of official delegation or welcoming party. After all, they had been away for about a year, were combat veterans, and were coming back to report on the war.

No one greeted them and nobody paid any attention as they made their way through the Navy Yard to catch a cab for a short ride to the War Department building on Pennsylvania Avenue. Washington looked about the same. Workmen were still working on the capitol dome, delivery carts crowded the streets, and newspaper boys hawked their wares. Nothing much had changed.

They sauntered into General Macomb's office. He was shocked. "What are you doing here?"

"Came back to talk about the bloodhounds."

"What about the bloodhounds?"

"We're the guys who bought them?"

"Oh, shit!" General Macomb blurted. "Poinsett's not going to like this."

Secretary Poinsett was already unhappy about the bloodhounds and the newspaper articles. He was even more distressed when he discovered that his nephew was somehow involved. "How did you get mixed up in this thing?"

"Don't know," Captain Cotesworth murmured, "just happened."

"Diego," Harry suggested. "He told Sidney."

"Who's Diego?"

"The dog man," Captain Cotesworth explained. "He exaggerates a lot and dramatizes things."

"And who is Sidney?"

"Hangs out at the Groggery," Harry explained, "buys drinks for everyone."

"How did he get mixed up in this?"

"Don't know," Captain Cotesworth muttered, "just happened."

"Be that as it may," Secretary Poinsett concluded. "We've got to talk with the president.

Harry said, "Never met the man."

"And you're not going to meet him, now," Secretary Poinsett snapped. "Sit in my office and keep your mouth shut. Haines and I are taking care of this."

Harry asked, "Who's Haines?"

Captain Cotesworth said, "Me."

President Van Buren was becoming alarmed about his election prospects. The Whigs had nominated William Henry Harrison as their candidate. Mobs of irrational people were out and about, marching in torchlight parades, building log cabins, passing out jugs of hard cider, flying banners, and shouting "Tippecanoe and Tyler Too."

It was most distressing. Secretary Poinsett and Captain Haines Langston Cotesworth walked over to the Executive Mansion and went upstairs to find the president in his study. The president was reading a recent edition of the *Albany Evening Journal*. Caleb Conklin, the little man from the state department, was perched on the stool behind the door.

President Van Buren said, "Weed's doing a number on your greyhound fiasco! He won't let it go."

"I know," Secretary Poinsett conceded. "I brought Captain Cotesworth to explain the problem. He's back from Florida."

President Van Buren folded the paper, put it on the table, and waited for an explanation. Captain Cotesworth waited for a question. President Van Buren broke the silence. "Say something. What's going on?"

58

Captain Cotesworth said, "The dogs are no good."

"Agree on that," President Van Buren replied. "But how did it get blown up into this story?"

"The dog handler, he blabbed to someone at a tavern."

"Who was it?"

"Ed or Sid, something like that," Captain Cotesworth mumbled. "He hangs out at the Groggery, don't know much about him."

Caleb suggested, "Sidney Benson."

"Sounds about right," Captain Cotesworth replied. "Who is he?"

"Correspondent for Thurlow Weed," Caleb answered. "Sidney has a unique flair for transforming mundane bits of gossip into items of inflammatory fiction. It's a literary skill in some demand these days. You boys gotta be more careful."

Secretary Poinsett asked, "So what do we do?"

"Couple of things," Caleb insisted. "We'll impose a news blackout and you'll need to meet a few of the more influential policy players to get this thing quieted down."

President Van Buren asked, "Where you holding the meeting?"

Caleb said, "Mary Ann's place."

"Good. Keep it over there. I don't want those people over here. They'll start poking around in my business, scheduling hearings, and all that stuff."

"We'll head it off," Caleb promised. He told Secretary Poinsett and Captain Cotesworth, "I want you at the meeting. You'll have to talk to the boys, provide an explanation, and shift the blame."

"Stay on this," President Van Buren growled. "Get some intelligence assets down there. Do it. I can't have anymore surprises."

"I'll get on it," Caleb assured the president. He asked Captain Cotesworth, "Who's playing the lead in the Easter pageant?"

"What pageant?"

"Someone to take the blame, give me names."

"Call, he's the governor," Secretary Poinsett suggested. "He got the dogs."

"Was the governor," President Van Buren announced. "I've replaced him and given Reid the job. We can stick Call with some of the blame, but we need a low-lying nobody, some insignificant yahoo to take the full fall."

"Bemrose," Captain Cotesworth suggested. "He got the dogs. We can nail him."

President Van Buren asked, "Who?"

"Bemrose," Caleb explained, "a small-time operator from North Carolina. He got into some trouble with the authorities over a land deal, disappeared for awhile, and showed up in Atlanta with Atkins and Foster, slave merchants. They sent him to Tallahassee with a covee. Bemrose cut a deal with Eaton when Eaton was governor and opened an auction house. Eaton gave him a commission when he was giving them away. Don't know the particulars on that."

President Van Buren asked, "What's he done with the commission."

"Not much," Caleb insisted, "brought the dogs and four Spanish agents back from Cuba. That's about it."

"He'll do," President Van Buren concurred. "Nail his confounded hide to the wall, make an example of him."

"Will do," Caleb promised. "And you'd better do something about General Taylor. He's ineffective."

"Taylor wants to get relieved," Secretary Poinsett explained. "I'll recall him and send somebody else to Florida."

"That'll do it," President Van Buren concluded. "Run along now but keep your mouths shut. Caleb's setting up a meeting at Mary Ann's place to quiet this thing down, hustle over there, do a little groveling when you get there, and eat some crow."

Secretary of War Poinsett and his now rather subdued nephew left the meeting and plodded back through the poplar thicket to the War Department. A servant came by a couple of days later and summoned them to Mary Ann's place.

Secretary Poinsett and his nephew rode over in the secretary's new Rockaway Phaeton. The driver pulled up to the front of a rambling three story federal style brick building. A plaque on the gate identified the building:

Ambassador's Parlor and Lounge
329 Maryland Avenue

The two gentlemen strolled up a curved walkway past beds of blooming tulips. Captain Cotesworth asked, "What is this place?"

"It's an exclusive gentlemen's club set up for ambassadors, dignitaries, and influential businessmen. The state department runs it."

"Do you come here very often?"

"I'm not a member," Secretary Poinsett explained as he led the way up the steps. "I'm not that influential, but I've advised them on their plantings."

"The tulips are nice."

"Glad you like them, got them from the Dutch ambassador. He suggested mixing the *Saxatilis* with the *Fosterianas* and hyacinths. It works."

Secretary Poinsett rapped on the door with his cane and a black servant opened the door. A massive gold, crystal chandelier hung from the ceiling and multicolored carpets covered the hardwood floor. A crystal vase of cut flowers sat on a low oriental teakwood table.

Mary Ann rushed out to greet them. Red lip rouge and crimson scarf set off her bright yellow dress. "Glad you're here. Come with me. We're in the side parlor."

Mary Ann led the way through a front parlor, down a hallway, and into the side parlor. Women were serving drinks. Trays of cheese, crackers, and pastries sat on a buffet table. Captain Cotesworth recognized Senator Buchanan and Senator Webster. William King, the President of the Senate, was waiting. Caleb was perched on a stool behind the French doors.

Senator King said, "Let's get started."

Mary Ann nodded, closed the French doors, clicked the lock, and sat down on a nearby chair. Senator King huffed, "We're dealing with a sensitive issue. That being the case, this meeting must be kept a private matter conducted between gentlemen of honor and integrity. I trust it will be kept that way."

Secretary Poinsett said, "Certainly!"

Senator King proceeded. "Now, I'm given to understand the captain has accumulated considerable combat experience in Florida. How are things going down there?"

"Moving right along," Captain Haines Cotesworth mumbled. "We're implementing the Peace Accord, rounding up the savages, and putting them on their side of the Peace River Boundary."

"Glad to hear it," Senator King conceded. "There's been considerable uncertainty expressed by so much of the press and a number of accusations have been made about alleged atrocities involving dogs. Now, I understand that you might be in a position to know something about the business."

Captain Cotesworth said, "A little."

Senator King demanded, "Who thought up the idea."

Secretary Poinsett asked, "What idea?"

"Dogs," Senator King insisted. "Who came up with the scatter-brained idea of using dogs?"

Captain Cotesworth said, "Governor Call."

A few of the gentlemen exchanged knowing glances. A young brunette in a white muslin gown suddenly appeared on the other side of the French doors. She reached for the knob, but Mary Ann waved her away. The girl hesitated, turned, and walking away.

Senator Webster watched her go. Then he said, "Call's not the governor anymore. There's gotta be somebody else."

"General Taylor," Captain Cotesworth suggested.

"Figured as much," Senator Buchanan insisted. "This unfortunate episode constitutes a flagrant violation of all of the accepted principles of civilized warfare. We've got to make an example here."

There were shouts of, "Hear, hear!"

Secretary Poinsett said, "Taylor's gone. I've replaced him."

"That'll take care of part of the problem," Senator King surmised. "Even so, there has to be a scoundrel in the woodpile, some low level functionary who got those dogs and precipitated this travesty. Who is this man?"

"Bemrose," Captain Cotesworth replied, "he's your man."

Senator King nodded but appeared confused. He asked Secretary Poinsett, "Who is this man, this Bemrose?"

Secretary Poinsett explained, "A two-bit Tallahassee slave merchant. John Eaton made him a colonel back when he was giving away commissions. Bemrose isn't one of our people."

Senator King said, "But your people gotta know what to do with him. Call him up or something, whatever you do, and get him out of Tallahassee. Make an example. Send him into the swamps and feed him to the alligators."

Secretary Poinsett agreed, "Being done."

"That oughta settle it," Senator King concluded, "any more questions?" As there were no more questions, Senator King said, "Thanks for stopping. Now, if you'll excuse us, we've got a few other matters to consider."

That being said, Mary Ann stood up and motioned for Caleb, Secretary Poinsett, and Haines to follow her. She took them down a hallway and into a small conference room where the gentlemen gathered around a conference table. She said, "Wait here. I'll be back."

As the gentlemen sat, Secretary Poinsett asked Caleb, "What's happening?"

"Get rid of the dogs," Caleb insisted. "We'll hang Bemrose."

Mary Ann came back with the woman in the muslin gown. The woman sat on a nearby sofa, leaned forward, clasped her hands, and smiled.

Mary Ann said, "This is Amanda. She's going to Florida with you."

Captain Cotesworth asked, "Who's going to Florida?"

"You are," Secretary Poinsett insisted, "can't have you here."

Amanda insisted, "And I'm going."

Captain Cotesworth asked, "Why?"

Caleb said, "To keep track of things."

Mary Ann explained, "You people don't know what you're doing. Sidney Benson is a bigger problem for the president than all of your Indians put together. We've dealt with Sidney in the past and know how to handle him. I can't go so I'm sending Amanda and two other girls."

"Nicole," Caleb suggested. "She's had some management training."

"Good choice," Mary Ann replied, "and Roslyn."

Caleb agreed, "That'll work."

Captain Cotesworth said, "So, there'll be three."

"Seven," Amanda snapped. "There'll be seven. Three of us, three servants, and a porter, that's six women and a man. That's seven."

Captain Cotesworth protested, "Why servants."

"We're professionals," Amanda explained. "We don't do menial work. It's all of us or none of us, that's how it is!"

"We came on a dispatch boat," Captain Cotesworth pleaded. "They don't carry women."

"You're not getting the picture," Caleb insisted. "I'm not suggesting. I'm telling. Do it."

Secretary Poinsett argued, "This is getting complicated."

"Screw you and your complications," Mary Ann snapped, "Marty's in a jam."

Secretary Poinsett blanched. "We'll do what we can."

"You'd better," Mary Ann growled, "or you'll all be out in the swamps. Do I make myself clear?"

"Yes, ma'am, or no ma'am," Captain Cotesworth replied.

"Don't you dare call me that," Mary Ann frowned, "I'm not your mother or your nurse. Do you have any more questions?"

"Why are we doing this" Captain Cotesworth asked. "What's the idea? What do you want us to do after we get to Florida?"

"Set up a gentleman's club," Amanda replied. "That's the plan."

"Not a problem," Secretary Poinsett conceded. "Who's paying?"

Caleb said, "It's being covered as an off-the-books asset."

"Transportation," Secretary Poinsett asked.

"All of it," Caleb answered, "the whole thing."

A lot happened. Governor Reid denied any and all knowledge of the dogs. General Macomb banned reporters from Fort Brooke, issued a news blackout, and ordered a change of command. General Taylor packed up and left Florida.

Colonel Bemrose got called up for an extended tour of duty with the United States Army. Initially pleased, he became disillusioned when ordered to Fort King, and distressed when assigned to a roving patrol of swamp rats. The patrol was sent into the hinterlands to serve as an expendable decoy to entice wandering bands of hostiles to come out and fight. Few figured he'd survive.

Captain Haines Cotesworth received a more difficult assignment. "Go back to Florida and take the women with you."

CHAPTER NINE

Three Assets with Luggage

Washington City to Key West
May 1840 through October 1841

Harry didn't plan on going. He figured his army days were over until Secretary Poinsett told him, "I don't know how you got into the army but you did. You're going back to Florida and comply with every lawful order properly given or I'm putting you in the nearest stockade and have you making little rocks out of big rocks for the rest of your natural born life. Do you have any questions?"

Harry said, "Nope."

"Then get with the program."

After that, Florida didn't sound so bad. Harry checked with Captain Cotesworth, and Captain Cotesworth issued an order properly given. "Pick up a transport wagon at Fort McNair and bring it to 329 Maryland Avenue. We'll be waiting."

Harry did as directed but several hours transpired before Harry appeared with the wagon. Captain Cotesworth and Amanda were waiting on the loading dock at the rear of the building. Captain Cotesworth asked, "Where've you been?"

Harry said, "Getting the wagon."

"How come the hold up? Secretary Poinsett signed the requisition."

"They didn't believe it," Harry claimed, "had to check."

"Be that as it may, let's get going."

Harry slid off the wagon to secure the horses. That being done, Harry jumped on the dock to encounter a blonde with a crate. She said, "Hi! I'm Roslyn."

"Let me help."

"Oh," she said, "sure." Roslyn gave Harry the crate and dashed off to get another. Harry put the crate on the wagon. Crates, boxes, and barrels followed as Roslyn, Amanda, Captain Cotesworth, and the slaves brought them to the wagon.

Harry was arranging the load when a dark-haired nymph appeared with an armful of books and ledgers. She said, "Hi! I'm Nicole."

"Let me help."

"No problem," Nicole replied. "I've got it."

Nicole put her books and ledgers on the wagon. Harry asked, "What are you doing with that stuff?"

"Part of the job," Nicole explained. "Discounting banknotes and keeping records is part of what I do."

"I guess."

"Really," Nicole insisted before rushing off.

Captain Cotesworth surveyed the growing pile of boxes, barrels, and crates on the wagon with alarm before asking Amanda, "Gotta take all this?"

"Sure do," Amanda insisted.

"We're on a dispatch boat. They don't have much room."

"All of it," Amanda explained, "everything or nothing!"

"Gotta have our stuff," Roslyn pleaded. "It's our mystique."

"I guess," Captain Cotesworth mumbled. He didn't like the women, putting up with the women, and where this thing seemed to be going. Getting the women to the Navy Yard would be hard enough. Getting the women on the dispatch boat, all the way to Florida, and on to Fort Brooke was going to be a nightmare.

Captain Cotesworth decided to exercise the prerogative of command. He delegated responsibility by telling Harry, "Run this stuff to the harbor and make the shipping arrangements with Master Evans."

Harry pleaded, "Aren't you coming."

"I'll bring the women."

Being left with no other option, Harry untied the horses, got on the wagon, snapped the reins, and drove off. It took awhile for Harry to get through the streets of Washington, admitted to the navy yard, and to the pier where the *Pegasus* was moored.

Master Evans wasn't pleased. "What you got there?"

Harry said, "We're taking it to Florida."

"No way in hell, not on my boat."

"We're bringing people," Harry added.

"How many you bringing?"

"Six women and two men," Harry replied. "That's eight."

"Don't haul women," Master Evans grumbled, "not set up for them."

"Get set up," Harry insisted. "Captain Cotesworth says they're coming and that's how it is."

"Who are these women?" Master Evans blustered. "If you're talking about the kind of women I think you might be talking about, we've got a problem."

"What's the problem?"

"Not getting mixed up in that business," Master Evans sputtered. "No sirree, I'm running a reputable boat. I signed on to carry dispatches."

"Let me assure you these women are held in highest esteem by distinguished gentlemen," Harry insisted. "They're on a special mission that's been cleared by the Secretary of War. It's a matter of national security."

"Everything's a matter of security with you people," Master Evans blustered. "These women, who are they?"

"Don't worry about them," Harry insisted. "They'll be on good behavior."

"Not worried about their behavior," Master Evans argued. "I'm worried about my crew's behavior. I'm not taking any chances."

Harry said, "We'll work it out."

"No way in hell," Master Evans grumbled. He stomped off.

Harry went back to the club and talked with Captain Cotesworth. Captain Cotesworth talked with Uncle Leon, the

Secretary of War, and Secretary Poinsett called Master Evans to his office to explain the nature of the arrangement.

Master Evans asked, "What happens if I don't do it?"

Secretary Poinsett said, "Than I'll have to fire you and hire someone else."

Master Evans considered the option for a moment. Then he said, "Why didn't you explain it? I'll take them but I got a reputation to consider. They'll have to keep below deck so nobody can see them."

As the women and slaves boarded the boat, Master Evans told Harry, "You got them on board, but you gotta keep them below deck until we clear the harbor."

'I'll try," Harry offered. "But the ladies are expecting special consideration."

"What do they want?"

"Special meals and appropriate bathing arrangements."

"They'll get a water bucket," Master Evans offered. "That's the only bathing arrangement we got."

"What about food?"

"Salt pork, biscuits, and cabbage," Master Evans insisted. "They've gotta make do with the rest of us. I'm not running a restaurant."

"And they'll need a promenade along the deck."

"Bullshit!" Master Evans exclaimed. "They're staying below until I clear the harbor. I got a reputation to consider."

Amanda put up with the restrictions until they cleared the harbor. Then she came on deck, sauntered the length of the deck, and told Master Evans, "Go to hell!"

Nicole made herself at home. She struck up lengthy conversations with the crew and thoroughly enjoyed the adventure. Roslyn got seasick as soon as the dispatch boat cleared the river. She stayed below and left the deck to Amanda and Nicole.

Roslyn adjusted to life at sea on the third day out and appeared on deck with Amanda and Nicole. The women eventually took over the boat. Master Evans grumbled a lot about his petticoat passengers but spent a lot of time talking with Amanda as she helped him plot their trip south.

Nicole started wearing the abbreviated shirt and trousers worn by the crew. Roslyn complained but nobody listened. The voyage continued as they made their way down the coast, crossed the sea, and arrived at Key West.

Key West was a small island at the far end of a chain of reefs and islands extending back to the mainland. The little city was laid out in squares along a ridge overlooking the harbor. Shops, bars, warehouses, and a hotel were clustered along Front Street. Crushed shell streets and walkways led back to an ancient mangrove, mahogany, and palm forest covering most of the island.

The women went ashore, took rooms at the hotel, and checked out their situation. Amanda accepted the fact that they had to go to Fort Brooke but didn't seem to be in a hurry to get there. The short stay stretched into days as Harry and Captain Cotesworth scurried around trying to find a way to get to Tampa Bay. Captain Cotesworth figured he had a solution when the *Erie* sailed into the harbor.

Captain Cotesworth asked Lieutenant Farley, "Any chance of catching a ride to Tampa Town."

"What are we talking about?"

Captain Cotesworth said, "My sergeant, six women, and a slave."

"I've already pulled you fellows out of the river, hauled you to Tallahassee, and brought back dogs. I'm drawing the line at hauling women. Not doing it. It's against Naval Regulations."

They had to wait for Captain McRea. A week or so went by before the *Highland Princess* showed up. Captain McRea said, "I'm taking cows to Havana. I'll pick you up when I get back."

"When's that?"

"How do I know," Captain McRea grumbled, "depends on the weather."

Amanda didn't object. The girls went shopping and enjoyed life in a community where there were seven or eight men for every woman. Captain Cotesworth was concerned about the delay. Harry didn't care. He found lodging at the base and waited for the *Highland Princess* to get back from Cuba.

A late summer storm came through town around the middle of September, delaying the *Highland Princess*. Some seamen claimed that a hurricane passed to the south but didn't do much damage in Key West. Another week went by before the *Highland Princess* got back from Cuba.

CHAPTER TEN

The Eagle's Nest

The women put up a fuss when they saw the *Highland Princess.* Amanda said, "I'm not riding on a cow boat."

"All we've got," Captain Cotesworth pleaded.

"All right, but you've got to clean it up."

"What ya talking about," Captain McRae grumbled. "How do I clean a brig?"

Amanda asked, "What's a brig?"

Captain McRae said, "A two-masted vessel with square sails. I've been sailing my *Princess* for a dozen years now and she's seen me through hard times and rough seas. You've got no business putting down a man's possession and means of livelihood."

"Didn't mean anything," Amanda replied. "I was just wondering."

"At any rate, you've gotta clean her up," Captain Cotesworth insisted.

"So long as you pay me for my time and hire the cleaning crew, I've got no objection," Captain McRae conceded.

Captain Cotesworth had to dole out a few dollars for the lost time and hire a cleaning crew. Harry found some Bahamans who spent a week washing down the boat. Then Amanda checked out the accommodations. She finally accepted the captain's cabin provided they scrub it again and paint it.

Captain McRea demanded more dollars. Captain Cotesworth laid out money and Harry found a painter. The cleaning and painting took another week. Then Amanda checked out the brig and accepted the arrangements with misgivings. They were on their way.

The *Highland Princess* sailed into Tampa Bay in late October and drifted up to the pier. Amanda took a look at Tampa Town and gasped. The pier was jammed with Spanish fishermen, their wives, and their children. Stray dogs scurried about. Jake Sutherlin and a group of cow catchers were clustered around a herd of scrawny cows at the far end of the pier. Carey and his bullwhackers were out and about. Misfits lounged on the Groggery porch. An open sewer ran down the middle of the street.

"It's a mistake," Amanda blurted. "This can't be the place."

"This is it," Captain Cotesworth insisted. "You'll get used to it."

"Doubt it." Roslyn cried.

Spanish fishermen shouted lewd remarks as the women and slaves followed Captain Cotesworth down the gangway and into the crowd. The women ignored the shouts and taunts as they made their way through the babble, trudged up the dusty road, and walked to the fort. Harry tagged behind.

Captain Cotesworth led the entourage to the fort and the commander's office. Colonel Davers examined the group before gasping, "What's this!"

Captain Cotesworth snapped an academy style reply, "Reporting for duty, sir!"

"Dammit, I got rid of you and you're back," Colonel Davers grumbled. "Who are these people? Why are you here?"

Captain Cotesworth said, "War Department orders." He slapped a packet on the colonel's desk.

"Can't believe this," Colonel Davers grumbled as he tore open the packet and recognized the signature of the Secretary of War.

"Gotta keep these people here until I find a place for them," Captain Cotesworth insisted.

Colonel Davers read the orders. "You're not giving me much choice! I'll keep them for the time being. Put them in the empty unit in the married officer's housing, but keep it quiet. The wives over there will raise a fuss if they find out what's going on."

"Just for a few days," Captain Cotesworth promised. Then Captain Cotesworth rushed off to find Diego.

Diego, the dog man, was in his usual spot at the end of the bar at the Groggery. Captain Cotesworth slid next to him and ordered a round of drinks. Diego acknowledged his presence by taking the drink.

Diego asked, "So where'd you go?"

"Special mission," Captain Cotesworth replied.

"How'd it go?"

"Good," Captain Cotesworth insisted, "We're out of the dog business."

"Not me," Diego protested. "Not my dogs. I raised those dogs from little puppies. They're my good friends and loyal companions. What's happening to them?"

"Don't know, but I got a different job for you."

What's that?"

"We brought three women and four slaves back with us. We're setting up a gentleman's club and have to contract with a third party to own and manage the club."

"What's a third party?"

"You, you're the third party," Captain Cotesworth insisted. "Find a house or building where we can set up. Special sources will cover the rent or purchase price, remodeling, and your salary."

"Why?"

"Because we're doing it," Captain Cotesworth explained.

"About the salary," Diego asked. "Is it good?"

"Better than you're getting now."

"Twice as much," Diego suggested, "sounds right so long as you cover all my expenses."

"And your Groggery bill," Captain Cotesworth offered.

"Always a bill," Diego agreed, "different name sometimes. Gotta have tonics but perhaps this club might serve libations."

"Probably, if you wish," Captain Cotesworth replied. "It's special money."

"Silver, I presume," Diego insisted.

"Silver, it is," Captain Cotesworth agreed. "What do we do with your dogs?"

"How do I know," Diego replied. "They're your dogs. That's your problem. When do we start this club?"

Diego looked for housing, but Amanda said, "I want trees."

"What for," Diego demanded. "Why do you need trees?"

"Trees and a garden," Amanda claimed. "I want a nice location next to the fort."

Diego found an old cracker house on the main road a sort distance above the fort at the top of the ridge. It was a one-room shack but came with seven acres of oak and cypress.

Captain Cotesworth said, "It's got trees so it'll do."

Diego bought the house and Captain Cotesworth took Amanda to the site to show her the cabin. Amanda was appalled. "The trees are nice, but the house is a disaster."

Captain Cotesworth said, "Tell us what you want and we'll do it."

Amanda drew up the plans and Diego hired a construction crew. The crew went to work, tore down the old cabin, and put up a new post, beam, and plank structure. Captain Cotesworth grumbled. "This is getting expensive."

"To hell with the cost," Amanda replied. "We're not working in a shack!" Then Amanda sent Diego to Havana with Captain McRae to purchase furniture, furnishings, and fabrics. Diego came back with bolts of fabric, love seats, upholstered chairs, marble topped tables, bedsteads, and a red velvet courtesan's couch.

Carey's cart men hauled cartloads of furniture and merchandise to the fort and stacked it in an empty warehouse. The women sorted their furniture. Nicole claimed the couch. "I like it," she said, "I'm using it."

"Why," Roslyn asked, "velvet spots."

"So, it spots," Nicole argued.

"You're hopeless," Roslyn insisted.

Several weeks went by before the construction crew finished the job, put down their hammers, and took up paint brushes. When they finished, a new dwelling resembling a plantation house stood among the trees on the ridge. Porches extended across the front of the building and along the sides. Hewn cypress posts and beams supported the walls, roof, and ceiling. Two inch thick oak board and batten covered the building.

Roslyn said, "Gotta have a name."

"Eagle's Nest," Amanda insisted. "That's what I'm calling it."

Captain Cotesworth asked, "How come?"

"We take gold eagles," Amanda explained. "Every eagle needs a nest."

"That's us," Roslyn suggested.

"So it is," Amanda replied. She led the group into the front parlor. Four rooms opened off the parlor.

Nicole took the first room on the right, saying, "I'll put my couch in there." Roslyn grabbed the second room on the right and Amanda ended up with the left back room. Diego took the remaining room for his taproom.

The Eagle's Nest opened with a flourish. Two army colonels and eleven militia colonels came to the opening. Diego brought a couple of Spanish gentlemen who claimed they were merchants. Amanda greeted the guests while Nicole and Roslyn served tonics and other libations.

Amanda distributed membership applications. "Admission to the club is restricted to members and their guests. Appointments should be made a week in advance. Fill out our application and submit it with a gold eagle to cover our processing cost."

Diego owned the property, but Amanda ran the club. Diego tended bar, chatted with customers, and delivered dispatches. He gave them to Captain McRea who gave them to Master Evans at the port in Key West. Master Evans took the dispatches to Washington City. The Army imposed a gag order on talking with reporters, and that ended the Florida stories being printed in the *Albany Evening Journal*.

Diego chatted with Sidney at the Groggery and a few gold eagles changed hands. Sidney said, "I'll think on it."

Colonel Davers called Captain Cotesworth to his office. Colonel Davers said, "You could have saved all of us a bunch of trouble if you'd told us that Poinsett was your uncle."

Captain Cotesworth said, "Nobody asked."

"Be that as it may," Colonel Davers replied. "I'm promoting you to major and making you my aide."

"Why?"

"Gotta keep you around where I can see you, that's all."

"Makes sense," Major Cotesworth agreed. The war continued. The army sent out a few patrols from time to time, and some of the Seminole moved to the reserved land south of the Peace River Boundary. A few went west. Others vanished.

President Van Buren got the Democratic nomination for a second term, but Harrison, the Whig candidate, received 234 electoral votes to Van Buren's 60. Harrison came to Washington and Van Buren went home to Kinderhook.

The Harrison administration replaced most of the Democrats who had worked for the Jackson and Van Buren administrations. Not being burdened by excessive party loyalty or suffering from unrealistic ethical constraints, Caleb covered his options by working both sides. Caleb survived.

CHAPTER ELEVEN

Tippecanoe and Tyler Too

Washington and Tampa
1841 through August 1842

William Henry Harrison was sixty-eight years old when he became president. He had been a militia officer during the early Indian wars and won fame as a relatively successful general during the War of 1812. He went to congress after the war as the delegate from the Northwestern Territory. This was followed by a stint as governor of Indiana Territory, several terms as a congressman from Ohio, and finally a single term as senator. He completed his career by being the ambassador to Columbia.

Having completed forty years of public service, General Harrison retired and went home to North Bend, Ohio. The Whigs disrupted his plans by nominating him for president, and he was swept into office on wave of popular enthusiasm. The Whigs made an issue of President Van Buren's aristocratic pretensions and condemned him for his costly Florida Indian war.

Thurlow Weed, editor of the *Albany Evening Journal,* was instrumental in exposing the details of the Van Buren administration and vowed that the errors of the past would be corrected. Mr. Weed was certain that President Harrison would lift the ban on his access to the news and events of the Florida war. Thurlow dashed to Washington to greet the president-elect on his arrival and greeted him by asking, "What about the Florida news blackout?"

The old man being confused and overwhelmed by the persistent demands of his supporters said, "Don't know about it, but I'll do what I can."

Not being satisfied, Thurlow demanded, "You've got to rectify the Van Buren administration's interference with the fourth estate."

The president-elect tried to figure out what Thurlow was talking about but couldn't remember Thurlow's question. He said, "I'll do what I can."

President Harrison was sworn in on March 4, 1841. It rained and snowed, but the old fellow stood outside on the portico delivering a two hour inaugural address. He didn't wear a hat or coat. Then he dashed off to three receptions and two balls. The president moved into the Executive Mansion but dallied before naming Daniel Webster as his secretary of state and selecting John Bell as his secretary of war.

Weed dropped in on President Harrison. "What are you doing about the Florida situation?

"What ya talking about?"

"Censorship," Thurlow sputtered. "The army's blocked all my access to information."

"Having Injun trouble," President Harrison replied. "Talk with Bell about it. It's his department."

Thurlow didn't know Bell that well but caught up with him at the War Department. Bell said, "Haven't heard about it, but I'll look into it."

Thurlow had better luck with Daniel Webster. Secretary Webster called Caleb to his office. "We've got a Florida problem."

Caleb suggested, "The war."

"Censorship," Secretary Webster replied. "Know anything about it?"

"Not much."

"Do something," Secretary Webster insisted.

"What?"

"Get Weed off my back. Work out something, schedule a meeting with him, or something."

"I'll get on it." Caleb talked to Mary Ann, but she wasn't concerned. Thurlow had printed unflattering allegations about her and her alleged relationship with the former president.

"Maybe, later perhaps," Mary Ann suggested.

President Harrison cherished simplicity. Complicated charts, long meetings, and lengthy reports bored him. He told his cabinet, "You fellows are making this job more difficult than it has to be. You talk too much and spend too much. Whoa it up! Keep it simple."

This generated some anxiety, but the cabinet members relaxed when they found out that President Harrison wasn't able to remember much of anything. He offered the same jobs to different people and even kept offering the jobs after they were filled. The president frequently appeared dazed or confused.

When people started asking for money, President Harrison started writing hand-drawn drafts on his accounts. As this became common knowledge, the president was overwhelmed by demands. He started overdrawing his accounts, over promising his constituents, and over-feeding anyone who happened to stop by at mealtime. The treasury secretary panicked and clerk quit.

Cost cutting became a matter of concern. The federal army had grown from fewer than six thousand men before the war to over fifteen thousand. A couple of thousand Florida militia men were being paid by the federal payroll and hundreds of war contracts had been issued to dozens of suppliers. Nobody knew where the money was going. The war was consuming over ten percent of the entire federal budget, but there didn't seem to be anything to show for it.

Then Mary Ann said, "Gotta have more money."

"Haven't got it," Caleb replied. "Webster's cutting my budget. You'll have to see the president."

"How do I do that?"

"The guards are gone," Caleb replied. "I'll take you over and we'll tell him you're part of security. He'll never know the difference."

President Harrison was nursing a cold and lounging on a sofa in his upstairs study. Caleb said, "Good afternoon, Mr. President. I trust you're doing well. This is Mary Ann. She's part of security."

President Harrison sniffled. "Don't think we've met."

Mary Ann said, "We have now."

"That's true," President Harrison conceded. "What can I do for you?"

"I need money."

President Harrison coughed a rasping cough. "How much do you need?"

"Couple of hundred will do."

"Got a pen?" President Harrison asked as he reached for a draft.

Mary Ann discovered that it was possible to bypass the cabinet, but then the president came down with pneumonia. He suffered a relapse and died after being in office for about four weeks.

John Tyler, the vice president, became president. President Tyler kept Daniel Webster on as his secretary of state but replaced his secretary of war. He gave the job to John Spencer. Mary Ann was pleased because John was an old friend.

Secretary of War Spencer and his Whig colleagues tried a different approach to solving the Florida Indian problem. They tried bribery. They gave $5,000 to every Seminole chief who brought in a band of sixty. Lesser chiefs got $200 and every warrior got $30 and a new rifle. A one way trip to the west was thrown in as part of the bargain.

Over four hundred Indians trooped into Fort Brooke, collected their bribes, and went west. General Jessup, a good Democrat, was recalled and replaced with Colonel William Worth, a good Whig. Colonel Worth took on the job with three goals: (1) reduce costs, (2) end the war, and (3) put the remaining Seminoles on the reservation south of the Peace River Boundary.

Colonel Worth stopped giving rations to the refugees. Then Colonel Worth dismissed the militia and sent them home. The federal government had paid out over three and a half million dollars since the beginning of the war. That ended.

Then Colonel Worth took on the war. He had about five thousand regular army troops in Florida but most of them were holed up in their forts and stockades. He ordered them out to round up the Indians. Several claimed they were sick and rushed to seek refuge in the hospitals.

Colonel Worth solved the problem by closing the hospitals. He claimed the malcontents were suffering from a lack of excitement and their sedentary lifestyle. That being the case, the men were sent into the swamps to round up the Indians. Some of the Indians moved deeper into the swamps and lakes of the interior.

Hundreds of disgruntled Florida residents were deprived of their salaries, rations, and handouts. Dozens descended on Tallahassee, complained to the governor, and lobbied the legislature. The *Tallahassee Floridian,* a Democratic newspaper, printed the complaints and distributed the news. The *Albany Argus*, a leading Democratic newspaper and Thurlow Weed's long time competitor, picked up the story and ran a series of articles on the Whig administration's highhanded tactics.

Thurlow Weed, shocked by the competition, called upon his friend John Spencer, Secretary of War. Thurlow told John, "Do something. The Democrats are raising a ruckus."

"What do you want me to do?"

"Close the Tallahassee rag!"

"Can't do that," Secretary Spencer insisted. "News is your problem. You do something."

"What?"

"Start a Whig paper in Florida. Give them some competition."

"But I'm not there."

"You got a man down there. Tell him to start a paper."

"Could do that," Thurlow agreed. "Send him a correspondent's commission, but he'll need a press and printer. How do I do that?"

"We've got a printing setup at Fort Brooke. They're not doing much with it, but we can't print a Whig newspaper on federal property using federal equipment. However, I can put the equipment up as surplus and sell it to your man."

"That'll work."

"But we'll need to cover our tracks," Secretary Spencer insisted. "You'll need to work out some details. I'll talk with Webster."

Secretary Spencer talked with Secretary Webster. Daniel Webster talked with Caleb, and Caleb set up a meeting at the Ambassador's Parlor and Lounge. A week or so later John Spencer, Thurlow Weed, and Caleb stopped at Mary Ann's place.

Mary Ann wasn't that pleased about the arrangement, but politics are politics. She greeted Thurlow and chatted with him. The gentlemen enjoyed tea, coffee, cookies, and conversation while they worked out a deal.

The Fort Brooke printing equipment was declared surplus and put up for sale. The War Department transferred the money required for the purchase of the press to the State Department and the State Department sent a dispatch to their off-the-books Florida asset. Amanda got the dispatch, walked over to the Fort Brooke bursar's office, and cashed a draft enclosed within the dispatch for a stack of sub-treasury bills. That being done, she beckoned Diego.

Diego asked, "What's up?"

"You're starting a newspaper."

"Not me," Diego blurted, "don't read the things."

"I'm not talking about reading. We're talking about buying."

"Can't," Diego claimed. "I don't have any money."

"I've got money." Amanda dropped her stack of sub-treasury bills on the table.

Diego scooped up the bills. "Don't know anything about newspapers."

"You don't have to know anything," Amanda insisted. "Sidney will do the writing and Harry will do the printing. It's been arranged."

"I'll do it for a piece of the action." Diego counted the bills. "I've got expenses."

"So I gather." Amanda pulled a $50 sub-treasury bill from the stack. "We've got to account for expenses.

"Why should I do this?"

"Because I'll kick your butt if you don't."

That settled the matter. Sidney had already received a dispatch from Thurlow Weed, so he was waiting. Diego rented a shack behind the Groggery and purchased the printing equipment. Harry wasn't declared surplus but got sent down as part of the deal.

Sidney received his correspondent's commission, got access to Fort Brooke, and provided with items of crafted information. Harry started printing the *Tampa Weekly Journal*.

Joint army-navy expeditions were sent into the Everglades to secure the hammocks, waterways, and canals. Sailors patrolled the waterways while marines and soldiers set up camps on the hammocks. Indian communities and settlements outside the reserved lands were burned and destroyed.

The combined operation continued until most of the hostile Seminoles were rounded up. The small group left in Florida was restricted to the reserved lands south of the Peace River Boundary. Colonel Worth figured he'd be able to keep these Indians on the reservation and enforce the peace agreement with three regiments. The war was over.

Washington welcomed the news. Hundreds of men were discharged and dumped on the streets of Tampa Town. Most officers were sent to new assignments, but Major

Cotesworth was left in charge of the token force remaining at Fort Brooke.

Harry printed the *Weekly Journal.*

CHAPTER TWELVE

Troubled Times

Tampa
May 1842 through September 1845

Captain McRea stomped into the Tampa *Weekly Journal* office late one afternoon, yanked out a chair, and helped himself to one of Sidney's cigars. He lit the cigar and puffed on it before saying, "Everything's going to hell!"

Sidney asked, "What's the problem?"

"The wife," Captain McRae grumbled. "She's been on my back since the war ended."

"Didn't know you were married?"

"Sure am, for about twenty years now, seems longer."

"Where's the wife?"

"Running the business in Key West," Captain McRae replied. "Sells stuff in her store, keeps the books, and cuts a few deals on the side."

"Other than being married, what's the problem?"

"Money," Captain McRae insisted. "The army left me high and dry when they pulled up stakes and moved out."

"What's that got to do with being married?"

"Told you," Captain McRea replied, "the wife. She's threatening to come with me to see why I'm not making more money."

"You're hauling cows so what's her problem."

"Not making anything," McRea complained. "Still getting a hefty price for cows but not making anything when I get back. Cuban merchants have upped their prices for everything I buy in Havana and nobody wants to pay a halfway decent price for anything after I get back here."

"That's how it is," Sidney suggested. "Business has gone downhill for everyone since the war ended. Guess we gotta make do with what we got."

Diego came in from the press room, grabbed a chair, and sat down. "Been hearing what you been saying. I can help."

"How," Captain McRae asked.

"Like my old dog business," Diego explained. "You gotta get people to want what they think you got. Set a price and cut a deal. That's how it works."

Captain McRae grumbled, "What's that got to do with anything."

"I've been watching," Diego continued. "The prices for what you got start dropping as soon as you get here. Everybody knows you've got to sell your stuff before you can load the cows. They just wait until you drop your price. That's when they buy your stuff."

Captain McRae said, "So."

"Keep the price up," Diego insisted.

"How can I do that when I'm not here," Captain McRae demanded.

'I'm here," Diego suggested. "I'll rent the army storage shed by the bay and buy your stuff as soon as you get here. I'll sell if after you leave. We'll both make money."

Captain McRea asked Sidney, "What do you think?"

Sidney said, "Might work."

Diego negotiated a deal with Major Cotesworth and took possession of the storage shed. Then he set up his store. Captain McRea went back to making regular runs between Tampa Bay, Key West, and Havana. Diego cut a few deals with the Spanish fishermen living nearby and made a few arrangements with the settlers. Then he got Diggory to help at the store. One way or another, Diego made a profit.

Otherwise, not much was happening. Harry printed the paper and took notice when he received a legal notice about the pending militia reorganization. The Tallahassee politicians were petitioning congress for admission to the Union as a state. The territory needed to comply with a number of requirements and one was reorganizing the old territorial militia to comply with the terms and conditions of the Federal Militia Act.

The legislature was offering a stipend and rations as an inducement for enlistment. Harry read the notice, printed it, and decided to take advantage of the opportunity. Sidney didn't pay much of a salary and he could use the rations.

When enlistment day arrived, Harry put on a new hat and strolled over to the Groggery. Being first man on the porch, he staked out a claim on the bench by the door. Jake Sutherland, the cow catcher, and Rube Riley, Jake's foreman, strolled over.

Jake asked, "Signing up?"

"Sure am," Harry replied, "figured I'd get a story for the paper."

"Came for rations," Jake announced. "We're not making anything with cow catching. Rube and I figure we'll sign up the rest of the gang after we get in. Maybe get a bonus or something."

"Run our own company," Rube insisted. "I'm not puttin' up with another Yankee runt strutting around, telling me what I got to do. No sirree! Not again!"

Harry didn't mention his background. He had shed his upstate New York origin somewhere along the way. Everyone in Florida had come from somewhere else, being considered a Florida native had its advantages.

Sixteen men showed up over the course of the next hour. They waited for the recruiter and finally, a much leaner and somewhat meaner Colonel Beauregard Bemrose limped through the swinging doors. Gold eagles were clipped to the collar of his shirt. The pallor and protruding gut of the dog days were gone. Beauregard had picked up a stiff leg and pronounced limp along the way but had obviously survived his years of decoy duty in the swamps of central and southern Florida.

"Sumabitch," Bemrose grumbled as he looked at the men on the porch. "About time you got here. I've been waiting inside fer a good half hour, but none of you people had sense enough to come in and tell me ya were here."

Jake said, "Nobody told us."

"You should have knowed enough." Beauregard stuck out his chest. "I'm Colonel Beauregard Bemrose. I'm a ring-tailed wild cat and half an alligator. Don't you forget it? I got sent down here to sign you fellows up and swear you in. That's what I'm gonna do."

Harry recognized Colonel Bemrose but didn't say anything. Nobody else did either. Bemrose fumbled around with hand in his trousers while he grumbled, "Got a piece of cigar here, someplace."

Nobody said anything. Colonel Bemrose cussed, "Dammit it! Thought I had it there fer a minute but got something else."

A few boys snickered. Bemrose pulled a bent cigar out of one pocket and tried to straighten it. He glowered at his malefactors. "What are you boys laughin' at?"

"Nothing," one replied.

"Nothing aint no laughin' matter," Bemrose growled as he fumbled around in his other pocket. "Oh, what the hell!" he grumbled. He limped toward the swinging doors before turning to say, "Stay where you are and wait. I'll be back." Bemrose limped off.

Rube muttered, "I remember him. We pulled him from under a log in the Ahapopka swamp."

Jake asked, "Doing what?"

"Getting ambushed," Rube replied. "Bemrose ran his boys right into an Injun setup. A lot of his boys didn't make it. Old Bemrose was hiding under a log when we got there. The Indians shot him in the ass, but it didn't improve his attitude."

"That's why he's limping?" Jake suggested.

"Probably," Rube replied, "didn't reckon I'd ever see him again."

Colonel Bemrose limped back out on the porch followed by Brinton Hooker, the Groggery owner. The colonel appeared to be in a better mood as he was now puffing on a cigar and lugging a mug of tonic. Colonel Bemrose surveyed the band of recruits and drew a few puffs on his cigar. He took the cigar out of his mouth and waved it around as he told Brinton, "This all you could dig up?"

"Guess so," Brinton replied.

"They told me you'd be raisin' a company."

"This is what you got," Brinton replied. "We'll get more after we get going."

"If this is what you got, it'll have to do." Bemrose drained his mug and handed it to Brinton before shouting, "On your feet, boys! Don't sit there. Get up and raise your right hand. This is it. I'm swearing you in."

The men jumped up, raised their right hands, and promised to defend Florida and do whatever else they were told. That being done, Colonel Bemrose grumbled, "Pick out your officers. You gotta have a captain, a lieutenant, a sergeant, and a corporal. I'll be inside." The assignment being given, Bemrose grabbed his empty mug and limped back between the swinging doors.

As Brinton owned the Groggery, he called the meeting to order and was duly elected captain. Carey Hayes, the cart man, had brought seven bullwhackers with him, so he got eight votes to become lieutenant. As Harry had been a sergeant in the army, he was elected sergeant. Jake Sutherland only brought Rube, so he ended up as corporal. Bemrose came back with a filled mug and surveyed the company before asking, "Get it done?"

Brinton snapped to attention. "I'm captain. Carey's my lieutenant and Harry's my sergeant."

Colonel Bemrose limped over to take a look at Harry. "Sumabitch, boy; I know you from someplace."

Believing a continuation of their original encounter might complicate matters, Harry said, "No, sir. Don't believe so."

"Maybe not, but ya look familiar." Bemrose shook his head as he stepped back to take another look at the company. "You fellows only got about a half a company here, but I guess half is better than nothing."

90

"We'll get more," Brinton promised. "Do you have any orders?"

Colonel Bemrose looked a bit perplexed. He drained his mug and waved it around before announcing, "Bigger mugs! We gotta have bigger mugs. That's it. I've been draining this one a good half dozen times and it aint done me nothing. That's your order. Get bigger mugs."

The troops whooped and hollered, "Bigger mugs." Bemrose led the way into the taproom and the troops followed. Colonel Beauregard Bemrose drank several tonics while he entertained the half company with exciting tales of his exploits on the grasslands and in the swamps of the territory during the Indian war. Nobody mentioned dogs or Lake Ahapopka.

Over thirteen hundred settlers from states to the north took advantage of the Armed Occupation Act and came to central Florida over the course of the next year. Some moved into the area around the headwaters of the Peace River. The army wanted this land occupied to keep the Indians on south side of the Peace River Boundary. Southwestern Florida was becoming absolutely crowded by pioneer standards.

A twenty mile strip of land west of the Peace River and as far north as Ahapopka Creek was maintained as a buffer between the settlers and the Seminole. President Tyler brought Texas into the union, served out his term, and was replaced by James Polk, a former congressman and governor of Tennessee. Florida was brought into the Union as the twenty-seventh state on March 3, 1845. President James Polk was inaugurated as the eleventh president the next day.

It took a couple of weeks for the news of these events to reach Tampa Town but most residents didn't much care, one way or another. State politics were not a burning concern and federal politics didn't much matter so long as the Seminole stayed on their side of the Peace River boundary. The cattle business and trade with Key West and Havana were more significant.

President Polk won the election with the slogan "Fifty four forty or fight!" He picked James Buchanan, the bachelor senator from Pennsylvania, for his Secretary of State and selected Bill Marcy, a senator and former governor of New York, to be his Secretary of War. That being done, President Polk started the Mexican War.

CHAPTER THIRTEEN

Nature's Fury

Tampa Town
October 1845 through early September 1848

Texas and Mexico disagreed on the border. Texas believed the Nueces River was the border, but Mexico considered Texas a breakaway province and didn't believe there was a border. Then the United States complicated the situation by annexing Texas.

Mexico appeared to accept the annexation so long as the Nueces River became the border between the two countries. President Polk disagreed. He ordered General Taylor to hold all the land north of the Rio Grande. General Taylor told General Worth to take his troops across the Nueces to establish a border at the Rio Grande.

The Mexican government protested this incursion and moved their troops up to confront the invaders. An armed engagement followed. The Americans claimed they were defending American soil, but the Mexicans knew they were defending Mexican soil. Congress declared war.

The federal government increased the army from 6,000 men to over 115,000 men. Major Cotesworth was promoted to Colonel and rushed to New Orleans to command an infantry regiment. Colonel Johnston came to Tampa to reactivate Fort Brooke and turn it into a supply depot and major embarkation point. Prosperity came back to Tampa Town.

The Mexican War continued for about two years until the Americans seized Mexico City and dictated the terms of the Treaty of Guadalupe Hidalgo, a treaty of everlasting peace, friendship, and tranquility between the United States and Mexico. After Mexico agreed to the terms of the treaty and gave up half of Mexico, some in the federal administration decided to explore other Latin American and Caribbean options.

Cuba was the closest option. It had fertile soil and a slave economy. The United States, the world champion of black servitude, could bring Cuba into the Union as another Slave state. This would help maintain the balance between Slave and Free states in the senate. Spain possessed the island but that wasn't considered a problem. Robert Johnson, the United States consul in Havana, sent Secretary of State Buchanan a dispatch telling him that the island was a likely prospect for acquisition. Cora, the Havana asset, agreed.

Secretary of State Buchanan set up an off-the-record meeting at Fort Brooke to consider options for the seizure, annexation, or purchase of Cuba. Diego figured something was amiss when the *USS Erie* sailed into the Tampa Town harbor late one afternoon, tied up at the pier, and dropped off Robert Johnson. Then, the *USRC Taney*, a federal revenue cutter, arrived on the scene and tied up behind the *Erie*. Having one of these ships in the harbor was unusual; having both was extraordinary.

Jefferson Davis, the hero of the Battle of Buena Vista, now a United States Senator from Mississippi, got off the cutter with General Quitman, and they swaggered up the road to the Eagle's Nest. John O'Donnell, a New York newspaper man, left the cutter somewhat later, and made a beeline to the Groggery for a drink. Then he walked up to the Eagle's Nest. Diego rushed out. "What's up?"

"Not much," John answered as he continued on his way. A somewhat upscale fishing smack, the *Chabella Fomosa*, arrived as it was getting dark. Diego stood on the pier and watched Jose Diaz, a leading Havana Creole, step off the smack followed by Cora, the asset. Three gentlemen tagged behind. One happened to be a former Spanish army officer, Narisco Lopez. They gathered at the Eagle's Nest.

Diego scurried to the club to confer with the servants. They couldn't tell him anything. Hector ignored him. Amanda

94

listened but shrugged her shoulders. "They're sportsmen and we're a sporting club."

The guests left a couple of days later. The ships sailed away and nothing happened. Diego shipped off a few dispatches on a fishing smack and scurried about. He appeared agitated, but nobody else cared.

Senator Davis, General Quitman, John O'Donnell, and the three Cuban gentlemen rode back to Washington on the *Taney* and met with President Polk to lay out the scenario for a possible Cuban insurrection. President Polk heard them out before asking them to hold off their plans while he pursued options for buying the island.

The *Taney* took the Cuban gentlemen back to Key West. Then they caught a ride to Havana on a fishing smack. As Spanish officials had somehow heard about them and their meetings, officials were waiting in Havana. The officials seized two gentlemen, but Narisco escaped.

When Narisco appeared in Rhode Island about a month later, the Spanish officials sentenced him to death in absentia. Very few people in Tampa Town knew anything about the activities taking place in Havana and probably, most wouldn't have cared if they did. Jake was catching cows. Captain McRae was taking the cows to Key West and Havana. He was bringing back merchandise for Diego and an occasional dispatch for Amanda.

August of '48 was hot and humid with showers. September was hotter, but that was the norm. A phosphorescent glow pulsed across the western horizon one evening, but nobody thought much about it. Intermittent winds gusted from the south when Diego stepped out of the Eagle's Nest the next morning.

Low dark clouds raced across the sky. Rain, whipped by wind gusts, started falling. The roar of crashing surf caught Diego's attention as he walked down the ridge to the harbor. Having grown up on Cuba, he was familiar with the storms of summer. The Spanish word was *huracan*. The English word was hurricane. The storms were the same.

Wind rattled the trees. Diego trudged on his way. Waves, as high as a man, were crashing against the shore. Water plunged over the pier, flowing off the sides as it receded. Men were trying to secure a coastal schooner. Spanish fishermen were dashing around.

A squall knocked Diego off balance. He twisted around to regain his stance, tasting salt on his lips. Diego struggled to catch his breath. He pushed into the wind to get to the newspaper office. Forcing the door open, he stumbled inside, and pulled the door shut. Sidney and Harry were printing the *Journal*. Diego yelled, "Get out!"

"What," Sidney asked.

"It's coming," Diego shouted.

"What are you talking about?"

"*Huracan*," Diego shouted. "It's a hurricane. Get out of here. Get to high ground."

A sudden blast rattled the building. "Maybe so," Sidney replied. "Where do we find high ground?"

"Eagle's Nest," Diego shouted as he slammed his body against the door, forcing it open, stumbling into the storm. Harry and Sidney followed Diego out the door and up the ridge. Horizontal sheets of water pelted them. Hector and the slaves were nailing on the last of the storm shutters as the men stumbled into the club. The slaves followed. Diego pulled the door shut and barred it.

Roslyn rushed out of her room. "What's going on?"

"Hurricane," Diego shouted over the sound of the wind driven rain pelting the building. "We've got to wait out the storm."

Nicole emerged from her room. "What storm?"

"Hurricane," Sidney said. "It's bad out there."

"Sounds like it.' Nicole settled on the sofa.

The wind roared, rumbled, and howled. Objects pounded the walls. A sudden crash shook the building. Roslyn screamed. Amanda gasped. "What's that?"

"Something big," Diego shouted. "Maybe a tree, but we're standing."

Roslyn sobbed. "You wanted those trees."

"Done in by a tree," Nicole muttered. "What a way to go."

Pounding, screeching, incessant sound drowned out everything. The wind stopped but returned with a vengeance. Water shot under the door and around the edges. Beams groaned and cracked but held. The wind eased off later that afternoon. Diego opened the door to find the porch crushed by a cypress.

There was a light rain. Water stood around. A storm surge receded down the ridge, back to the bay. Water was carrying broken trees, remnants of buildings, dead horses, an ox cart, and portions of the stockade. The storm surge had come up the ridge and over the porch. It seeped under the door, must have been fifteen or sixteen feet high.

Sidney gasped, "Oh, my God!"

Amanda pushed by Diego and Sidney. She stepped onto the wreckage of the porch to survey the devastation. One look was enough. Amanda said, "That's it! We're out of here!"

Diego led the way out of the club and down the road to what was left of the harbor. Sidney and Harry tagged behind. Stockade walls were blown asunder, demolished, and destroyed. Cypress trees and oaks were torn up, broken, and smashed. Debris littered the roadway. Battered soldiers crawled from the wreckage. They stumbled and blundered about.

Tampa Town was gone. The pier was gone. A wrecked fishing smack was stacked on the debris where the Groggery had once stood. Harry made his way over piles of trash and timbers. He started digging in the refuse searching for his press. He couldn't find anything. The press and type were gone.

Sidney asked, "What do we do?"

"Clean up," Diego replied.

It took several days to sort out trash and debris. Some people were missing and never found. The *Highland Princess* sailed into the harbor a few days later, anchored in the deep water of the bay, and Captain McRae rowed ashore. "Looks like you got the hurricane."

"Sure did," Sidney replied. "The girls and I want a ride to Key West. Harry's in the militia, so he's gotta stay and help pick up."

Harry would just as soon have gone along, but he was part of the militia. The militia had to hold the fort.

Captain McRae got Bill Simon, his mate, to help. They loaded the women, their slaves, Diego, and Sidney on the brig. That being done, they sailed away.

CHAPTER FOURTEEN

Gentlemen of Leisure

Washington City
September 1848

James Buchanan, President Polk's secretary of state, was an amiable sort of man. He usually spent an hour or so most mornings tending to the affairs of state. Then he strolled up Pennsylvania Avenue, stopped private citizens along the way, chatted with them about public issues, and enthralled them with the attentive tilt of his head.

Secretary Buchanan was near-sighted in one eye and far-sighted in the other. This allowed him to see both sides of most issues while appearing to agree with whatever point of view being expressed. Completing his official duties for the day, Secretary Buchanan sauntered over to 329 Maryland Avenue. He spent most afternoons taking his leisure seated in his favorite leather chair in the side parlor at Mary Ann's *Parlor and Lounge.*

Senator Lewis Cass was a sometimes companion. On this particular afternoon, the two gentlemen sat next to each other in twin leather chairs. Secretary Buchanan took a dispatch off the stack on the table between the chairs, read it, and handed it to Senator Cass. Secretary Buchanan was working his way through the dispatches in short order, but Senator Cass was taking his time. After all, Senator Cass had the world at his finger tips. He had locked up the Democratic nomination for president and favored to win the election.

Mary Ann brought in a tray of scones. She put the tray on the table between the two gentlemen and sat down on the straight chair next to the door. Secretary Buchanan reached for a scone. "This all you got."

"Come on, Buck," Mary Ann snapped. "I've brought you a pot of coffee, broke out a box of cigars, and baked a dozen scones. What more can you want?"

"Cuba," Senator Cass intoned, "Cuba on a tray. That's what I want."

"Dispatches," Secretary Buchanan asserted. "Don't you have anymore?"

"That's it," Mary Ann replied. "Cora's on top of things in Havana but we're not getting her dispatches in a timely fashion. She sends them to Tampa on a cow boat, and our Tampa assets send them to Key West. Sometimes they miss the dispatch boat and the assets get delayed on Key West. Sometimes, they get lost. It's a problem."

"Tampa's off the track," Senator Cass insisted. "Why don't you send them directly to Key West?"

"We don't have anyone on Key West," Mary Ann explained. "Our assets are in Tampa."

"Nothing's happening in Tampa," Senator Cass asserted. "They pretty much closed Fort Brooke. Reposition the assets."

"I'll talk with Caleb," Secretary Buchanan suggested, "get him to reposition the assets, move them to Key West."

"Speaking of Caleb," Senator Cass replied, "where is he? Caleb was supposed to bring a Cuban over. What's his name?"

"Narisco," Mary Ann said, "Narisco Lopez. He got here yesterday."

"Where is he?"

"With Caleb in the billiards room," Mary Ann answered. "I'll get them."

Mary Ann left and came back a few minutes later with Caleb and a short man sporting a big mustache. The man was wearing a military style jacket. Caleb said, "This is Narisco."

Narisco clicked his heels together, stiffened, and stuck out his hand. As Senator Cass stood up to shake Narisco's hand, Caleb said, "Narisco was an officer in the Spanish army, but he's seen the light."

"What light?"

"The glorious beacon of liberty," Narisco replied. "I' m lifting the burden of Spanish oppression from the backs of the people."

Senator Cass asked, "How are you going to do that?"

"Scheduling popular uprisings to coincide with an invasion," Narisco explained.

"How's that gonna happen?"

Caleb explained, "Cora's organizing the opposition, John O'Donnell, the newspaper man, is raising money, and Narisco's raising the army."

"How'd O'Donnell get involved?" Senator Cass asked. "What's his scheme?"

"Complicated," Caleb suggested. "Cora worked for O'Donnell when he published the *New York Review*. He's got family in the Cuba sugar business and owns a tobacco company outside Havana."

Senator Cass said, "So, he's got reasons."

"Sure has," Caleb agreed. "He's put a bunch of money in Cora's Havana Club and opened branches of the club in New York and Boston. We're setting up braches in Baltimore and Philadelphia and started selling bonds."

"Based on what," Senator Cass demanded

"Land," Narisco explained. "Bond holders will be able redeem their bonds for Cuban land after I return the island to the people."

Senator Cass asked, "If investors get the land, what do the people get?"

"Free," Narisco replied.

"Free of their land," Senator Cass suggested. "Guess I don't want to know much more about these shenanigans."

"Nobody will know anything," Caleb assured Senator Cass. "We're keeping it under wraps."

"Make certain you do," Senator Cass insisted.

Secretary Buchanan said, "It's a private matter, more of a humanitarian venture."

"Precisely," Caleb agreed.

Senator Cass asked Narisco, "So what are you doing?"

Narisco said, "I've raised a regiment of volunteers in New York and am raising another in New Orleans. We'll rendezvous on Key West and go to Cuba to restore order after the insurrection."

"Public safety sort of thing," Caleb suggested.

"It is," Narisco agreed. "Thousands will rush into the streets to join us. We'll support them and set up a governing council."

Senator Cass asked, "What do you want from us?"

"Approval for our rendezvous," Narisco suggested, "and support to get to Cuba."

"What kind of support? What are you talking about?"

"Gunboat or maybe, couple of frigates," Narisco suggested. "Station them along the way."

"Naval escort," Senator Cass grumbled. "Don't know about that."

"Might be a few problems," Secretary Buchanan claimed, "but we'll see what we can do."

"Diplomatic recognition," Narisco added, "with humanitarian assistance."

Senator Cass grumbled, "What are we getting?"

"Cuba," Narisco asserted. "I'll request immediate annexation after I've stabilized the population, but there are provisions."

"What provisions?"

"Citizenship for nationals upon annexation and guaranteed property rights, the same with Mexico," Narisco replied. "It's reasonable."

"Reasonable," Senator Cass replied. "And what do you expect to get out of this?"

"Adequate compensation," Narisco insisted. "Million or so in gold should suffice."

It was quiet. Mary Ann asked, "When is this supposed to take place?"

Secretary Buchanan suggested, "After the election."

"After the inauguration," Senator Cass insisted. "I don't know if I'm going to be elected, but if I am, I don't want something coming down if I'm not in any position to do anything about it."

"Makes sense," Secretary Buchanan replied. "Nothing happens until after we get the ducks lined up."

"Ducks," Narisco agreed.

Mary Ann asked, "Anything else?"

"That's it," Narisco replied

Senator Cass shifted in his chair. He asked Secretary Buchanan, "Where does Polk stand on this?"

"Polk's on board," Secretary Buchanan assured Senator Cass. "He just wants us to hold off until after he's out of office."

"And ducks are lined up," Narisco suggested.

Senator Cass ignored Narisco to ask Secretary Buchanan, "What about England and France?"

Secretary Buchanan answered, "We're at peace with both although I believe that England and France have their own aspirations. They've moved some of their operatives to the area."

Senator Cass said, "Sounds risky."

"Not so risky," Narisco insisted, "Maybe I should talk with the British. Lord Renfrew's on Key West. He's willing to take risks.'

"No need for that," Senator Cass growled. "We're with you on this. Just gotta take our time and be careful, that's all."

Secretary Buchanan told Narisco, "Wait until we're ready. Don't rile the waters."

"Won't do that," Narisco agreed. "I'll wait."

Secretary Buchanan said, "Well, that oughta cover it. Thanks for stopping over. We'll take it from here."

Caleb said, "Gotta be running. I'll keep everyone informed."

"Do that," Senator Cass replied. "Keep it quiet. I don't want to read about it in the Whig papers."

Mary Ann left with Caleb and Narisco. She came back as Senator Cass grumbled, "That scoundrel tried to threaten us. He said he was going to talk to the English."

"Talk, that's all" Secretary Buchanan replied. "We're just using him to put a little pressure on the Spanish authorities. We've got a carrot; he's our stick."

Mary Ann asked, 'What's the carrot?'

Secretary Buchanan said, "Cora's cut a deal with the Cuban Creoles. They've offered us a hundred million to buy the island. If we can get Spain to sell it to us, we'll get the island and keep their money. We're using Narisco to put a little pressure on Spain so they'll go along with the deal. It's a replay of our old Florida scheme.

Mary Ann asked, "What happens to Narisco?"

Secretary Buchanan said, "Who knows."

"Never heard of him," Senator Cass insisted. "What about Renfrew? What's he doing on Key West?

"Don't know," Secretary Buchanan admitted. "I'll get someone on it."

CHAPTER FIFTEEN

Jacaranda Club

Key West
October 1848 through June 1849

The *Highland Princess* was a mess but Amanda didn't complain. She wanted to get out of Tampa and was willing to settle for anything. Captain McRae was even softened a bit by their plight. He helped Amanda and the girls aboard the brig and took them down to his cabin. He told them, "You'll have to stay over with the wife for a few days when we get to Key West."

"What wife," Amanda demanded.

"My wife," Captain McRae replied.

"Didn't know you were married," Amanda muttered.

"A good twenty years now," Captain McRae replied. "We got a couple of about grown kids. Isobel runs our store and keeps the books."

"She's a business woman," Amanda noted. "We should get along."

"She is," Captain McRae agreed. "But she's in a different line of work than you folks."

"Business is business," Amanda insisted. She stepped aside to make room for Roslyn and Nicole as they lugged a crate of clothing and personal items aboard the brig.

Roslyn grumbled, "Not much room."

Amanda said, "We'll manage."

"Expect so." Captain McRae left the girls to work out their own arrangements. He went on deck, issued orders to Simon, his mate. Simon relayed the orders to the three man crew and the *Highland Princess* got underway, coming about, and heading for Key West.

Isobel McRae was waiting on the pier as Captain McRae eased his brig up to his usual mooring spot. Isobel glanced at the empty deck before complaining, "Where are the cows?"

"Couldn't get any," Captain McRae explained. "A hurricane wiped out Tampa Town. There aint nothing left."

"I've got buyers," Isobel insisted. "You gotta go back."

"They'll have to wait," Captain McRae grumbled. "I brought some people with me and we gotta find a place for them."

Amanda, Nicole, and Roslyn appeared on deck followed by Diego and Sidney. Isobel checked out the group before asking, "Anymore?"

"Four slaves," Captain McRae replied. "The rest are cleaning up. I told ya the place is a mess."

Isobel shrugged her shoulders but suggested, "We've got room in the loft above the store. The women can camp out there until they get established."

Isobel took them to the two story wooden building on Front Street that housed the McRae Market. The market with its attendant warehouse and cattle stockade constituted her business enterprise. Captain McRae kept the business alive by hauling in cows from Florida and merchandise from Havana. Isobel sold the cows to the Bahamans who ran a local slaughter house and marketed her merchandise while she tried to manage Sarah, her fifteen year old daughter, and Angus, her thirteen year old son.

Sarah was not a homebody. She knew her way around Key West, greeted the incoming ships as they tied up at the piers, frequented the ethnic neighborhoods on the island, and spent most of her time out and about, enjoying the attractions of Key West. The small city, largest in Florida, was perched on a coral island about a hundred miles south of the Florida mainland. It was the crossroads of the Caribbean.

About three thousand people lived on the island. Most earned their livelihood by trade, smuggling, piracy, and ship-wrecking. Others worked in the shops, taverns, and bawdy houses along Front Street. Sarah frequented the shops, visited the taverns, and spent some time contemplating the traffic flowing in and out of the bawdy houses.

Being interested in such matters, Sarah took an active interest in the women who moved into the loft above her mother's store. Nicole turned out to be a kindred spirit. As they got to know each other, Sarah took Nicole on outings to show her the island. They chatted with sailors on Tift's Wharf, struck up conversations with painted ladies behind the bawdy houses, walked by the Watlington House, toured Jungletown, and visited an old Haitian Voodoo Lady on Petronia Street.

The Voodoo Lady took an interest in Nicole. The Lady held Nicole's hands in her hand and gazed into Nicole's eyes as she proclaimed, "You have an ancient soul. It harbors secrets from the distant past and will champion your quest for riches."

"Not that old," Nicole protested.

"Be that as it may," the Voodoo Lady replied. "Your incarnation is but a manifestation of the eternal. The essence of eternal mystique descends through the maternal lineage."

"Grandmother raised me if that's what you mean," Nicole suggested. "Maybe that's got something to do with it."

"Your mother's mother," the Voodoo Lady insisted. "The essence descends from mother to daughter, generation to generation. It's our precious fountain of eternal wisdom. What do you know of your grandmother's mother?"

"She was Abenaki," Nicole revealed. "I never knew her. Grandmother said her father was a Frenchman."

"Such is immaterial," the Voodoo Lady claimed. "Your mother, your grandmother, and your great grandmother manifested the spirit."

"Probably," Nicole agreed. "I'm here."

Sarah laughed. They left the Voodoo shop and continued on their journey. They explored the African Cemetery, watched a funeral procession, broke through a mangrove thicket, and came out on the beach. The women walked along the beach until they came to a weatherworn mahogany log.

Nicole sat on the log and gazed at the sea. She said, "This would be a perfect place for an assignation."

Sarah asked, "What's that?

"It's a secret meeting."

"Just us," Sarah replied.

"Just us," Nicole agreed. "Sit on the log. Try it."

Sarah did as she asked, "Was your grandmother an Indian?"

"About half," Nicole replied. "Her mother was Abenaki. My grandmother's father, my great grandfather, was a Frenchman from Quebec."

"You're a French Indian."

"I guess," Nicole agreed. "Mostly French though. My grandfather and great grandfather were French. Father might have been."

Sarah said, "My parents are from Scotland so that makes me a Scot. I guess that's good."

"A Key West Scot, but you're probably more Key West than Scot. That's how it goes. I've worked with a lot of people and they're about the same."

"Men," Sarah suggested.

"Mostly men," Nicole agreed.

"Than you're a fallen woman," Sarah asserted. "That's what mom said."

"Fallen from what," Nicole blurted. "I'm an independent woman, if that's what you mean. I do my own thing."

"With men," Sarah suggested.

"Sometimes," Nicole admitted, "part of what I do."

"Wow," Sarah replied, "that's interesting."

"But there's more to it," Nicole insisted. "I maintain financial records, manage accounts, redeem banknotes, and do a whole lot of other things."

"With men," Sarah persisted.

"Sometimes," Nicole repeated. "Let's talk about something else."

Sarah shrugged her shoulders before glancing at the sun, now over the water. "It's getting late. We'd better go."

"Sure enough," Nicole replied. She slid off the log and they made their way down the beach, through the cemetery, into the street, and back to the McRae Merchandise Market.

The dispatch came the next day. Amanda was directed to (1) close the Tampa club (2) relocate to Key West, (3) open a new club, (4) Collect information on events transpiring in Cuba, and (5) wait for the next dispatch. Nicole said, "Guess we're going back to work."

"Guess so," Amanda replied as she hustled off to confer with Isobel about business opportunities on the island.

Isobel heard her out before saying, "I don't know much about selling what you're selling. We already got a bunch of places on Front Street."

"We serve a more discrete clientele," Amanda insisted. "We only entertain gentlemen of distinction."

"Aint many fancy fellows on the island,'" Isobel claimed. "You can set up a hoity-toity place if you want, but it'll cost a bunch."

"No problem," Amanda replied. "We're on assignment."

The next dispatch conferred their status. Mary Ann was pleased they were on the island and explained that funds would be transferred through the Navy Department. The Navy would be funding an import-export contract with Sidney Benson and the contract would fund their club and other assets on the island. They were directed to do four things: (1) form an import/export company, (2) purchase a facility, (3) open the club, and (4) wait for further orders.

Sidney said, "Let's do it."

Forming the import/export company was easy. Diego found an empty office on the corner of Front and Duval Streets, and Sidney drew up the contract. It took Commodore Perkins awhile to figure out why he needed the contract, but he signed it when the money came. That being done, Amanda and Sidney started searching for a site for their gentleman's club. Diego checked with a few acquaintances in the Cuban community and came up with a two story house on Caroline Street.

Sidney took Amanda, Nicole, and Roslyn over to check it out. Sarah tagged along. Amanda liked the house. It was close to downtown but situated on a side street where gentlemen could come and go. Moreover, tropical foliage grew in front of the house and along the sides. This would shield the gentlemen as they walked up the walkway leading to the front porch. Jacaranda trees grew around the house.

Amanda looked at the trees. "I'm calling it the Jacaranda Club."

"Nice name," Sidney said. "I've gotta have a name for the import/export company so I'll call it the Jacaranda Company."

"That'll work," Amanda agreed. "We'll support each other."

Sidney took them on a tour of the house. French doors opened into a spacious front parlor where a grand stairway led to the second floor. There was a small library on the left and a dining room on the right. Amanda loved the parlor. Roslyn pranced up and down the stairs. "This is great. It's elegant. I love it."

Money flowed to the Navy Base and from the Navy Base to Sidney Benson. Sidney gave Diego some money, and Diego bought the property.

Amanda moved to the house, and Diego took the girls shopping. They purchased chairs, tables, bedsteads, and sofas from the warehouses and shops along Front Street but Nicole couldn't find another couch.

Roslyn said, "Get something else."

"I liked my couch."

Diego said, "I'll get one in Havana."

Diego ordered the couch and the girls opened the club.

CHAPTER SIXTEEN

Swamp and Overflowed Lands Act

Washington City
July 1849 through November 1850

The 1848 presidential election didn't go as planned. Martin Van Buren, the former president, entered the fray as a candidate for a third party called the Free Soil Party. Martin didn't get elected but took enough votes from Cass and the Democrats to throw the election to Zachary Taylor and Whigs.

The outcome caught everyone by surprise, especially General Taylor. When General Taylor received a letter from the United States Senate telling him he had won the election, he refused to accept the letter because it wasn't stamped. He sent it back and this created some consternation. The senate finally sent a messenger to tell General Taylor that he had won the election.

General Taylor accepted the decision by resigning his military commission. He left Baton Rouge, traveled up the Mississippi and Ohio on several steamboats, and got to Wheeling in the middle of a snowstorm. He traveled overland by sleigh to Pittsburg where he caught a coach to Cumberland, Maryland. Then he took a train to Baltimore and on to Washington, getting to Washington on February 25, 1849.

Dozens of office seekers and onlookers rushed to greet the new president. Most were disappointed. One observer described General Taylor as being, "plain and undistinguished at best." Another said, "He looks like an old farmer hauling a load of hay to market."

Mary Ann was dismayed but recovered her composure when President Taylor selected John Clayton as his secretary of state. John was a senator and old friend from Delaware. He would do.

President Taylor was inaugurated on March 4, 1849. The new president then threw the political establishment into turmoil by urging the residents of New Mexico and California to draft state constitutions and set up state governments without going through the traditional congressional oversight and approval process. California drafted a constitution prohibiting slavery.

The South was appalled. John Calhoun, representing South Carolina in the United States Senate, convened a southern caucus to oppose the initiative and filed a letter of protest. President Taylor ignored the letter while California adopted its constitution and set up its state government. This was done without any congressional oversight, review, or approval.

Senator Calhoun and his South Carolina colleagues threatened secession, but President Taylor told them, "I'll lead the army against you and hang you quicker than I hanged the deserters and spies that I caught in Mexico."

The South believed that the Mexican War had been fought to maintain the balance between the Free and Slave states by bringing more Slave states into the Union. The North rejected this position and accused the south of attacking the spirit of compromise that had long sustained the Union. Chaos loomed but President Taylor stuck to his guns.

Secretary Clayton sought assistance to fashion an equitable solution. Secretary Clayton, Buck Buchanan, Senator Webster, and Senator Clay met one afternoon in the side parlor at 329 Maryland Avenue to discuss the issue. Buchanan was off the federal payroll but managed to retain his favorite leather chair.

Secretary Clayton started the meeting. "The California fiasco has stirred up a bunch of problems and we gotta find a fix."

"Astute observation," Senator Webster suggested. "What about Texas? They're threatening war with New Mexico."

"That's a problem," Secretary Clayton agreed. "It goes back to the land we picked up. New Mexico and California pretty much ran their own business when they were part of Mexico, so the president figured they could just keep on running their business. They wanta come into the Union as Free States, but the South wants them admitted as Slave States."

"Mexico already abolished slavery," Senator Clay pointed out. "New Mexico and California were Free. You're not going to get them to change their minds."

"Don't forget Deseret," Buck Buchanan warned. "The Mormons want to come in as a separate state and bring all their wives with them."

"So I hear," Secretary Clayton conceded.

Senator Clay insisted, "It'll take a bunch of compromises to address these issues. We've got to give the South something to get them to go along with anything, and we've got to deal with President Taylor. I hear he's pretty adamant on this thing."

"Pretty adamant on most things," Buck insisted. "But there are ways around obstacles. I'd try Caleb Conklin if I were you. He's got a way of doing things."

Senator Webster said, "Sounds like an idea."

Senator Clay cautioned, "Conklin can help but we've got to get a package together. Getting something through the House won't be a problem. We'll pick up enough northern Democrats, Whigs, Free Soil delegates, and American Party votes to offset the southern caucus."

Buck said, "There's the senate."

"That's the problem," Senator Clay agreed. "We'll need at least six Southern votes to get anything through the Senate. Won't be easy, but we'll get it."

The meeting ended and Secretary Clayton put Caleb to work. Secretary Clayton called a follow-up meeting a few days later. Senator Webster, Senator Clay, and Buck were in the side parlor. Senators Downs and Soule from Louisiana came with Senators Clemens and King from Alabama. Senator Calhoun was ailing but came anyway. He brought Vice President Millard Fillmore.

The group waited for Caleb to show up with the Florida delegation. Several minutes passed before Caleb showed up with Jackson Morton and David Yulee. Senator Morton was a Pensacola lumberman and Senator Yulee was an attorney and railroad man from St. Augustine. Mary Ann shut the French doors and the group got down to business.

Secretary Clayton said, "We're close to an agreement. Perhaps Senator Clay can bring us up to date."

"Glad to," Senator Clay insisted. "We've agreed on the main points. We'll be introducing a series of bills that will admit California as a free state, provide Texas with adequate compensation for giving up their New Mexico claim, organize the New Mexico territory without regard for slavery, close down the Washington slave trade while permitting slavery, and pass a law requiring everyone in every state to aid and assist property owners in seizing and returning their runaway slaves."

Senator Webster said, "That'll protect the slave holders and their property rights."

Senator Calhoun conceded, "Everyone gets something."

"Except Florida," Senator Morton protested. "We're not getting anything."

"Getting your slaves back," Senator Clay insisted. "That's something."

"Not a major concern," Senator Morton replied. "Most of us don't own that many slaves. If we do and they go anywhere, they just run into the nearest swamp. Send in the dogs and drag them out. We don't share the common misfortune of bordering a Free State."

Senator Webster asked, "So, what do you want?"

"Special considerations," Senator Morton insisted.

"Perhaps you can be more specific."

114

"We told Caleb," Senator Morton replied. "He can do the talking."

"What's up?"

"Land," Caleb replied.

"What do you mean?"

"Florida's a small state in terms of population but a big one in terms of land, but the federal government owns most of the land."

"Our common affliction," Senator Soule asserted. "Louisiana shares the same misfortune."

Caleb said, "Florida got five hundred thousand acres when it was admitted the Union but federal government kept seventy percent of the land. Although much of this land is under water for all or part of the year, it retains an element of potential value."

"It can be drained, cleared, and sold," Senator Morton insisted. "But we've got to own it before we can develop it."

"What's the problem," Vice President Fillmore grumbled. "Guess I don't know what you follows are talking about."

Some looked askance. Vice President Fillmore didn't spend much time in Washington and it showed.

Senator Webster said, "We can get a package through the house without much of a problem, but we're going to be about six votes shy in the senate. We'll need six Southern votes and it appears we've got to get Florida, Alabama, and Louisiana to go along with us. Otherwise, we're screwed."

Buck suggested, "I'm pretty much out of work, but I guess you fellows will be joining me if you don't work this out and hold the federation together."

"Good God," Mary Ann blurted, "don't have room enough for all of you."

There was laughter before Buck suggested, "So why not trade some worthless swampland for a few votes."

Senator Clay asked Senator Morton, "How much do you want?"

"Much as I can get," Senator Morton replied.

Caleb pointed out, "A considerable portion of the federal land in Florida and a substantial portion of the federal shore lands along the Alabama and Louisiana coast are partially covered with water for much of the year. We can transfer these lands to the respective states with the provision they drain the land and develop it. The land doesn't have any commercial value at present but might have some value after being drained and developed."

"But we'll need enough to make it worthwhile," Senator Morton insisted.

Caleb said, "Florida gets twenty million acres, Alabama gets about eight million, and Louisiana gets eighteen million."

Senator Morton asked, "What do we have to do?"

Senator Clay replied, "Vote to save the federation."

"What about South Carolina," Senator Calhoun asked. "What are we getting?"

"Something," Caleb answered. "We'll work it out."

Senator King from Alabama said, "Count us in."

Senator Downs from Louisiana said, "Sounds fair."

Senator Clay announced, "That'll get us through the senate provided we can count on the Vice President's vote in the event of a tie."

Vice President Fillmore said, "I'll go along."

"We still got the president," Secretary Webster cautioned. "He's threatening a veto."

Caleb said, "We'll get around it."

President Taylor attended the dedication of the Washington Monument on July 4, 1850. He sat on a shaded platform in front of the unfinished monument while Senator Foote delivered a lengthy main address. Then the president stayed to listen to the other orators before taking a long walk along the Potomac River.

The president drank iced water, chilled milk, and ate a basket of fresh cherries when he got back to the executive mansion. He had a late dinner and spent an uncomfortable night. He felt better that morning but complained of nausea and discomfort that afternoon. His physician prescribed calomel and opium. The president's condition deteriorated and he died the next day.

A hundred thousand came to Washington for the funeral. Vice President Fillmore was sworn in as the thirteenth president. Several bills were debated in the senate the following week. Florida, Alabama, and Louisiana broke from the Southern caucus to support these bills and President Fillmore signed the Compromise of 1850. The senate passed the Swamp and Overflowed Lands Act the next day, and President Fillmore signed it.

The Swamp and Overflowed Lands Act gave Florida Twenty-one million acres of land. The Florida Legislature created a Board of Trustees to control and regulate the development of this land. Draining and developing wetlands became official state and federal policy, but there was a problem. Indians were living on the wetlands south of the Peace River boundary.

Something needed to be done with the Indians, but Charlie Conrad, Secretary of War, insisted, "After we get Cuba."

CHAPTER SEVENTEEN

Spies and Paramours

Key West
November through January 1850

It took the authorities awhile to agree upon the policy and course of action regarding Cuba. Then it took the clerks several days to prepare their dispatches and send them out to their various agencies and assets. It took a good month for the dispatches to get to Key West, but their intent wasn't always clear. Sidney and Amanda read the dispatches when they came in and did their best to use them to their advantage.

The club was a priority. It took Amanda awhile to set up the club and longer to attract a paying membership. Diego brought over some prospects and others sauntered up the walkway. A few signed up.

The club intrigued Sarah. She stopped by almost every day. It was fun. Hector, the doorman, announced the callers. The girls rushed out to greet their guests, escorted them to the parlor, spent time with them in the library, and entertained them in the dining room. Sometimes they went upstairs. They usually came down looking somewhat disheveled but generally appeared pleased. Then they tried to schedule another appointment as they escorted their gentleman companion to the back door. It was peculiar.

Sarah was there when Nicole received the letter of referral from Juliet. Juliet wrote that Lord Gordon Renfrew would be on Key West and wanted an appointment. Nicole said, "Wow, nobility!"

A week or so later, Sarah and Nicole were sitting on the sofa in the parlor, leafing through Amanda's new leather bound *Antiquities of Athens* when Lord Renfrew walked in. He didn't knock. He just walked in like he owned the club. Fixing his gaze on Nicole, he said "I believe you must be Nicole."

"I am." She closed the book.

"An old friend suggested I know you."

"And who is this friend?"

"Juliet," Lord Renfrew stated in a matter of fact manner.

"You've gotta be Lord Renfrew."

"Lord Gordon Clifton Renfrew, to be precise. I find that I'll be spending some time on this rustic but rather quaint island, so I decided to look you up. Juliet assured me that you'd provide an interesting experience.'

"Perhaps," Nicole suggested, "so long as you make it interesting."

"That's a rather cheeky response, my dear, but nevertheless a challenge."

"Could be," Nicole replied. "Come, we'll discuss arrangements."

Sarah was left with the *Antiquities of Athens* on her lap as Nicole led Lord Renfrew to the dining room. She decided to leave. Sarah got up, put the book back on the shelf in the library, and nodded to Hector on her way out the door.

She was sauntering down the walkway when a portly gentleman approached. "Excuse me, but I was wondering if this might be the Jacaranda Club."

"It is." That being said, Sarah continued on her way.

Sarah stopped at the club the next morning to find Nicole sitting in the dining room munching on a piece of toast. Nicole called, "Hey! Come in. Join me for coffee."

Sarah went into the dining room and pulled out a chair. "Guess, I will." Sarah sat down. The serving girl brought coffee.

Nicole asked, "What's up?"

Sarah tried the coffee. Then she asked, "So, how'd it go?"

"How did what go?"

"Lord Renfrew."

"Oh, that," Nicole answered. "Good, didn't get much information but he made another appointment. He's coming back."

"When's he coming back?"

"This afternoon, I believe."

"He's not very nice."

"He's not, but he's a man with a purpose."

"So how come you're doing him?"

"I'm a woman with a purpose," Nicole replied. "I need to get information and make money while I'm doing it."

"That's your purpose," Sarah insisted. "What's his?"

"Cuba," Nicole explained. "He wants Cuba. Spain's going down and the vultures are sniffing over the island's breathing carcass, interesting but lucrative."

"How so?"

"Money, it's interesting. Renfrew gave me Guineas. They haven't been minted for awhile so it'll be interesting to figure out where he got them and how he got them. Money tells stories."

"What's that got to do with anything?"

"Finding the funding source," Nicole explained. "We've got British Guineas, Spanish Doubloons, Pieces of Eight, American dollars, Gold Eagles, banknotes, and who knows what else floating around on this island. They all come from somewhere. Tracking them down generates information and exchanging them generates profit. How does that sound?"

"Complicated," Sarah suggested.

"Not so, John's helping."

"Who's John?"

"New York banker," Nicole answered. "He was here yesterday."

"Heavy set fellow?"

"Yes, why?"

"Saw him when I was leaving."

"Probably," Nicole replied. "We're setting up a currency exchange. I'm managing the exchange."

"How come?"

"I'm a bookkeeper. Exchanging currencies is part of what I do."

Sarah said, "When you're not doing your other part."

"When I'm not doing that," Nicole agreed.

"I don't know about that part."

"Know what," Nicole teased, "bookkeeping?"

"I know about bookkeeping. Mother runs a store."

"You mean the upstairs part."

"Yes, that part," Sarah insisted.

"You oughta try it," Nicole suggested. "You're old enough. You'll like it."

"Not now," Sarah blurted, "maybe later."

CHAPTER EIGHTEEN

Dispatches and Contracts

Key West
February through March 1850

Diplomats, spies, and agents of several nations stalked the streets of Key West. Much of the world's commerce flowed in and out of the Caribbean and the island occupied a key spot on the shipping lanes. Santo Domingo was up for grabs. Puerto Rico and Cuba appeared ripe for taking although Spain was still clinging to the last vestiges of its once vast colonial empire.

Sidney and Diego had time to spare as not much was happening at their Import/Export Office. The next dispatch changed everything. They were directed to (1) contract with a shipping company to improve shipping and enhance the flow of dispatches between Key West and Havana, (2) open a subsidiary office in Havana, (3) establish a relationship with the *Club de la Habana*, and (4) support resistance activities as warranted. A postscript scratched at the bottom stated:

We're sending a steamboat. Use as needed
to effectuate the terms of this assignment.
  C. Conklin

Sidney asked, "What's this about?"
"Cora and her Havana club," Amanda replied.
Who's Cora?"
"One of us," Amanda explained. "She worked Texas before being given the Havana assignment. We're forwarding her dispatches but she needs to get more in and out of Havana and do it more quickly."

Sidney said, "We'll work out an agreement with McRea. He's the only one who can get in and out of Havana without raising the hackles of the Spanish authorities. He's been doing it for years."

"Let's do it."

As Captain McRae happened to be in town, Sidney and Amanda walked over to Isobel's store. Amanda told Isobel, "We need to work out a business relationship."

"What you got in mind?"

Amanda said, "Improve transportation between here and Havana."

Isobel grumbled, "What's wrong with what we got."

"Nothing, but we've got to get more stuff between here and there and get it done more quickly."

Sidney suggested, "Perhaps a schedule."

Captain McRae grumbled, "Aint got nothing to haul so I aint been making many trips."

Sidney said, "We might have some freight."

"What you got?"

"Nothing yet," Sidney conceded, "but we might get something."

"Not doin' gun running or that sort of thing," Captain McRae grumbled. "A bunch of Creole hotheads been trying to stir up trouble, but I don't want any part o' that."

Isobel said, "Damn it, James; hear them out. You aint been hauling anything since the hurricane took out the cow business. You'd better get back to haulin' or I'm gonna have to close up."

"This'll work," Amanda assured Isobel. "We're talking about dispatches, light freight, and an occasional passenger. We'll cover your expenses, pay you enough to make it worthwhile, and cut you in on any windfalls that might fall our way."

Captain McRae listened. "What do you wanta do?"

Amanda said, "Start making regular runs between Havana, Key West, and Tampa Bay. Carry a few passengers, some dispatches, and light freight. That's it."

"Nothing left at Tampa Bay," Captain McRea grumbled. "No sense going there."

"That'll change," Amanda replied. "The federal government's rebuilding Fort Brooke."

"How'd you hear that?"

Amanda said, "I've got sources."

"Expect you do," Isobel replied. "If we can keep the store open and make some money on the side, I don't have any problems with your deal." Captain McRae shrugged his shoulders. "If they're gonna rebuild Fort Brooke, maybe you can get us a contract to haul some of the freight."

"Work on it," Amanda promised.

Captain McRae grumbled, "Can't haul big stuff on my brig."

"Not talking about a brig," Amanda announced. "You're using a steamboat."

"What steamboat! What are you talking about?"

Sidney said, "We're getting a steamboat."

"Don't know about those things," Captain McRae grumbled. "I've never been on one."

Isobel said, "You'll learn."

"What do I do with my brig?"

Amanda suggested, "Make delivery runs along the coast. Haul cotton and stuff. There's a market for it."

"Maybe so," Captain McRae conceded. "Guess I could send Simon out with the brig. He's been my mate for years. Angus can go along. That'll keep Bill on his toes and Angus might learn something. He's plenty old enough."

"But you're hauling our merchandise on the steamboat," Isobel insisted.

"Gotta have coal," Captain McRae protested. "Where do I get that? Wind's free. Never cost me anything."

Sidney said, "We'll get it from the navy yard."

"How you going to do that?"

Amanda warned, "Don't ask!"

Isobel gathered her wits. "Let me get this straight. You're giving us a steamboat and coal and paying us for the privilege."

"That's it," Amanda agreed

"Sounds pretty good to me," Isobel concluded. "When do we start?"

Amanda said, "When we get the steamboat."

Sidney added, "After the election."

But General Taylor won the election. It didn't make much difference to the people on Key West as most weren't concerned about such things. Even so, a bureaucracy is a marvelous thing. Once arrangements for something have been made, the arrangements take on a life of their own.

A refurbished schooner rigged steamboat chugged into the Key West harbor late one afternoon about a month later and tied up at the pier. Sidney was working in his office when the door opened and a grease-spattered, little man stuck his head in the door. The man said, "Hi! I'm Willy Fairchild. I brought your boat down."

"What boat?"

"Skinner's Shipyard sent it," Willy answered, "said you ordered it."

Sidney replied, "Don't know about that."

"Oh, yes," Diego barked. "We sure did!" He admonished Sidney, "Don't you remember?"

"I guess."

"The dispatches," Diego insisted.

"Oh, yes! Havana dispatches," Sidney replied. He asked Willy, "Where's the boat?"

"In the harbor."

"Let's go see," Sidney shouted. He jumped up and led the way out of the office.

The *Salvor* was a reconditioned coastal paddle-wheel steamer, a little over a hundred foot long and about thirty feet wide. She was powered by a Novelty Iron Works engine and listed as a salvage boat to be operated by the Jacaranda Import/Export Company. The *Salvor* was a sight to behold.

125

There was room for cattle on the deck, passengers in the cabin, and freight in the hold. Captain McRae took a look before grumbling, "Don't know if I can run it."

"Nothing to it," Willy insisted.

"Then you can help me run it."

"Sure thing," Willy agreed. "Need a job. Glad to help out."

Now that they had Willy and the steamboat, Sidney and the girls were ready to follow through on the requests. Diego offered, "I'll catch a ride to Havana on the *Salvor*, open a branch office, and check out the Havana Club while I'm there. What do I do about this resistance thing?"

"Damned if I know," Sidney replied. "Something will turn up."

Something turned up a couple of days later when a little man sporting a big mustache sauntered in the front door. The man stopped, looked them over, and announced his intentions by barking, "Senior Benson!"

"That's me," Sidney answered. "Who are you?"

"Narisco Lopez."

"Senior Lopez!" Diego scrambled to his feet. "Heard you might be coming this way."

"And who are you?"

"Call me Diego," Diego asserted. "That's me. What can I do for you?"

Narisco said, "I'm here to see Senior Benson."

"Who said?"

"The big little man in Washington City," Narisco replied. "He told me you'd get my dispatches to Havana."

Sidney asked, "What's this man's name?"

"Konkleen or something like that."

Sidney said, "Close enough."

Diego offered, "I'll take the dispatches. I'm going to Havana on the *Salvor*."

That's our steamboat. They're getting the boat ready and I'll deliver your dispatches as soon as I get there. It's on my way."

Narisco insisted, "I was told to deal with Senior Benson."

126

"We're the same," Diego assured Narisco.

"Wouldn't go that far," Sidney protested. "But Diego can deliver your dispatches. Anything else we can do for you?"

"Maybe a place to stay," Narisco suggested. "I'll be here a couple of days and be on my way."

Diego said, "I've got a place."

"Is it nice?"

"Nicest on the island," Diego insisted. The gentlemen struck up a conversation in rapid Spanish as they left the office. Sidney sat at his desk. It was getting confusing.

Narisco spent a few days at the Jacaranda Club. Amanda took Narisco under her wing as soon as he walked in the front door and spent a lot of time with him. When not otherwise engaged, Narisco spent some time chatting with Diego and a few other Spanish speaking gentlemen.

When Diego was boarding the *Salvor*, he told Sidney, "They're sending money."

"Who's sending money?"

"Money for Narisco."

"I don't know what you're talking about."

Diego explained, "Nicole has a friend. He was here and talked with Nicole. He's raising money for Narisco. They're holding rallies on the streets in the cities up north and selling bonds. He's sending us banknotes."

"How many?"

"Thousands."

Sidney said, "They have to be redeemed at the issuing bank. They're not worth much down here."

"Nicole's redeeming them."

Sidney sputtered, "How's she doing that."

"Don't know," Diego replied, "but she's doing it."

CHAPTER NINETEEN

Banknotes and Steamboats

Key West and Cuba
March through June 1850

Amanda fired off a dispatch to Mary Ann as soon as Narisco left. She wanted clarification of the situation with Narisco and needed additional staffing. Sally Sue came to Key West about a month later, bringing a dispatch with her. This one said: (1) The United States and Spanish empire remain at peace. (2) Peace must be maintained while the United States pursues options for the purchase of Cuba. (3) Civil insurrections may facilitate the consummation of such sale. (4) Covert support and assistance should be provided as deemed appropriate.

The note scrawled at the bottom of the dispatch requested:

Forward any and all pertinent
information derived from N. Lopez
C. Conklin

This sort of clarified the situation. Amanda wrote a lengthy report on the items of information that she had derived from Narisco and sent it back on the dispatch boat. Then she walked over to the office of the Jacaranda Import/Export Company to talk with Sidney. Sidney appeared perplexed.

Amanda asked, "What's up?"

"Dammed if I know. I got a banknote from some Boston bank for five thousand and another from a New York bank for eight thousand. They're made out to the Jacaranda Sporting Association."

"That's us," Amanda insisted. "Give me the banknotes and I'll give them to Nicole. She's taking care of business."

Sidney said, "Putting them in your club account?"

"They're going in our New York Branch."

"What are you talking about?"

"A chartered bank," Amanda replied. "Don't ask so many questions. Nicole's handling it but we're collecting transaction fees. It's legal."

"Perhaps," Sidney conceded. "What does Nicole know about banking?"

"More than you think."

"I thought this was Narisco's money," Sidney insisted. "How does he fit into this?"

"He's raising the money but not getting it."

"What do you mean?"

"Narisco's a pawn. He can take a step to the left or a step to the right. That's it, but he has to keep going. Narisco thinks he's using Washington to get what he wants, but Washington's using him to get what they want. Everybody's using Narisco. I used him to get more staffing. That's how it is."

"What's Narisco getting?'

"Used," Amanda revealed. "That's it."

Sidney toyed with the banknotes. "These things have a combined face value of over thirteen thousand dollars. They're not worth that much here, but they're worth something."

"Give them to me. I'll give them to Nicole."

"Hold on," Sidney insisted, "I got a dog in this fight. I don't mind being a fall guy or designated receiver, but it ought to be worth at least a portion, maybe five or ten percent of whatever value these have."

"One or two at most. I'll talk with Nicole. Give me the notes."

"Amanda, you're hard nosed," Sidney grumbled. "But give my regards to Nicole. I'm sure she'll be generous."

Contributions kept coming. Sidney collected one percent, gave Amanda the banknotes, and she gave them to Nicole. Nobody heard anything from Narisco, but there were rumors that he had signed up six hundred volunteers in New Orleans. A Cuban fisherman told Diego that Narisco had moved his volunteers out to Round Island, a windswept crescent of sand located along the Gulf Coast. The banknotes kept coming.

One afternoon Hector announced, "Mr. John for Miss Amanda." Amanda rushed to the door to find John O' Donnell, the New York newspaperman.

"Hey John, how come you're back?"

"Passing through," John explained. "I got a ride this far on the dispatch boat and I'm catching the packet to New Orleans. Narisco's in jail. Gotta get him out."

"How'd that happen?"

"Taylor won the election," John explained. He pulled the plug, sent in the Navy, rounded up Narisco and his volunteers, and threw Narisco in jail. We've got rallies planned in the south but can't raise a cent with Narisco in jail. I've got to get him out."

"What do you want me to do?"

John said, "Get a couple of thousand from Nicole. I'll need the money to pay off a few people. That's what I gotta do."

"I'll get it," Amanda replied, "anything else?"

"A place to stay," John insisted. "The packet's not leaving until tomorrow."

John spent the night and left the next morning. Amanda didn't think much about the visit, but John sent a package with a letter and another fifty thousand in bank notes a couple of months later. Narisco was signing up volunteers and appearing at fund raising rallies. John wrote that he had picked up an old steamboat, the *Creole*. Amanda gave Nicole the banknotes.

The *Creole* chugged into the Key West harbor a couple of weeks later. John and Narisco swaggered into the club. John set up an appointment with Roslyn. Amanda set aside time for Narisco. Lord Renfrew appeared and was going up the stairs with Nicole when they encountered Narisco and Amanda coming down the stairs. Lord Renfrew nodded but didn't say anything. It was a busy day.

CHAPTER TWENTY

Narisco

New Orleans to Cuba and Key West
May and early June 1850

John and Narisco left Key West on the *Creole*. They went back to New Orleans, gathered up a hundred or so Kentucky riflemen, a hundred and thirty Louisiana Cajuns, twenty-seven former pirates, and ninety-eight other volunteers to launch a pre-emptive invasion on the north coast of Cuba. The group rushed ashore at Cardenas at daybreak. They tried to seize the town but were confronted by thousands of Spanish troops.

Narisco and his men took a look at their untenable situation and scrambled to safety on the *Creole*. The *Pizarro*, a Spanish gunboat, fired at them as they steamed away. The *Pizarro* gave chase and chased them all the way across the channel and into Key West harbor. Narisco and his troops abandoned the *Creole*, jumping ashore as the steamboat approached the pier.

Some of Narisco's men milled around in confusion on the pier and the rest fled up the street. The Spanish gunboat sat about a quarter mile offshore and there were rumors of a bombardment. Sidney paced the floor of his office and sent Diego to the harbor to deal with the problem.

Hundreds of Key West residents rushed to the harbor to watch the bombardment. Flags were run up flag poles and dozens took to rooftops to get a better view of the confrontation. Diego pushed his way through the crowd until he found Narisco. They embraced and disappeared into the crowd.

A dozen or so elderly veterans of the Seminole Wars mustered on Mallory Square to defend the city. Younger men went to the trouble of pulling two old cannons out of the fort and setting them up on the beach. They got ready to repel the invasion, but nothing happened. The United States Navy roused from its slumber to send the *USS Water Witch*, an American gunboat, out to confront the Spanish gunboat. The *Pizarro* backed off and anchored in deep water. The event settled into a stalemate.

Narisco's troops vanished in the crowd. Narisco and Diego sought refuge in the Jacaranda Company office. Sidney wasn't happy. He growled at Narisco, "What in hell do you think you're doing!"

"They knew I was coming," Narisco shouted. "They knew about me. They knew where I was going and what I wanted to do. The Captain General had five thousand men, his whole army. They were there, they were waiting for me."

Diego asked. "What happened to your insurrection?"

"Don't know," Narisco blustered. "They rounded up all my people, took them out, and shot them like dogs. They knew everything."

Sidney asked, "Who knew?"

"How do I know?" Narisco blustered. "Somebody does."

Sidney asked, "So, what are you going to do?"

"Raising another army, a thousand men, and going back."

"You said they had five thousand."

"Five thousand, ten thousand, how do I know," Narisco grumbled. "But I'm going back!"

Sarah walked in. She said, "They're taking the boat."

"What boat," Narisco demanded.

"Your boat," Sarah replied. "The Navy's taking it. They got Marines all over the place."

"They can't do this to me," Narisco dashed out the door. Diego and Sarah followed.

Commodore Franklin Farley, commander of the Gulf Coast Squadron, was on the pier with his marines. The marines had taken possession of the *Creole*. Some were standing around, and others were unloading crates of arms and ammunition.

133

Narisco stormed down the pier. "Get off my boat! I own that boat. Leave it alone."

Commodore Farley said, "This vessel and its cargo are being seized."

Diego pushed his way forward. "Why? The boat hasn't done anything."

Commodore Farley explained, "This craft is being operated by a foreign national who has engaged in an unprovoked criminal action against another nation. We're holding the vessel until we determine ownership."

"Please, pardon me Mr. Commodore," Diego pleaded. "There's been a mistake. It's my boat. I own the boat."

"You're the dog man."

"A long time ago," Diego stammered.

So it was," Commodore Farley agreed. "What are you doing now?"

"I'm with the Jacaranda Company. We do imports and exports."

"And other things, I hear."

"What about my boat?"

"I need ownership papers."

"I'll get the papers," Diego assured the commodore. Commodore Farley called off a few Marines. Diego, Narisco, and Sarah waited around until the Commodore left. Then they went back to the office.

Sidney asked Diego, "What's happening?"

"We've got to show papers to get the boat. What do you want to do?"

"I'll take care of it," Sidney insisted. He asked Narisco, "What are you doing now?"

"Going to the club," Narisco replied. "I'll be there until things quiet down."

"Good idea," Diego agreed. "Do that. I'll be over."

Narisco hesitated before asking, "How do I get there?"

"Walk," Diego replied. "You've been there."

"Marines are out there. I'm not armed."

"I'm going," Sarah said. "Come along. I'll save you."

134

"But of course," Narisco replied as he shrugged his shoulder. He followed Sarah out the door and onto the street. As they walked along, Narisco asked Sarah, "Do you work at the club?"

"Not today."

"What's the mean?"

"I'm busy today," Sarah teased. "Maybe some other day though."

"Maybe," Narisco insisted.

"Perhaps," Sarah replied.

Hector greeted them. Sarah took Narisco into the library to see Amanda. Amanda said, "Heard you were back."

"Didn't go so good," Narisco replied. "But I'm back."

"Glad you're here," Amanda told Narisco as she motioned for Sarah to leave. "Tell me about it." Amanda closed the door.

Sarah sauntered into the parlor to find Sally Sue on the sofa. Sarah asked, "What's up?"

"I'm waiting for an appointment."

"Who with?"

"Ricardo," Sally Sue replied, "Diego's friend. He's a merchant."

Narisco's riflemen and Cajuns swarmed the streets of Key West. A bunch seized the tavern next to Isobel's store and burned down a bawdy house. Isobel spent the afternoon and much of the evening sitting on a chair in front of the market holding a musket on her lap.

Narisco left on a fishing smack. Nobody knew where he was going. It took a few weeks for the news of his failed invasion to reach Washington. As the Spanish government believed the United States was responsible for the attack, they filed a protest. Spain demanded reparations for damages, the apprehension of the individuals participating in the attack, and their transportation to Cuba for trial and possible execution.

Narisco riled the waters.

CHAPTER TWENTY ONE

Complications

Washington City
July 1850

Millard Fillmore never planned on becoming president. He wasn't there when President Taylor ate the cherries and drank the milk. Millard didn't know much about Spain, little about Florida, less about Key West, and nothing about Narisco. President Fillmore didn't figure he'd be the president for very long so he kept his full-time Chancellor's job at the University of Buffalo. He didn't know what to do about the Spanish problem so he gave it to Daniel Webster, his Secretary of State.

Secretary Webster was comfortable with the decision. He discussed the problem with Caleb. Caleb said, "We can use it."

"What for?"

"Secure your presidential nomination."

"How are you going to do that?"

"Manifest destiny," Caleb insisted, using the term crafted by Cora and popularized by John O'Donnell. "We need a national issue to get beyond regional interests. The North and South don't agree on much except expanding our borders. Jefferson, Madison, and Polk used national expansion to their advantage. Van Buren didn't use it. That cost him the election."

"What's Spain got to do with anything?"

"Cuba," Caleb replied. "We can get the island."

"Maybe," Secretary Webster mumbled. "Thought Taylor closed that thing down?"

"Delayed it," Caleb insisted. "That's all. The people and plans are still in place. Cora's in Havana, O'Donnell's raising

136

money, Quitman's raising troops, and Narisco's still our front man. We can patch it up and put it together."

"Suppose," Secretary Webster replied, "But how's that going to get me the nomination?"

"Mass hysteria," Caleb suggested. "We'll organize rallies all over the country to free Cuba and cap them off with a massive demonstration in front of the Baltimore Convention Hall. We'll put you on the speaker's stand with Narisco and bring in a few old generals. That'll stir up the enthusiasm needed to get the nomination."

"Might work," Secretary Webster suggested. "What about Spain?"

"What about Spain?"

"They're not going to like this. They filed a protest."

"Tell them there's been a misunderstanding and we're investigating the allegations. That works, and it'll hold them off until after the election. Then we'll decide what we want to do. If this Cuba thing works, that's good. If not, we'll drop it."

"Makes sense," Secretary Webster conceded.

"Cuba's got something for everyone," Caleb declared. "New York sugar merchants want the cane fields. Massachusetts shipping interests want access to Havana harbor. The South wants another Slave state. We've got unemployed veterans. This will give them something to do. It's a winner and good for business."

Secretary Webster said, "Let me think on it." He pondered Caleb's suggestion for a day or two. He discussed the concept with Jeff Davis, a senator from Mississippi, and his old colleague and occasional adversary, John Calhoun from South Carolina. Both agreed. It was an idea worth considering.

Secretary Webster gave Caleb the go-ahead, so Caleb scheduled a meeting with John O'Donnell, the New York newspaper man, and General John Quitman, the war hero and former governor of Mississippi. John O'Donnell brought Narisco. The gentlemen met in Caleb's corner office on the second floor of the State Department building.

Caleb said, "This will be a short meeting."

"Sounds good to me," General Quitman replied. "What's up?"

"We've got the go-ahead for Cuba."

"What about Fillmore?" John O'Donnell asked. "Where does he stand?"

"Don't have any idea," Caleb replied. "Fillmore's in Buffalo. Nothing's going to happen anyway until after the Whig convention.

General Quitman asked, "How come?"

Caleb said, "Webster's going for the nomination."

"Why do we have to wait?"

"Because Webster wants us to wait," Caleb said. "He's using our Cuban initiative to build support for his candidacy. We've got to be ready to activate the plan as soon as he gives us the go-ahead, but nothing happens until after the convention. That's next year."

"Gives us time," John O'Donnell suggested. "Maybe we can sell bonds at the convention."

"Probably," Caleb replied. "How are your bond sales and fund raising progressing?"

"Good," John O'Donnell replied. "I'm selling bonds in Baltimore, Boston, Savannah, and Charleston. Calhoun's with us on this thing."

"Great!" Caleb insisted. "Start organizing rallies in Boston, Buffalo, Pittsburgh, Cincinnati, Philadelphia, Charleston, and Savannah. I want a really big rally on the street in front of the Convention Center in Baltimore to stir up the delegates. We've got to generate enthusiasm for an expansionist plank in the Whig platform. Some of the Democrats will go along with us. How are you doing with your donors?"

John O'Donnell said, "Sam Colt's giving eight thousand and I'm hitting up the New York sugar merchants. They're good for another ten or twelve thousand."

"Good!" Caleb asserted. "And you're clearing the money through our Key West branch?"

"Absolutely," John O'Donnell replied.

"Sounds good but keep it under wraps," Caleb insisted. If anybody asks why you're raising money, tell them it's for sporting ventures, buffalo hunting or something like that. Caleb asked General Quitman, "How's the recruiting going?"

"Slacked off," General Quitman mumbled, "figured we weren't going."

"We're going," Caleb said. "Get on it. We need to have a reasonable force in place to establish our credibility."

"I'll get on it but I've got a question?"

Caleb asked, "What?"

General Quitman said, "We've trotted out on this limb before but then someone comes along and chops it off. Is it for real this time, or are we playing games?"

Caleb glanced at Narisco. "It's for real so long as nobody screws up."

Narisco mumbled, "Who screwed up."

Caleb asserted, "Your unauthorized, pre-emptive invasion was a screw-up."

Narisco mumbled, "Didn't know they knew I was coming."

"Shouldn't have gone," Caleb insisted. "But you did and we're dealing with result. Raise troops but don't take anyone anywhere until I give the word. Do you understand? Do you have any problems with it?"

Narisco muttered, "Nope."

It was quiet. John O'Donnell said, "Maybe Narisco can help sell bonds."

"Remember, keep it quiet and low key," Caleb warned. "I don't want any trouble with anyone, not now." The gentlemen nodded. "We're set," Caleb concluded. "Sell bonds, schedule rallies, and raise an army, but nobody goes anywhere until I give the word." The purpose of the meeting being achieved, John O'Donnell went back to New York.

General Quitman sent Narisco to Key West.

CHAPTER TWENTY TWO

Sidney and the Buffalo Hunters

Key West
July through August 1850

Sidney grabbed the old dispatch from the War Department granting him his correspondent's commission and walked over to the Navy Yard. He met with Commodore Farley, displayed his credential, and managed to convince the commodore that keeping track of the *Creole* was a matter of significant concern. "It's a matter of credibility. That's what's at stake here," Sidney claimed. "One can't be endangering the public's perception of a potential loss of sovereignty over these issues. Your reputation's at stake."

"How so," Commodore Farley demanded.

"The boat," Sidney insisted. "She's secured in the harbor. You've done your job. It's the army's domain. The army should be taking responsibility for it."

Sensing an opportunity to be rid of a potential problem, Commodore Farley said, "You've got a point."

Following up, Sidney suggested, "Release it, and I'll work out the details with the army."

"Makes sense," Commodore Farley concluded. "How do I release it?"

"In my name," Sidney suggested. "I'll be responsible."

Once that was done, Sidney left Commodore Farley's office, walked over to Fort Taylor, and talked with Captain Hunt about securing a contract for running a shuttle boat between Tampa and Key West. Captain Hunt asked, "Got a boat?"

"Responsible for one," Sidney claimed. "For a small fee, say a couple of hundred a month, I'll make the *Creole* available as a shuttle boat. You'll need it while you're rebuilding Fort Brooke."

"Good idea," Captain Hunt agreed, "Any special conditions?"

"No, not really, register it and we'll run it under your flag."

"That'll work," Captain Hunt concluded.

On his way back to the office, Sidney stopped at the Merchandise Market to see Isobel. As Narisco's ruffians were out and about, Isobel suggested, "Come inside. I'll lock up. I'd like to talk."

Sidney followed Isobel into the store and waited while she locked the door and pulled the blinds. Isobel asked, "How about a coffee."

"Sure." Sidney followed Isobel to the back room where he told her, "I got the boat."

Isobel poured coffee. "What are you going to do with it?"

"Leasing it to the army," Sidney said. "They're rebuilding Fort Brooke and going to need a shuttle."

Sidney pulled out a chair to sit at the table. Isobel placed Sidney's cup of coffee beside him and leaned against, partially sitting on the table "That'll work. Gonna carry passengers?"

"Some, I guess," Sidney answered. He reached for the coffee.

Isobel tugged her skirt back a little. "That's good. Maybe I can hitch a ride from time to time."

"Probably," Sidney replied. "What did you want to talk about?"

Isobel suggested, "Things we can do each other."

Sidney looked up. "Got anything in mind?"

"Oh, come on. I locked the door. Use your imagination."

Sidney did until they heard a loud commotion coming from the street. Isobel slid off the table, rushed to the window, and opened the shade to find a crowd gathering in front of the building. People were pushing, shoving, and shouting. Shots were being fired.

Sidney yelled, "What's going on?"

"Goddam riot," Isobel shouted as she grabbed a musket, loaded it, and pushed the door open. She grabbed a chair and dragged it in front of the store. Sidney did likewise and sat next to Isobel. The crowd milled around the tavern next door. Some were carrying torches. Sidney said, "I'd better check the office."

"Go ahead! I've got this place covered."

Sidney pushed through the crowd and thoughts of the evening. Nevertheless, Isobel strolled into his office the next morning, saying, "I gotta talk with you about something."

"What's that?"

"I want you to cut a deal with the army to buy cows," Isobel insisted. "I've been talking with Jake Sutherlin, the cow catcher. We've got to get the captain hauling again and figured you'd know how to get a contract."

Having nothing else to say, Sidney said, "I'll work on it."

Narisco came back a few days later, gathered up his Cajuns, and took them back to New Orleans. Diego fluttered around, but for the most part, the island quieted down. Captain Hunt registered the *Creole,* and the Army Engineers started running the boat between Key West and Tampa Bay.

Diego stirred up a storm a week or so later when a bunch of Kentucky riflemen arrived on a fishing smack. The riflemen swaggered around for a couple of hours before camping on the beach by the African cemetery. When asked what they were doing, they said, "Buffalo hunting."

Diego brought his friend Ricardo to the office. Sidney asked, "What's up?"

Ricardo said, "These are Narisco's people."

"Probably," Sidney replied.

Diego said, "They're up to something."

"Buffalo hunting," Sidney replied.

"Not here," Ricardo insisted.

"No buffalo on the island," Diego asserted. "Let's ask Amanda. She might know something." They rushed to the club and Diego asked Amanda, "What's going on with Narisco?"

"I don't know," Amanda replied. "I haven't seen him. Why are you asking?"

Ricardo said, "We got buffalo hunters on the island."

"Gotta be someplace," Amanda replied. "Maybe they're going hunting."

"Not here," Ricardo grunted. "Narisco's going for another invasion."

"Can't happen," Diego assured Ricardo, "Narisco's got no way to get there. That's the agreement."

"For what it's worth," Ricardo protested. "I tell you, he's up to something."

"Don't ask me," Amanda insisted, "I don't know anything."

Diego said, "We've got to find Narisco, get him back. That's the only way we can find out what's going on." Diego left Ricardo and rushed back to the Import/Export office. Sidney fired off a dispatch to Washington and another to General Quitman in New Orleans. They didn't hear anything, but Narisco showed up a few days later. He brought more Buffalo hunters.

Diego and Ricardo watched as Narisco paraded his buffalo hunters up Front Street. Then Narisco sauntered into the office. Sidney asked Narisco, "How's it going?"

"Good. And you?"

Diego demanded, "What are you doing."

"Hunting," Narisco suggested. "That's what I do."

"You've got over hundred men on the island," Ricardo blustered. "Why are they here?"

"Two hundred forty, I believe," Narisco replied. "They're getting ready."

Sidney reminded Narisco, "Nothing happens until you get the word."

"From the big little man, I know," Narisco conceded. "I got more men coming. Then we'll leave."

Ricardo demanded, "Where you going?"

"Hunting," Narisco replied, "already told you." Then he asked Diego, "What about Amanda? Do you think she's busy?"

"You gotta ask."

Diego did. More men arrived. Nobody paid much attention until Lord Renfrew showed up on an old Bahaman steam powered ferry boat. The Bahaman deck crew scurried about as the ferry tied up at the pier. Narisco and his buffalo hunters boarded the ferry sometime after midnight. The ferryboat got up steam and chugged out of the harbor just as the sun was coming up. Lord Renfrew watched them leave.

Isobel asked Sidney, "What's going on.

Sidney said, "Don't know."

Information trickled back over the course of the next few weeks. The ferryboat deposited Narisco and his buffalo hunters on the northern coast of Cuba. They stormed ashore and seized a village before the Spanish army chased them into the mountains. Narisco was captured, taken to Havana, and strangled in a public execution.

CHAPTER TWENTY THREE

Tampa Town Recovery

Tampa to Key West
September 1851 through June 1852

The Great Gale of '48 wiped out Fort Brooke and most of Tampa Town. The Eagle's Nest, three other buildings, and a barn were left. Clean up and recovery was slow until the Army Engineers got the order to rebuild Fort Brooke. They leased the *Creole* and started making shuttle runs between Key West and Tampa Town hauling freight, passengers, and building supplies.

The Army sent General Twiggs to Tampa and he brought Colonel Garland and two regiments of engineers. Harry and Rube got a job working on the new army pier. Jake dashed off to Key West to see about getting the cow business started again. Jake came back to report, "We're in business."

Harry and Rube were hammering the last plank in place on the pier when the *Salvor* made its initial run into Tampa Bay. The steamboat drifted up to the end of the pier before the paddlewheels brought the boat to a halt. Captain McRae stepped out of the pilot house and tossed a line. Rube caught the line and wrapped it around the nearest post.

Captain McRae glanced around before grumbling, "You boys gotta get a better setup here if you want me to start haulin' cows."

"Working on it," Rube replied. "Where've you been anyway?"

"None of your business," Captain McRae insisted as he stepped off the boat and onto the pier. "Where's Sutherlin?"

"Coming," Jake yelled as he sauntered down the pier.

Harry stood off to the side and looked on as Captain McRae and Jake Sutherlin held a short conference. Captain

145

McRae said, "I'll haul your cows if you fellows put up a decent sized paddock to hold 'em and build me a building big enough to store my stuff and sell some merchandise when I'm not here."

Jake asked, "How are you gonna sell something when you're not here?"

Captain McRae said, "I'll get someone."

"How big do you want the building?

"Big enough," Captain McRae insisted. "I'm bringing a bunch of stuff."

"Figured as much," Jake replied as he eyed the boat. "We'll put up a post-beam-and-plank building, say forty by sixty, but you gotta finish it off the way you want it. How does that sound?

"So long as she's got a decent roof," Captain McRae insisted. "Don't want anything getting wet."

"Cedar shakes," Jake suggested. "We'll cut them at the mill."

"That'll work."

"Sounds like a deal," Jake concluded. "I'll send some boys out to start catching cows and we'll put up your building."

"Cedar shakes," Captain McRae insisted. "Get your cows ready and I'll be back in a couple of weeks." With that being said, Captain McRae boarded his boat and shouted at someone. Dark smoke poured from the stack and billowed over the harbor as Rube released the lines. The paddle wheels lurched into reverse, backing the steamboat from the pier. It made a wide turn as it got out into the harbor and started splashing across Tampa Bay.

When Captain McRae got back to Key West, he walked over to the store to tell Isobel, "We're moving."

"What are you talking about?"

"We're moving the business to Tampa Town."

"No way," Isobel replied. "Not me. I'm staying here."

Captain McRae said, "Can't stay on the island. We got to get out from under the Jacaranda outfit. They're taking over everything."

146

Isobel insisted, "I've got that outfit right where I want it. Don't you go getting everything all fouled up. I'm staying here. I'm not going anywhere."

"But I'm building a setup at Tampa Town."

"Fine, use it."

Captain McRae asked, "How we going to do that?"

"Sarah," Isobel said. "We'll send Sarah. She's plenty old enough to run the operation. I've got to keep track of things here, but I'll keep my eyes on Sarah by going back and forth on Sidney's shuttle."

"Might work," Captain McRae agreed. "Sarah's not doing much around here.

"Hanging out at the club, that's all," Isobel insisted. "Getting her off the island might be a good idea."

"Give her some responsibility," Captain McRae insisted. "It'll be good for her."

"Sure will," Isobel agreed. But Sarah was shocked when her mother told her, "You're going to Tampa Town."

"What for?"

"Running our store," Isobel insisted. "Someone's gotta do it."

"But, I'm busy."

"Doing what," Isobel demanded. "Hanging out at that club's not getting you anywhere. You need to settle down and find a man."

"What for," Sarah demanded. "The girls at the club use protection. They don't have husbands and they're doing things."

"Sure are," Isobel agreed. "But a husband's about the best protection you can get."

"What do you mean?"

"If you get in trouble, just say it's his. That's how it works."

"Oh, my God!"

"That's it," Isobel concluded. "You're going to Tampa."

The girls at the club were sympathetic, but Roslyn said, "Your Mother's right. Products are good but don't always work."

"I guess," Sarah conceded

"Besides," Nicole insisted, "you're the marrying type."

"What do you mean?"

"If you were going to do what we're doing, you'd be doing it."

"Probably."

"Go to Tampa, check it out," Amanda urged. "Come back and see us when you can. Maybe, you'll find a man."

The matter being decided, Isobel, Sidney, and Sarah took a trip to Tampa on Sidney's shuttle to check the situation. Jake, Rube, and Harry were putting up a two story building on the waterfront. The walls were up and roof was on. Isobel said, "My God, it's big."

"Gotta be," Jake insisted. "It's what McRae wanted."

"You've got enough room for a store, bar, and warehouse," Sidney noted. "Put rooms upstairs and we'll call it a hotel."

"Good idea," Isobel conceded. "But we've got to finish it."

"We will," Sidney promised, although he wasn't doing the work.

Isobel glanced at Sarah. "Sarah's gonna run it."

"It's too big," Sarah protested. "I can't do everything by myself."

"Hire Harry," Jake suggested. "He can help."

Sidney asked Harry, "Interested."

Having no other options, Harry said, "I guess."

Isobel said, "That'll work."

As the hotel wasn't finished and there was no place to stay, Sidney took Sarah and Isobel up to the Eagle's Nest. Isobel, Sarah, and Sidney spent the next two days working out their plans for the hotel before catching the shuttle back to Key West.

Sarah fled to the club. Amanda consoled her. "It won't last. You'll be back. Make the most of it."

148

"I guess, but I'll miss you."

"Don't worry," Amanda insisted. "You'll be back."

Sarah and Isobel took the furnishings for the hotel back with them on the shuttle about a month later. Harry carried everything to the building and Captain McRae arrived on the *Salvor* a couple of days later. Captain McRae took a quick look at the building project before loading Isobel and Jake's cows on the *Salvor*. Sarah watched them leave before taking charge of the project.

Sarah put Harry to work painting. Isobel didn't show up for a couple of weeks. There weren't any guests, but Sarah was getting the place in order. Harry stocked shelves in the store and did this while trying to stay out of the mother/daughter arguments. Isobel eventually gave up arguing to spend time with Jake before leaving on the shuttle.

Isobel came back about a month later but she spent most of her time at Eagle's Nest. Isobel arrived and departed over the course of the next several months. Nobody knew when she was coming and nobody knew when she would be leaving. That kept everyone on their toes. Working for an irrational woman and her demanding daughter was a new experience for Harry.

Even so, it was better than being unemployed. Sarah had Harry set up the bar and position chairs and benches on the front porch. That brought in a few customers. Then she had Harry carry furniture up to the bedrooms on the second floor. That being done, she told Harry, "Wall off a section in the warehouse."

"How big," Harry asked.

"Ten by twelve, maybe twelve by fifteen," Sarah insisted.

"What for?"

"My space when mother's here," Sarah explained. "And put up shelving while you're at it." Harry didn't know he was "at it," but he put up the walls and built the shelves. Otherwise, the hotel got off to a slow start.

Brinton moved his bar and business to the old barn on Washington Street and got most of his old drinking crowd, but the Tampa Bay City Hotel managed to attract the better sort of visitor. Sarah sold merchandise while Harry tended bar and counted the cows in the paddock. Sarah kept a tally of the cows that Captain McRae loaded on the *Salvor* once or twice a month.

Captain McRae dropped off boxes and crates of merchandise when he arrived at the harbor, and Harry stocked the store. Otherwise, Captain McRae didn't take much interest in the activities. Isobel did.

CHAPTER TWENTY FOUR

Matters of Selection

Baltimore and Tampa Town
June 1852 - October 1855

The Whigs convened in Baltimore in early June to nominate a candidate for president. Daniel Webster's New England supporters turned out in force to secure his nomination but the southern delegates wanted to keep Fillmore. Fillmore had gone along with the South by signing the Compromise of 1850 with its fugitive slave provision and the Swamp and Overflowed Lands Act that gave vast tracts of land to several southern states. Otherwise, Fillmore didn't bother anyone. A nonfunctioning presidency had its advantages.

The Whigs took fifty-two ballots to reject Webster and Fillmore and select Winfield Scott as their compromise candidate. General Scott was a war hero from two wars so the Democrats figured they'd lose the election when they gathered in Baltimore. The Democrats were divided over slavery and the provisions of the 1850 Compromise so it took forty-nine ballots to select Franklin Pierce. He was a former congressman and senator from New Hampshire.

Caleb and Mary Ann were disappointed with the outcome of the Whig convention, so they took an active interest in the Democratic convention. They supported Bill Marcy. Bill was a safe candidate. He had served as governor of New York and been the Secretary of War in the Polk administration. More important, Bill was part of the old Van Buren entourage. After Frank Pierce got the Democratic nomination, he selected Bill to become his Secretary of State. Caleb and Mary Ann decided to back Frank.

Caleb went to work. General Scott's campaign train was derailed and delayed. Hecklers harassed General Scott at every whistle-stop, and he lost support with every appearance. The nickname of "Old Fuss and Feathers" stuck and General Scott, the hero of two wars, was defeated. Frank Pierce was elected.

Tampa Town residents didn't much care. Their local election was more interesting. City fathers had filed incorporation papers and scheduled an election. Diggory and Brinton were running for mayor.

Sarah had her own concerns. Although she was adjusting to her change in circumstances, she missed hanging out at the club. Perhaps her mother was right. Maybe, she needed a man. There were a lot of men in Tampa Town but most were too crude or too independent.

She wanted an attractive man, but more important, she wanted an attentive man, one who would listen to her every whim and respond to her every desire. That being the case, Sarah focused her effort on the man most available, her handyman. Harry listened, did what he was told, and sought her approval.

Sarah didn't exactly know how to go about transforming their employer-employee arrangement into a romantic relationship, so she fell back on what she had observed at the club. This required a proper arrangement and an appropriate setting.

Sarah told Harry, "There's an old couch in the Eagle's Nest. Bring it down."

"How big is it?"

"It's pretty big."

"What for?"

"Mom wants it out of the house."

That being the case, Harry said. "I'll get Carey to help."

"Please do."

Carey came over and they dragged the couch out of the corner room at the Eagle's Nest. They were pushing, shoving, and dragging it into the warehouse when Sarah said, "Put it in my space."

"What for?"

"Do it."

Harry and Carey lifted, lugged, and dragged the couch to get it through the door and into Sarah's space. Harry shoved it against the wall. Sarah examined the room. "I've got my space."

"What for?"

"Privacy," Sarah replied. "I never know when mother's going to show up or how long she's going to be here."

Her explanation made sense in a way, so Harry went back to tending bar. They were locking the store a couple of days later when Sarah said, "Come and look at my couch. I cleaned it up."

Harry said, "I've seen it."

"I fixed it and cleaned the room."

Harry gave in and followed Sarah to her space. It was different. A piece of carpet covered the floor and drape hung over the window. A pewter candle holder and stack of books were piled on a marble topped table.

"It's my reading nook." Sarah closed the door. "You like it?"

"Nice, I guess."

Sarah lit the candle. "It is." She sat on the couch. "I cleaned it."

"That's nice."

"Come on, sit down." Sarah ordered. "I want to tell you about the couch. It's a special couch."

"It's heavy." He sat down.

"This was Nicole's couch."

"Probably," Harry said, glancing toward the door.

Sarah moved closer. "Let me tell you about it."

"I gotta go." Harry stood up, "got things I gotta do."

"Later," Sarah suggested.

"No, now," Harry insisted. "I gotta go." Harry opened the door and left, leaving Sarah sitting on the couch.

Things hadn't worked as planned, but Sarah accepted the disappointment with grace. Her "club" approach hadn't worked, so Sarah decided to hold off for a while and try a "business" approach.

When Harry came to work in the morning, Sarah sauntered over. "Sorry about last night."

"No problem."

"We gotta talk business."

"What kind?"

"Newspaper," Sarah suggested. "I hear you were a printer."

"I was."

"We'll have to talk," Sarah insisted, "when we get a chance."

"Let's."

But Isobel arrived. She put Harry to work. Sarah didn't pursue her business with Harry while her mother was around, but she caught up with him again as soon as her mother left. Sarah said, "We gotta talk about starting a paper."

"When?"

"After work," Sarah suggested, "in my office."

That evening Harry followed Sarah to her reading nook that had become an office. There was a desk and chairs, but the couch was there. Sarah lit a candle and pulled out a bottle of wine. She popped the cork.

Harry said, "Thought we were talking business."

"We are." Sarah poured the wine and pulled out a block of cheese. Just figured we could share a little wine and nibble on some cheese while we talk. I've got cheddar."

Harry sat on the couch. It was firm. Harry said, "Nice couch."

"That's why I kept it," Sarah handed Harry a glass of wine. They spent an hour or so sipping wine and nibbling cheddar while they talked about Tampa, the couch, and starting a paper. They finished the first bottle and started another. Harry shared some of his printing experiences.

"It'll work," Sarah insisted. "Mother has influence with business people on the island, and there's the Jacaranda outfit. They've got connections."

The candle was sputtering when Harry put down his glass. He got up to leave, but Sarah reached over. "Glad we talked." She planted a quick kiss on Harry's lips. Harry returned her kiss; then started to pull back. Sarah said, "Gentlemen finish what they start."

CHAPTER TWENTY FIVE

Tampa Town Commerce

Southwest Florida
October 1854-January 1855

Sarah and Harry forgot about the newspaper. Nobody mentioned the paper that night or the next. But Sarah recalled the overt reason for her prolonged dalliances in the stockroom when Isobel showed up on the shuttle boat, stayed over for a few days, and asked her, "What's going on at the store? You're spending a lot of time down there."

Sarah said, "Talking with Harry."

"What about," Isobel demanded.

"Newspapers," Sarah blurted, "talking about newspapers."

"Three nights in a row," Isobel grumbled. "What about newspapers?"

"Starting one," Sarah insisted. "They had a paper before the hurricane. Harry printed the paper. We could sell advertising, print papers, and sell them. We could make a lot of money."

Isobel found it surprising that her otherwise impractical daughter was suddenly excited about making money. Isobel considered the matter before telling Sarah, "I'll talk with a few people about it."

Business picked up at the store and hotel as men came from Georgia, Alabama, and the Carolinas seeking land under the terms of the Armed Occupation Act. The newcomers took rooms at the hotel while they staked out land claims along the Hillsborough and Myakka Rivers.

The traffic energized the local economy. Doc Dunfield opened a new clinic and apothecary shop. Diggory Dunigan was so excited about being elected mayor that he expanded

156

his casket business. Brinton Hooker recovered from the disappointment of not being elected mayor and fixed up his barn on Washington Street. Then he put up a new eating and drinking emporium, the Buccaneer Bar, in front of the barn.

Isobel took a look at the improving economic situation, cut a deal with Sidney to watch over her Key West operation, and started spending more time in Tampa Town. Then the federal government gave the Florida legislature twenty million acres of wetland under the terms of the Swamp and Overflowed Lands Act. The legislature was glad to get the land but didn't know what to do with it. After due consideration, they decided to give land grants to private individuals who submitted plans for draining and developing the land.

Speculators rushed to Tampa Town to take advantage of the opportunity. They took rooms in the hotel and spent hours at the bar. Then they sent out survey parties to tramp over the hinterlands.

The surveyors didn't do manual labor. They demanded black field hands to carry loads and chop survey lines. As black field hands were in short supply in Tampa Town, Brinton Hooker dashed off a quick letter to Beauregard Bemrose in Tallahassee urging him to bring down a boatload. Beauregard, sensing an opportunity for profit, followed up on Brinton's letter by picking up a dozen slaves on consignment, loading them on an old coastal schooner, and hauling them to Tampa.

The hulk struggled into the Tampa Town harbor late one afternoon and tied up across the pier from the *Salvor*. Captain McRae wasn't much concerned, but Willy sniffed the air, saying, "We got ourselves a slaver."

Captain McRae said, "Don't worry about it. It's just another merchant trying to scratch out an honest living by doing a little business."

Willy shook his head. "Don't much cotton to that kind of business." Willy went below and didn't come up for the rest of the day.

Brinton came down to the harbor a little later and boarded the schooner. He found Beauregard on deck and the slaves in the hold. Brinton asked Beauregard, "How many you got?"

"A dozen," Beauregard told him. "I gotta get them off the boat."

"Where you gonna put 'em?"

"Your place," Beauregard insisted. "Where else am I gonna put 'em."

"Aint got a place fer them," Brinton complained. "I don't want them in my bar or my barn."

"Why can't I put them in the barn," Beauregard grumbled.

"Running my other business in the barn," Brinton blustered, "can't mix sugar and molasses."

"Aint you got any other place where we could put them," Beauregard asked. "It won't be long."

"There's a shed behind the barn. I don't know if you want to put your negras in there. Used to keep mules in there"

"It'll do. I gotta put them someplace."

"If you say so," Brinton grumbled. "Figured you was gonna sell them."

"I'll hold an auction but I gotta get the word out." Beauregard shrugged his shoulders. "Sumabitch, let's get this show on the road!"

Beauregard herded his little covee of dispirited field hands ashore and chained them up in Brinton's shed. Then Beauregard limped over to the Tampa Bay City Hotel and rented a room while he worked out the details for his auction. Once he had his room, he settled on a stool at the corner of the bar and ordered a rum tonic. Having completed his thinking on the matter, Beauregard asked Isobel, "How about me running a slave auction off your front porch?"

Isobel said, "Aint ever done anything like that."

"Figured you'd probably say that," Beauregard replied. "I'll make some different arrangements."

"Now, hold on," Isobel snapped. "I never said I wouldn't do it. How much do I get out of this auction of yours if I do?"

"Four bits a head. How does that sound?"

"Not too bad if you got enough to make it worthwhile," Isobel replied. "I'm running a business and not taking this on just fer the fun of it."

"I got a dozen negras chained up over in Brinton's shed."

Isobel calculated her take. "A dozen will do."

Beauregard cleaned up his twelve field hands as best he could and lined them up in front of the hotel. Several local residents, a few speculators, and a bunch of fishermen showed up to check out the merchandise. Then they waited around until Beauregard got enough of a crowd to start the auction. When the bidding was done and the slaves were sold, Beauregard counted his money. He handed Isobel six dollars.

Beauregard said, "We did pretty damn good. I'd have done better if I had a bigger turnout. I'll bring in another load but we gotta stir up more interest."

"I'll help on that," Isobel told Beauregard. "We're starting a paper."

"Sumabitch, that's a good idea," Beauregard blustered. "I'll run a couple of ads. That'll bring them out."

As the newspaper idea appeared to have merit, Isobel talked with Captain McRae about it. Captain McRea listened to his wife, thought about the idea for awhile, and talked with Willy about it. Willy shook his head as he grumbled, "Don't know a helluva lot about that business. You'd better talk with someone who does."

Isobel said, "I'll talk with Sidney. He'll know what to do." Isobel rode back to Key West and looked up Sidney.

"We had a paper up there awhile back," Sidney allowed. "Let me talk with a few people about it." That being decided, Isobel caught the shuttle back to Tampa Town. When she got back, she was so busy catering to the demands of the entrepreneurs and speculators at the bar in the hotel that she forgot about the newspaper.

Land speculators were mapping out their expeditions while they sent survey parties into the wetlands of South Florida. The surveyors ignored the Peace River Boundary as they crossed the river to conduct surveys on the Indian lands. The Seminoles filed protests with the War Department, but nobody paid much attention.

Charlie Conrad, the secretary of war, decided to do something about the Indians. He ordered General Twigs to clear a wagon road across the Florida peninsula from Fort Brooke to Fort Pierce. Secretary Conrad claimed the road would mark the northern boundary of the Indian lands to ensure the terms of the peace agreement. Others believed the road was being built to provide military access to the region to get rid of the Indians.

Tampa Town residents liked the road. The road brought money. Contracts were issued for surveys, labor, and cartage. Carey picked up a couple of contracts. Engineers started surveying the route and labor parties started clearing a path.

The road from Fort Brooke to Fort Pierce was completed in record time. General Twiggs then ordered his men to build stockades along the route and open a supply depot on the Peace River. This required more manpower than he had available, so General Twiggs called up the local militia unit for ninety days of service.

Harry was still a sergeant but the summons caught him by surprise. Harry put on his uniform and reported for duty. He figured he'd probably be assigned to garrison duty at Fort Brooke but once again discovered that realities of military service frequently differed from the expectations for such service.

Harry's squad was assigned to a thirty-four year old engineering lieutenant named George Meade. Lieutenant Meade loaded the squad on Carey's freight wagon for an unexpected jaunt to the old Indian ford at the headwaters of the Peace River. It took three days to get there and there wasn't much to see when they got there.

The Peace River was only about a hundred feet wide and a couple of feet deep but it was the dry season. Lieutenant Meade paced off a two acre parcel under the oak and pine trees. "This is it, boys. We're building Fort Meade."

The name made sense in a way. Harry and his men cleared the land. It took a good week to chop down the trees and cut them into logs. Then they had to build saw pits and saw the logs into posts, planks, and boards. Engineers and slaves started putting up buildings while Harry and his men sawed the timber. Several wooden buildings were constructed.

The enlisted men's quarters were positioned along the road and the officer's cabins were set back in the remnants of the oak grove. Stables were built along the river and a hospital building, consisting of "a room for the sick of all diseases," stood apart from the other buildings.

Although the river was relatively shallow and narrow, the engineers wanted to make certain they could cross the river during the rainy season. They built a huge log raft to carry freight wagons and coaches back and forth across the river. Harry's men got to haul the ropes that pulled the raft.

About two hundred regular army troops came to Fort Meade. About a third took sick with malaria, cholera, and other fevers as soon as they got there. About half of these men died. As Florida natives were considered resistant to tropical disease, Harry's men got the job of burying the dead. They worked at this detail until they completed their ninety days of duty. Then they were released.

Harry jumped on Carey's freight wagon to catch a ride back to Fort Brooke. Harry jumped off the wagon as soon as it rolled into town and dashed down the road to the hotel. Sarah rushed out. "You're a mess!"

"I'm back."

"So I see. Get cleaned up."

Harry spent the next few days recovering from the deployment. Then General Twiggs decided to build a stockade at the mouth of the Caloosahatchee River. The Seminole sent a letter of protest to the War Department, but nobody answered the letter.

Congress debated the matter for awhile before passing a military appropriations bill that authorized building a fort on the Caloosahatchee River. The Seminoles sent another letter. Getting tired of receiving the complaints, Secretary Conrad ordered General Twiggs, "Get rid of them."

Colonel Garland sent Lieutenant Hartsuff out with a survey party. Lieutenant Hartsuff and a handful of men struggled back to the Caloosahatche a few days later. Lieutenant Hartsuff had been wounded and three men killed by what Lieutenant Hartsuff claimed was an unprovoked attack by Billy Bowlegs and his braves.

Reports of the massacre were sent to Washington and Tallahassee. The Florida Legislature responded with glee. A good little Indian war would get rid of the Indians and open the lands south of the old Peace River Boundary. The governor called out the militia and Beauregard Bemrose, the militia's ranking colonel, put on his uniform.

Colonel Garland gathered up three hundred mounted infantrymen and rode out of Fort Myers to round up the Injuns, but warriors were waiting. The Indians launched an ambush and casualties were inflicted. Colonel Garland backed off and scrambled back to the fort. Chief Bowlegs, having made his point, withdrew and vanished into the Big Cypress.

About a week later a bunch of Indians attacked the Tillis family homestead on the north bank of the Peace River. The family held off the attackers until a militia unit from Fort Meade arrived to drive off the Indians. The militia pursued the Indians through the brush and across the river. Three whites and an Indian were killed.

Homesteaders living across central and southern Florida fled to the forts. Then a war party attacked the blockhouse that guarded the entrance to the Caloosahatchee River. A soldier was killed and another wounded. General Twiggs called Colonel Garland back to Fort Brooke. "Hold that stockade until we finish the fort."

Colonel Garland didn't want to take his engineers off the construction project so he decided to reinforce the stockade with militia. He called in Sergeant Harry Lane. "Get your boys together, run down to the Caloosahatche, and reinforce the stockade at the mouth of the river. We're running supplies up the river and need to keep the river open until we finish the fort."

Harry asked, "Who's running the operation?"

"You are. I'm promoting you to lieutenant and putting you in charge. Get your boys down there!"

"Yes sir!" Harry tried to assume a military stance.

"And get a proper uniform."

"Yes sir! Right away, sir," Harry snapped, imitating Captain Cotesworth. "One more question, sir."

"What's that?"

"How do we get there?"

"You work for McRae. He's got a steamboat. Get him to take you."

Harry accepted the shock of being promoted to officer. He rushed to the uniform shop where he purchased a field blouse and silver bars denoting his rank. Properly attired, he swaggered to the Tampa Bay City Hotel to find Isobel. He had to make transportation arrangements.

Isobel took a look. "I can get you on the *Salvor,* but you'd better tell Sarah."

"Won't be long," Harry insisted, "just until they finish the fort."

"Never know, do what you gotta do."

Harry didn't know how much Isobel knew about his relationship with her daughter but didn't want to ask. Isobel said, "Run along. I'll talk with Captain McRae. We'll fit you in."

Harry dashed to tell Sarah. "I'm a lieutenant!"

"Is that good?"

"Sure is. I'm taking my men to the Caloosahatche."

"You'll be gone."

"A short while but I'll be back."

"Sure hope so."

CHAPTER TWENTY SIX

Bemrose and the Swamp Rats

Southwest Florida
January 1855 - March 1858

It took Harry and fourteen men a couple of hours to get their equipment and supplies together and on board the *Salvor*. Sarah rushed to the boat and scrambled aboard for a prolonged farewell. Captain McRea put up with the delay for a half hour or so before kicking off his daughter. Willy got up steam to get underway.

The steamboat backed from the pier, made a great sweeping turn, and chugged across the bay. They were on their way to the Caloosahatche. When they arrived, the boat anchored in deep water while the crewmen rowed the dinghy back and forth taking Harry, his troops, and equipment ashore. Then Harry led his fourteen stalwart warriors up a narrow path to the stockade to reinforce the sergeant and ten soldiers who survived the Indian attack. The Indians were gone. Harry, being the only officer, took command.

Harry was familiar with the area as the stockade stood less than a half mile from the site of Dallam's store. Harry wasn't taking any chances this time. He sent out his men cut away the trees and brush growing around the stockade. He posted guards. Harry prepared for action but it never came. Steamboats towing barges chugged up and down the river. Material and supplies were being hauled to the new fort being built upstream.

A couple of weeks passed before a messenger floated down on a barge. The messenger told Harry, "They want you at the fort."

"What about my men?"

"Bring them."

Harry and his men abandoned their stockade, boarded the barge, and rowed it up the river. It took awhile to get to Fort Myers as they were not accustomed to carrying out such tasks of a nautical nature.

Fort Myers, the nation's newest military depot, was rising on disputed territory. The army engineers weren't that concerned as they were busy supervising the gangs of slaves clearing land and building buildings. A few cabins stood around a partially cleared parade ground. Larger structures were being constructed. Fort Myers wasn't much of a fort but looked like it might become one.

A sergeant greeted them. He put Harry's men in a partially completed barracks and took Harry over to a roughhewn command center to meet Colonel Garland. Colonel Garland said, "Glad you made it. We're bringing in the rest of our militia and consolidating them for an operation with the navy. Tallahassee's sending the ranking militia colonel down to take charge. We'll go over details as soon as he gets here."

Harry moved into a log building and waited for the ranking colonel. Other junior militia officers arrived. They waited for the colonel. A week or so later, Colonel Beauregard Bemrose limped ashore. He complained about the lack of proper military etiquette being extended on his arrival but otherwise seemed content.

Colonel Garland introduced Colonel Bemrose, "We're in luck boys. Colonel Bemrose is here to lead us. He was a swamp rat in the last war and came out of retirement to do it again."

The officers jumped to their feet as Colonel Bemrose limped to the front of the room. "Sumabitch boys," he shouted. "We're gonna have ourselves one hell of a good rip-snorting time!"

Limping back and forth, Beauregard spotted Harry. "Sumabitch boy, I've seen you before, know you from someplace."

"Groggery," Harry insisted, "you swore me in."

"Maybe so...but there was something else. Don't worry. It'll come to me. Mark my words, I never forget a face." That being said, Beauregard pivoted and went back to lecturing, "And for the rest of you, I'm bringing good news. You're gonna be just like me."

This provoked a few grunts, but Beauregard prevailed, "I'm a mean old alligator, a genuine ring-tailed swamp rat, and I'm gonna turn you boys into swamp rats just like me! You're gonna go out in those swamps, grab those Injuns where they live, and drag them in here. It's a simple job but fun, anybody got questions?"

A lieutenant asked, "How we doing this?"

Colonel Garland explained, "We're running a combined operation with the navy. Captain Farley's sending marines into the Everglades. They'll chase the Injuns out and we'll catch 'em."

A man protested, "What about the regulars? What are they doing?"

Colonel Garland said, "Holding the fort."

"How come they're not going?"

Colonel Garland said, "The fort's a priority. The regulars are here to build it. That's their job. Besides, you fellow live here, know your way around, and are acclimated to the climate. You're more for the job."

There was grumbling. Bemrose shouted, "Stop your bitchin! We're better at being swamp rats than they are. I told ya we're gonna have fun. You're gonna have more fun than a one legged pirate sporting a wooden prick in a bawdy house. What the hell more can a man want?"

Grumbling gave way to laughter. Colonel Garland said, "Listen up! Rathborne's taking the lead. I'm sending him up the Caloosahatchee and over the ridge to Okeechobee. Lane's following. The rest of you are going down the cost. Work your way into the Big Cypress. You'll run into the marines out there."

"There's a mix-up," Harry argued. "I'm a printer...don't know anything about this."

"Sumabitch," Colonel Bemrose shouted. "You're a lucky boy. You're gonna get more to print than you ever thought you'd ever get. Get with the program."

Colonel Garland said, "You've had combat experience."

Harry blurted, "Where?"

"Dallam's store," Colonel Garland replied. "You were there."

Being again confronted by the irrational whims of fate, Harry sat down. A lieutenant asked, "The rules of engagement, do we just shoot 'em or bring them in?"

Colonel Bemrose said, "That's a stupid question. If someone shoots at you, shoot him. We're not running a Sunday School picnic!"

Harry wasn't particularly pleased with the situation, but the assignment would get him out of Fort Myers and away from Bemrose. He walked down to the river to check out his boat crew and found Sergeant Jake Sutherlin waiting with a bunch of cow catchers.

Rube Rigby, Jake's foreman, spoke up, "I'll be damned. Where'd get those lieutenant's bars?"

"Not from some mouthy cowcatcher," Harry blustered, trying to emulate the language of command. "You mean, I've got to put up with you people."

"Your lucky day," Rube insisted. "We'll save your butt."

Harry was relieved to discover Sergeant Sutherland, Corporal Rigby, and twelve cow catchers constituted his boat crew. They knew their way around. Maybe they could keep him out of trouble.

The boat was a shallow draft thing, more of a barge. They were sent up the Caloosahatchee into the heart of the Seminole homeland to seek out Indians, burn their settlements, and destroy their crops. The trip wasn't too bad at first. They were able to row and pole their way up the river, but then, it went downhill.

They had to drag the loaded boat over sandbars and other obstructions in shallow water. The men floundered up to their waist. They fought off mosquitoes and other insects while they kept a wary eye for snakes and alligators. They encountered a few snakes, but the snakes didn't bother them so long as they gave the snakes time to get out of the way. They came upon several abandoned huts and a few hideouts along the way. They burned the dwellings but didn't see any Indians.

They stumbled upon an inhabited log dwelling the fourth day out. Harry positioned his men around the hut and advanced upon the structure. A shot rang out, and Harry's men responded by firing round after round into the dwelling. No other shots were received. It was quiet. Then Corporal Rigby shouted, "I'm going in!"

Rube lit off a torch, dashed through the grass, and tossed the torch into the building. The building burned to the ground. The men waited for the fire to run its course before dragging a couple of corpses out of the ashes. They left the corpses and continued on their way. Harry had no way of knowing if the shot came from the dwelling or if it had been fired by one of his men.

The 1856 presidential election was held while the war continued. None of the boys in the swamp knew anything about the election and wouldn't have much cared if they did. The Democrats were running James Buchanan. The Whig Party had collapsed and the American Party was running Millard Fillmore. There were rumors of a new Northern abolition party, but nobody knew much of anything about that.

The Big Cypress operation continued through the winter and into the spring and summer of 1857. The boat crews made long treks along the Caloosahatchee and Alafie Rivers with an occasional jaunt up the Peace River. It was dreadful duty. Harry and his boat company were crossing over the headwaters of the Caloosahatchee one spring day when they came upon an old Indian man, three women, four children, and a black man. The Indians couldn't peak English, but the black man surprised them.

The black man said, "Figured you boys might come along this way. The old man is sick and the rest of us aint had nothing to eat for the last four days."

Jake asked, "What do we do with them?"

Harry said, "Take them back."

The black man said, "I'd appreciate that."

Then Harry recognized the man. Harry blurted, "Damn! You were with us at Dallam's store. What was your name?"

The black man looked them over and nodded. "Think you called me Floyd. I believe that was the name."

"What are you doing here?"

"Making do with what I got. I came from Georgia to get free. The Seminole took me in and made me a slave. Then you people took me and made me a slave. Then the Calusa got me and made me a slave. Now you got me again."

Harry's boat company fed the captives and took them back to Fort Myers. Floyd was turned over to the army and put to work at the saw mill. The war sputtered along for a few more months. Then the nation's new president, President Buchanan, stopped the war.

President Buchanan figured it would be cheaper to ignore the remaining Indians than fight them. There were only a few Seminoles left in Florida and they had been pushed out of the way. The desirable lands south of the Peace River were available for development and settlement. Besides, President Buchanan had other interests.

It took time for the new administration's policy to trickle down to the swamp rats. When General Twiggs got word of the change, he told Colonel Garland and Colonel Garland told Colonel Bemrose. It took a couple of more weeks for Beauregard to round up his swamp rats. Beauregard called them in. "Go home, boys. The war's over."

Jake said, "Just getting used to chasing Injuns. Now, I gotta go back to cow catching."

"Not me," Rube insisted. "I'm raising a little hell. Then I'm grabbin' some of that free land they're giving away."

Harry said, "I'm going home."

169

CHAPTER TWENTY SEVEN

Pursuing Manifest Destiny

Washington City
April 15, 1858

By all accounts, James Buchanan was the most qualified candidate to ever become president. He spent two or three hours working in his office on most mornings. He read his mail, wrote out lengthy longhand responses, read a few newspapers, and chatted with whoever happened to stop by. Then he left the Executive Mansion to stroll along Pennsylvania Avenue. He stopped people along the way and chatted with them about domestic issues and foreign affairs. Then he walked over to 329 Maryland Avenue.

Lewis Cass, the secretary of state, was there to update the president on the Cuban situation. Mary Ann brought an asset from Key West, and Caleb was bringing Congressman Quitman. The Buchanan administration had already closed down the Florida Indian operation, secured its mainland base, and was getting ready to turn the Caribbean into an American lake. Cuba was the first step.

Spain's hold on the island was tenuous at best. Great Britain was threatening to seize the island under the semblance of a financial pretext. France was lurking around the edges of the controversy and there were a few wealthy Creoles living in Havana who had the temerity to suggest breaking away from Spain to become a separate and independent nation. The United States needed to make its move and do it quickly.

When the Spanish war frigate *Ferrolana* fired on the American Mail Steamer *El Dorado* in March 1855, the public clamored for revenge, but President Pierce dithered, dallied, and delayed. He squandered the opportunity. James Buchanan promised to correct this oversight and was about to do so. Cuba was the agenda.

Mary Ann brought her asset into the room. "Perhaps you remember Amanda."

"I do," President Buchanan replied. "You were here awhile back."

"I was." Amanda curtsied. "It's good being back."

"Glad you're here," President Buchanan claimed. "We need someone who's familiar with Florida."

"She's familiar with the region," Mary Ann insisted, "and the players."

"Probably," President Buchanan replied. "Where's Quitman? He said he'd be here."

Secretary Cass nodded toward the door. "They're here."

Caleb opened the French doors and came in with Congressman Quitman, chairman of the military affairs committee. Quitman glanced around the room before selecting the upholstered chair by the window. Caleb sat on a straight chair.

"Let's get started," President Buchanan insisted. "How's it going?"

"Coming along," Quitman replied. "The committee's on board but our field people are running into problems."

Secretary Cass asked, "What's up?"

"Matter of commitments," Quitman explained. "We had everything lined up and ready to go a couple of years ago when Frank Pierce pulled the plug. Now we're running into a wait and see attitude. Nobody wants to rent anything."

"That's a shame," President Buchanan grumbled. "We had a clear shot at the time, could have picked up Cuba, and probably Puerto Rico, but Frank lost his nerve."

"That's it," Quitman agreed. "Six thousand men locked and loaded, but Frank sent in the navy and cleaned us out."

Amanda said, "Cora was fit to be tied."

"Britain," Secretary Cass insisted, "They sent the boat."

"Renfrew," Amanda blurted. "He slipped by us."

"That's history," President Buchanan insisted. "What's done is done. Let's get to the issue at hand."

Quitman said, "Cora's stoking the Havana connection. She needs a little more money to wrap it up, but she'll have her creoles out on the streets of Havana kicking up a storm as soon as we give the word."

Secretary Cass turned to Amanda. "Aren't you collecting money?"

"We are. Nicole's got it in a special account."

"None of ours, I hope," Mary Ann murmured. "Don't want anyone tracing anything back to us. Wasn't a Cuban collecting the money?"

"Collecting it but not holding," Caleb insisted. "He's a front man."

"It's a New York bank," Amanda explained. "We got a branch on the island. O'Donnell set it up."

Secretary Cass suggested, "You'll need collateral."

"Got it," Caleb replied. "We filed a hundred thousand in federal bonds with the state comptroller. We're using them."

President Buchanan asked, "Where'd you get the bonds?"

"Treasury," Caleb said, "discounted by half."

"Sounds risky," Secretary Cass grumbled. "Don't you need New Yorkers as trustees?"

"Got 'em," Caleb insisted. "O'Donnell and I are from New York, and Nadeau's from the Adirondacks. That's New York."

"Who's Nadeau?" President Buchanan asked. "He sounds like a Frenchman."

"Not he," Amanda answered, "she's single and over twenty-one, so it's legal."

Mary Ann said, "Nicole."

"Precisely," Caleb asserted. "We had to have an on-site trustee. Nicole's on Key West and able to do the job."

Secretary Cass asked, "What does a woman know about money?"

"A lot," Mary Ann insisted. "She's a trained bookkeeper."

"And earmarked the funds," Amanda added.

Secretary Cass blurted, "What do you mean?"

172

Caleb said, "Sporting ventures, buffalo hunting, that sort of thing. It worked before and it'll work again. Consistency ensures credibility."

"Probably," President Buchanan agreed. "I'm not that concerned about your financial shenanigans. I've got more important concerns."

Quitman said, "Such as?"

"Managing the operation," President Buchanan insisted. "We've got the groundwork in place but we can't make a final offer until we wrap up a few more of our details. It's a matter of timing."

"Guess I don't have the whole picture," Quitman grumbled, "figured we were just going for an insurrection and invasion."

"Part of the plan," Secretary Cass explained. "We're trying to buy the island. We've got a thirty million offer on the table and we're buying up the two hundred million dollar debt that Spain owes Great Britain. We're picking up the English notes for about twenty-five cents on a dollar and once we have them, we'll put the squeeze on Spain. Spain will have to pay or give us the island."

"That's why we need the invasion threat," Caleb explained. "If Spain faces a financial crisis at the same time as it confronts the possibility of insurrection and armed invasion, they're more likely to sell the island."

"I see," Quitman conceded, "might work."

Caleb said, "It will."

"Keep it moving," President Buchanan insisted. "But keep it quiet."

"It's moving," Secretary Cass insisted. "The army's pulling their troops out of Fort Brooke and redeploying them to Fort Taylor on Key West. We're beefing up our naval presence in the Caribbean. We'll have a credible military presence in the area and have it ready if the buffalo hunters go for a frolic."

"Public opinion," President Buchanan cautioned.

"Working on it," Caleb replied. "We're setting up a newspaper in South Florida, proximity lends credibility. We'll feed the printer inflammatory articles to influence public opinion and build support for the endeavor."

Secretary Cass told Quitman, "Get your boys ready."

"They're ready. Just need a way to get them there, that's all."

President Buchanan asked, "What's your problem?"

"That's what I started to say," Quitman sputtered. "Nobody will rent us anything after the navy took their boats the last time around."

President Buchanan told Caleb, "Get 'em a boat."

"Not a problem," Caleb replied. "I'll shift one over to the Jacaranda outfit. They're an import/export operation. Nobody will know the difference."

President Buchanan said, "Oughta work."

CHAPTER TWENTY EIGHT

Commercial Transactions

Tampa Town
May 1858 through January 1860

The army left Fort Myers after the Bowlegs War ended and closed Fort Brooke. The troops were redeployed to Fort Taylor, a new fort being constructed on Key West. Then the federal government canceled the Tampa civilian contracts, dismissed the laborers, and turned the slaves over to Beauregard Bemrose to be sold at auction.

Beauregard came to Tampa. Brinton moved his girls to a better location, and Beauregard turned Brinton's old barn into a slave quarters and auction house. Auctions were held on some Thursday afternoons, but Beauregard spent most of his time perched on a stool at the bar at the Tampa Bay City Hotel. Beauregard limped in early most days and hung around until Isobel kicked him out at closing time.

Carey Hayes stopped over from time to time to enjoy a few drinks. Jake stopped when he brought his cattle drives to Tampa. Diggory Dunigan, the postmaster and undertaker, now mayor of Tampa, stopped by on occasion.

Beauregard dominated the discourse. He recited rousing tales of his military prowess and valor, especially his significant role in the battle at Ahapopka. Beauregard claimed, "Sumabitch, boys! We jumped in that hell hole, grabbed 'em by their tails and hauled 'em out."

Jake asked, "What'd you do that for?"

"Had to get them to come out and fight," Beauregard shouted. "They nicked me in my leg during the fracas, but we got 'em!"

"Ass," Carey said. "They shot you in the ass."

"Sumabitch, it was the leg!" Beauregard shouted. "They shot me in my leg."

At other times Beauregard complained about being ignored by the army, being passed over for promotion, and otherwise, being treated in shabby fashion by the Tallahassee bureaucrats. "Politics," Beauregard claimed, "that's what it is."

"What are you talking about," Diggory grumbled. "Somebody made you a colonel. That's pretty damn good!"

"To hell too," Beauregard grumbled, "I should have made general. I got some opportunities along the way but got screwed every time. It started with the dog caper. A blue blood, high society city boy from South Carolina stuck it to me. He came up to Tallahassee with a scrawny little Yankee. Gave them a good deal, but they shot off their mouths to some big shots and I got screwed."

"Sounds like a Yankee," Carey insisted. "They're like that you know."

"Oh, I surely know," Beauregard agreed. "I've been watching for those two boys ever since and I'll string both of them up by their necks if I ever find 'em. The smooth-talking city boy was the one who did me in. Nothing good ever crawled out of the Carolina low country."

Jake said, "Thought you were from Carolina."

"North Carolina," Beauregard blustered. "That sumabitch who screwed me came from Charleston. That's South Carolina. Nothing good ever came out of Charleston. If I live to be a hundred, I'll never forget his smooth talking ways."

"What about the Yankee," Carey asked.

"Altogether different matter," Beauregard claimed. "Yankees look and sound pretty much alike. Never could tell one from another."

"That's a fact," Carey agreed.

Most of them generally went along with Beauregard on most things, but for the most part, they were more concerned about their own problems. Hungry, forgotten, displaced veterans stalked the streets of Tampa Town seeking shelter and sustenance. Burglary had become an accepted lifestyle.

Drunks camped in the thickets and under the trees. Ruffians tried to steal freight off Carey's ox carts.

Jake Sutherlin collected a few of the better class of vagrants and took them off to become cow catchers. Great herds of wild cattle roamed the grasslands of the Myakka, Peace, and Caloosahatche Rivers.

When Harry got home, Isobel said, "Glad you're back. We're setting up a newspaper."

"Where are you getting the equipment?"

"Don't know," Isobel replied. "Sidney cut a deal with someone. We just got to print the articles they send us. Otherwise, we can print whatever we want."

"Where's Sidney getting the articles?"

"Don't know," Isobel admitted. "We gotta print something in it if they're gonna gives us a paper and I figure if they give us something, we don't have to write it."

Captain McRae steamed into the harbor a couple of weeks later carrying a new Hoe Cylindrical-Bed Press, type, ink, reams of paper, and a file of prepared articles. Harry set up the press in a shed behind the hotel and started printing the first edition of the *Tampa Weekly Journal*. He placed the prepared articles on the first page. The articles provided lurid descriptions of the atrocities being foisted off on the Cuban people by the Spanish authorities in Cuba.

Harry filled up the rest of the paper with local news, Diggory's obituaries, and a few advertisements. Harry sold a few papers around town and shipped a stack to Key West on the *Salvor*. Captain McRae gave Sidney the papers and Sidney sent them to Washington. Caleb sent the papers to several Democratic newspapers scattered around the country.

Edition followed edition and every edition highlighted the deplorable details of daily life in Cuba. The nation assumed that these descriptions had to be accurate because Tampa was close to Cuba and able to obtain credible information. Harry went about his business printing his newspaper, selling a few local copies, and shipping the rest to

Key West. He didn't know that he was influencing public opinion.

Carey Hayes stopped by the print shop from time to time to pick up a paper and buy advertising. One afternoon he announced, "I'm taking over the army's old saw mill down on the river. There's a market for lumber and I'm filling it."

Harry asked, "Gonna run the mill with your bullwhackers?"

"Nope, Bemrose still has the boys who ran the mill for the army. I'm gonna go over there and see if I can get them."

"I thought Bemrose sold those boys."

"Not all of them," Carey insisted. "The big one, the one they call Samson, is pretty mouthy. Nobody wants him so Beauregard's keeping the other one until he can sell both."

"Doesn't make sense," Harry claimed. "Why doesn't he just sell the one?"

"You know how it is. It's all or nothing with Beauregard."

Harry said, "If you want them, you'd better get over there. Bemrose will be shipping them out if he can't sell them."

"Come along," Carey suggested. "Let's see what he's got."

"Don't know if I really want to go over there," Harry claimed. "Bemrose and I get along better if I keep some distance between us."

"Come on," Carey insisted. "You're just bothered about how he acted during the war. He's got a mouth on him but can't do anything now."

That being the case, Harry went along with Carey and they walked over to Beauregard's auction house. The barn had seen better days. Someone had kicked in the front door but that didn't bother Beauregard.

Cary picked his way around the broken door and they went into the barn. Beauregard limped out to greet them. Beauregard said, "Sumabitch! Come in, boys. Don't just stand there in the door blocking the daylight. I aint got many negras left but I got a few. There's an old field hand, couple of mill operators, and a cute little breeder if you're into that sort of thing."

178

Carey said, "Thought we'd take a look."

"Then hustle in and take a look. You can't see much if you're blocking the light coming in from the doorway."

"Got a point there," Carey conceded as he followed Beauregard into the dim interior of the barn. Beauregard limped along until they came to an elderly field hand chained to a post.

Beauregard said, "Got a few good years left and I can give you a good deal if you want him." Beauregard had cleaned the old fellow up a little and outfitted him with a relatively new shirt pulled over a patched pair of canvas trousers. Beauregard continued, "This boy has a little experience behind him. He knows what to do, when to do it, and how to do it. He's been broken in so he'll give you a damn good day's work without any sass!"

Carey said, "Heard you had the mill operators."

"Out back," Beauregard replied. "The big one's uppity but I been working on him."

Carey said, "I'd like to take a look."

"I'm a tellin' you, he's a mouthy sumabitch," Beauregard warned. "If you want him, I'll give you a good price but you got to take both of them. They go together."

"What's wrong with the other one?"

"Half Injun and a runner," Beauregard replied.

Carey said, "Thought the army used them at the mill."

"Oh, they did. You gotta watch 'em though."

"I see," Carey replied. "I don't know if I'm about to pay good money for uppity negras or runners, but guess I'll take a look while I'm here."

Harry and Carey followed Beauregard out behind the barn where they found a big black man chained to a post and another seated on a low bench behind the bars of an iron cage. As Beauregard pointed toward the man chained to the post, he said, "That's the mouthy one. Been giving him a little threshing now and then but hasn't helped."

A few welts crisscrossed the man's back. Samson demonstrated his uppity nature by ignoring them. Harry glanced at the cage. He recognized Floyd.

Harry walked over and asked, "What's going on, Floyd?"

Floyd said, "Gettin' by."

Beauregard asked Harry, "You know him?"

"Run across him a few times," Harry replied.

"He'll work out," Carey surmised. "Maybe, I'll take him."

"I'll sell you the runner but you got to take the other one too," Beauregard insisted. "They're a matched set, go together."

Carey checked out Samson. Samson ignored him. Carey finally said, "It don't look like you broke him up too much. He'll probably heal up pretty good. I'll take him off your hands, but you gotta give me a half-way decent price if I take both."

"If I can work you up to a half-way decent price, that oughta work," Beauregard replied. "We gotta dicker."

Carey and Beauregard dickered for an hour or so, came to an agreement, and Carey took the slaves. As they were leaving, Beauregard took a look at Harry. He grumbled, "You aint said a hell of a lot. What's your problem?"

"No problem." Harry replied.

"I know you from someplace."

"I'm the printer," Harry insisted. "I print the *Journal*."

"Yeah, I know," Beauregard conceded. "But I still think I ran into you before."

Harry said, "Fort Myers! I was a swamp rat. You chased my butt through the swamps down there."

"Had fun, didn't we." Beauregard chuckled at the thought. Then he said, "Oh, yeah! I remember. You're the one who dragged Floyd out of the swamp."

"That's right," Harry agreed.

"No wonder you knew Floyd," Beauregard blustered. "But still seems like there was something else. Let me think on it."

Carey put his two slaves to work at the mill. Harry continued putting out his paper and printing the articles that

Captain McRae brought from Key West. The articles talked about the civil unrest permeating the island and the opportunities that existed for men of destiny. Fame, fun, and good fortune for a few brave men to answer the call to arms, step forth, and rescue the Cuban people from oppression.

Some articles stirred up a little interest.

CHAPTER TWENTY NINE

Matrimony and Filibusters

Tampa Bay
January 1860 through June 1860

Harry churned out weekly editions of the *Journal* without thinking about it. He sold a few copies around Tampa and shipped the rest to Key West. Captain McRae took the papers and brought back articles, paper, and ink. Somebody appeared to be paying for the supplies, but Harry didn't ask. He had other concerns.

Sarah was taking more time. They chatted frequently during the day, met in the afternoon, enjoyed a late supper at the store, and explored the parameters of their developing relationship. Locking doors lost their urgency.

Isobel came down from the Eagle's Nest one evening, went into the store, walked to the stock room, and yanked the door open. A flickering candle provided the only illumination, but it generated more than enough to reveal the couple on the couch. Isobel said. "Guess, we gotta talk."

"Oh, my God," Sarah gasped. "Go away."

Isobel shut the door. "Figured this is what's been going on."

Sarah sat up. "How'd you know?"

"Not stupid, honey," Isobel replied. "Figured talking with you would be a waste of time, so I'll talk with Harry."

"What about," Harry mumbled.

"Doing what's right," Isobel insisted. "It appears you've been doing this for awhile now. About time you got married."

Sarah groaned, "Mother."

Harry said, "I guess."

Isobel told Harry, "You gotta talk with the captain."

"Probably so," Harry agreed. Marriage might have advantages. Harry didn't own anything. Sarah's family had ships and stores. It took Isobel longer to convince her daughter that marriage was a good and proper thing to do.

Isobel told Sarah, "Harry's dependable and a hard worker."

"I guess," Sarah conceded.

"Getting married is a good idea."

"Protection," Sarah suggested.

"Yes, there is that. Besides, I'd like a grandchild."

"Oh! My God," Sarah blurted.

A few days later Harry walked down to the pier to have his talk with Captain McRae. He boarded the *Salvor* and made his way forward to the wheelhouse where he found Willy with the captain.

Captain McRae interrupted his conversation with Willy to ask Harry, "What do you want this time?"

Harry said, "Gotta talk."

"Well," Captain McRae replied as he puttered around with the ship's wheel. "I'm not doing anything right now so let's talk. "What've you got to say?"

Harry glanced at Willy. "Alone."

"There aint nothing you can say that Willy can't hear."

"About your daughter," Harry pleaded.

"Gotta grease the main shaft," Willy mumbled as he turned and walked away. "Not getting mixed up in any o' that kind of stuff."

Captain McRea watched Willy depart. "What about Sarah?"

"Kind of complicated," Harry replied.

"Nothing complicated about diddling. She's plenty old enough."

"I guess," Harry replied. "How'd you know?"

"Twern't hard,' Captain McRae answered. "Sarah had that look about her when she got you to haul that couch down to the stockroom. Women get like that you know."

"How come you didn't say something?"

"Weren't any of my business," Captain McRae insisted. "Besides, I figured you might just as well be gettin' a little while you had a chance."

"We're getting married," Harry replied.

"That's what I meant," Captain McRea insisted. "Take it from me; you won't be getting a helluva lot after that happens. That's how it goes."

"Still getting married," Harry insisted.

"Probably so," Captain McRae replied. "Sarah's always been a headstrong sort of woman, but it'd be a good idea to make an honest woman out of her."

Captain McRae took them out on the *Salvor* and married them at sea on the way to Key West. Willy watched the wedding but didn't say much. Then the newlyweds spent a couple of days on Key West. Things were in a bit of a ruckus.

Congressman Quitman, who preferred being called "general," was on the island, running around, spending time at the Jacaranda Club, wandering in and out of Sidney's office, and talking with strangers. Diego said, "There's going to be a fight."

Sarah asked, "Where?"

"Cuba," Diego insisted.

"When," Sarah demanded.

"Don't know," Diego answered. "When they get ready, I guess."

Harry talked with General Quitman and Sidney. Sidney gave him articles to print in the paper. General Quitman said, "Good paper you got there. Keep it up."

"Oh, I will," Harry replied, not really knowing what General Quitman was talking about. The newlyweds caught the shuttle boat back to Tampa Town and Harry went back to setting type and printing the paper.

The first set of articles described Cuban atrocities. It talked about brutal slayings and executions. The second set presented lurid tales of enslavement and persecution. The third called for brave men of destiny to step forth and volunteer for a merciful mission to rescue the afflicted women and children of Cuba.

The call for volunteer's generated considerable interest at the Buccaneer Bar as it was the hangout for unemployed veterans. Activities picked up when General Quitman came to Tampa on the shuttle boat and opened a temporary recruiting station in an abandoned Fort Brooke guardhouse. A dozen or so veterans rushed up to the fort to sign up. They hung around for a day or so before Captain McRae showed up with a new steamboat.

The *Scottish Princess* sat low in the water. She looked powerful, sleek, and fast even when tied up. Willy said, "I got her up to eighteen knots and didn't even have to tie the safety valve down."

Jake Sutherlin took a look before asking Captain McRea, "What you hauling on that thing?"

Captain McRae said, "Buffalo hunters."

"Where'd you get the boat?"

"Don't be asking questions when you don't need to know the answers. Let's just say she came when needed."

Jake insisted, "A mite pretty fer cow hauling."

"Simon's hauling cows on the *Salvor*," Captain McRae grumbled. "I'm hauling dispatches and buffalo hunters."

"How'd you get mixed up in that business?"

Captain McRae growled, "Damn it! Don't be asking so many questions when you don't need to know the answers. That's all I'm gonna say."

General Quitman marched his volunteers down to the *Scottish Princess* and they boarded the vessel. That being done, Willy got up steam, backed away from the pier, and steamed away. The newspaper articles stopped coming.

This caught Harry by surprise and he had to scramble to find material to fill the paper. Word trickled back over the next few weeks that Congressman Quitman, the one time general, had suddenly taken sick, and died. Some suspected poisoning. Buffalo hunting plans were delayed and disrupted.

CHAPTER THIRTY
VIOLENCE AND VIGILANTES

Washington City and Tampa Bay
June through November 1860

Invasion rumors persisted. The presidents of Costa Rica and Nicaragua reacted by issuing the Rivas Manifesto that placed their countries under the protection of France, England, and Sardinia. Sardinia didn't do much, but England and France sent warships to the Caribbean. When congressional politics heated up over a slavery issue in Kansas, the Buchanan administration decided to hold off on implementing the Cuban plan until after the midterm.

However, the abolitionist opposition complicated matters by spreading malicious rumors to arouse the Northern electorate. The radical Republicans claimed the Buchanan administration was plotting to seize Cuba, Puerto Rico, Hispaniola, Nicaragua, and Costa Rica to bring them into the Union as Slave States. Such action would guarantee Slave State dominance in the senate and perpetuate the immoral practice of slavery.

The abolitionist Republicans held forty-four seats in the House of Representatives as an outcome of the 1856 general election. This increased to one hundred and sixteen seats after the midterm election. The Republicans used their new found power.

Pandemonium reigned. The House of Representatives took over two months to select a Speaker and then a fist fight broke out on the floor of the House that ended up with more than fifty congressmen fighting and wrestling. The Sergeant at Arms tried to stop the fighting, and the Speaker banged his gavel to no avail. The fighting continued until a Wisconsin brawler grabbed the hair of his Mississippi opponent and yanked off his wig. The fighting ended with the brawlers laughing over the scalping.

The legislative deadlock took its toll. Expansionist plans including the Cuban operation were placed on hold. Captain McRae parked the *Scottish Princess* and went back to hauling cows on the *Salvor*. The *Princess* was too expensive to operate and hauling cows was more fun.

Captain McRae hauled about seven hundred cows to market and increased this to over four thousand the following year. Jake Sutherland moved down to Fort Ogden on the Peace River to be closer to the cattle lands. Jake got the Jacaranda Company to put up a stockade and help him built a pier on the south side of the Peace River where it entered Charlotte Harbor. They now shipped their cows out of Charlotte Harbor rather than driving the cows all the way to Tampa.

Commerce dropped off in Tampa and gangs of unemployed ruffians started congregating at the Buccaneer Bar. Occasional fights, friendly stabbings, and a little maiming constituted the entertainment at the Buccaneer. It got so bad that the handful of self-respecting ladies who were living in Tampa Town went out of their way to avoid the area.

As it appeared that theft and corruption were becoming the primary means of livelihood, the few decent people who happened to live in Tampa Town became alarmed. Harry got his dander up when a group of hooligans confronted Sarah in the store and threatened her with bodily harm. Sarah went berserk and kicked their butts but Harry decided to take action. He printed an editorial in bold type on the front page of the *Journal* stating, ***"Vice has become triumphant and villainy is stalking the streets of our fair city. It stalks forth boldly and confronts us in our daily ventures in the bright light of the day."***

Something had to be done. Tampa Town didn't have a police force and even if it did, Tampa didn't have a court to maintain order. Harry, Isobel, Mayor Dunigan, Beauregard Bemrose, Carey, and a few others decided to take action. They held a meeting at the hotel, decided to get rid of the troublemakers, and gave the job to Carey and his bullwhackers. Captain McRae hauled a big iron cage or hoosegow up from Havana and the bullwhackers set the hoosegow up on the town square in front of the Tampa Bay City Hotel.

Carey and his bullwhackers became the Tampa Bay Regulators and set out to clean up the town. They started in a relatively moderate manner. If a culprit was observed disturbing the peace, a hickory switch was placed at the door of his cabin as a warning. If the problems continued, the malefactor was apprehended, taken downtown, tied to a post next to the hoosegow, and thrashed with the hickory switch.

This worked for awhile, but then the rabble started fighting back. The Regulators shot a ruffian, but the violence continued. The ruffians targeted Carey and jumped Carey's saw mill slaves as they attempted to deliver a load of lumber. Samson kicked the stuffing out of one vagrant and threatened another. The vagrants backed off, but the sight of a black slave accosting white vagrants bothered Brinton Hooker. He went looking for Beauregard.

Beauregard had strong opinions about such incidents. He trooped up the street looking for Carey. Beauregard shouted, "Sumabitch here, Carey! This town's going to hell. We can't have your negras beating up white men in the light of day."

"They was attacked," Carey protested. "They shouldn't have done that, but they was attacked."

"Bullshit," Beauregard snarled. "I told you that Samson was an uppity bastard but you took him anyway. "You gotta do something about this."

A crowd gathered and the situation was becoming a bit tense so Carey said, "We'll hold it over and check with the mayor."

"What are you doing with the negras," Beauregard demanded.

"Puttin' them in the hoosegow," Carey replied, believing this would keep them out of harm's way until the situation quieted down.

Then Carey went down to the saw mill followed by Beauregard and the mob. They gathered up Samson and Floyd and put them in the hoosegow. Carey figured the matter would probably be resolved in a day or so while he checked with Mayor Dunigan.

The mob followed Beauregard and Brinton back to the Buccaneer. The boys figured something had to be done. They waited until after dark. Then several hooded men marched down to the hoosegow, chased off the guard, broke down the door, hauled out Samson, and hanged him on the front porch of the Tampa Bay City Hotel.

The group hooted, hollered, and shouted as they hauled up Samson and watched him gasping out his life while he kicked and squirmed. Then they went to get Floyd but Floyd was gone. Beauregard said, "Dammit, I told you he was a runner."

Carey was upset. He walked over to the undertaker's shack, looked up Mayor Dunigan, and told him, "Somebody's got to pay fer my slaves."

Isobel told Captain McRea about the fracas and Captain McRae complained to Mayor Dunigan, "I can't have people hanging negras from my front porch. It's got my wife riled and it's bad for business. Somebody's gotta put a stop to it."

Mayor Dunigan was fighting mad. He said, "I do the hanging and burying in this town. We can't have a free-for-all."

Then Carey sent his Regulators out to pick up Beauregard. They threw Beauregard in the hoosegow when Mayor Dunigan charged him with disturbing the peace. A trial was held the next day. Mayor Dunigan found Beauregard guilty, fined him twenty-five dollars, and put him back in the hoosegow until he paid the fine. It took Beauregard a while to come up with the money. Beauregard was upset when he got out and Beauregard carried a grudge. Nobody paid Carey for the slaves.

Harry stopped worrying about local issues and turned his attention to covering national politics as another presidential election loomed on the horizon. The situation in Washington continued to deteriorate as congressmen armed themselves and threatened each other with bodily harm. The gentlemen politicians from the Southern states had always maintained a genteel style of governance that was now being overwhelmed and disrupted by the antics of the religious fanatics, grubby mechanics, and tradesmen from the north descending on Washington.

The national Democratic convention was held in Charleston on April 23, 1860, but the national party of Jefferson and Jackson split over slavery and other sectional issues. The Southern delegates left the convention in a huff while the Northern and Western delegates stayed behind and tried to select a nominee. They voted fifty-four times before they giving up and going home.

The Southern Democrats got together in Richmond on June 11th and selected John Breckinridge, the vice president, as their candidate. The Northern Democrats met in Baltimore on June 18th and nominated Stephen Douglas. The Whigs, a few disaffected Democrats, and some survivors of the American Party met in Baltimore. They formed their Constitutional Union Party and nominated John Bell

The radical abolitionist Republican mob met in a wooden structure in Chicago where they nominated a railroad lawyer. The man had only served a couple of terms in congress during the Polk administration. The Southern Democrats weren't that concerned as the man's name did not appear on any ballot in any southern state.

The Democrats split their votes three ways and Abraham Lincoln, the sectional candidate from the North, won the election.

CHAPTER THIRTY ONE

Threshold of Conflict

Tampa Town
November 1860 through April 1861

Fort Brooke was abandoned, the army was gone, and the navy didn't come around anymore. Jake shipped his cows out of Charlotte Harbor. A few neglected cows, some chickens, and an occasional hog wandered the streets of Tampa Town. Carey sawed a little limber at the mill on the Hillsborough River and shipped an occasional load to Key West. A few Spanish fishermen sailed out of the bay but most had moved to more lucrative locations.

About two hundred white residents and a handful of slaves were left in Tampa Town. A couple of hundred settlers and a few dozen slaves lived on the farms and plantations scattered across Hillsborough and Manatee counties. These folks came to Tampa Town on occasion.

Captain McRae still brought in supplies for his store and Isobel continued to run the hotel. Brinton Hooker served his usual clientele at the Buccaneer Bar. As undertaking had dropped off, Diggory spent most of his time at his post office. Beauregard sold an occasional slave and Harry ran the store while churning out weekly editions of his newspaper. Sales dropped off. Sarah was expecting a child.

The weekly stage from Gainesville brought shocking news that shattered the peace and tranquility of Tampa Town. Abraham Lincoln, the abolitionist candidate from Illinois, had been elected president. Waves of despair accompanied the announcement. The malevolent contagion of abolition had spread its tentacles into the very heart and soul of the confederation.

Mayor Dunigan called an emergency meeting. Settlers from the surrounding area rushed to town and over five hundred men, women, and children gathered on the square in front of the hotel. Diggory stood on the porch to deliver a lengthy but impassioned speech calling for strength and resolution to endure the grave threat to civil order. Then Beauregard Bemrose limped to the porch, got everybody's attention, and shouted out a call for secession. His resolution was adopted by acclamation.

The governor of Florida and legislature convened a state convention to consider all possible and appropriate courses of action. Sixty-nine delegates rushed to Tallahassee and sixty-two delegates passed the Ordinance of Secession. The seven delegates opposing secession were hooted from the hall. Florida was now a separate, independent, and sovereign nation. The Gainesville stage brought the triumphant news to Tampa and everybody rushed out to celebrate.

The Tampa Town Brass Band led a procession through the streets. A group of rowdies rushed to the fort. They loaded one old cannon and used it to blast out salute after salute. The excitement and festivities of secession persisted for several days.

Beauregard dusted off his uniform, limped up to the fort, and swore in a bunch of Brinton's rowdies to form the Tampa Bay City Home Guard. That being done, Beauregard called the boys together, mustered them on the parade ground, and regaled them with tales of glory.

"Sumabitch, boys," Beauregard shouted. "We're in business. We're the Tampa Bay City Guards and we're holding this bastion for the Lord and our separate, independent, and sovereign state of Florida. Any of you boys got any questions?"

Nobody had any questions and nobody in town thought it made much difference anyway. Florida had removed itself from the abolitionist frenzy sweeping the North and nobody figured there'd be any problems. After all, Florida had a long history as a separate principality. Harry was pleased that he had a topic for a special edition of the *Journal*. He needed more information.

The Gainesville stage only came around about once a week, so Harry figured Beauregard might know something. He had avoided Beauregard since the incident with the slaves but it was a new day. Harry walked up to the fort. He found Beauregard ensconced in Colonel Davers' old office and Beauregard was willing to talk.

Harry took out his pencil and started to take notes as Beauregard said, "Things are moving right along. We got the federal arsenals at Chattahoochee, Fernandina, and St. Augustine without firing a shot. We just marched in and took them. I've got Fort Brooke, lock, stock, and barrel, and we got the Yankees on the run."

Harry asked, "Think there'll be a war."

"No, no way," Beauregard insisted. "The abolitionists are nothing but a bunch of old preachers, women, and city boys. Preachers and women won't fight and city boys can't fight. They just aint got the stomach for a good old fashioned ass-kicking, eye-gouging, bare-knuckles brawl. We've got it covered."

"That's it?" Harry asked.

"That's it," Colonel Bemrose insisted. "Now, you can just hustle right on down to your print shop and print up a damn good story. Put it on the front page. Tell everyone that Beauregard Bemrose has everything under control in Tampa. I'm holding Fort Brooke, and I've got forty good, rip-snorting Home Guards set and ready to defend it."

"I'll do that," Harry conceded.

"Make sure you do." Then Beauregard said, "Been thinking about you."

"What about me?"

"Wondering where you came from." Then he asked, "Were you by chance a Yankee?"

"No way," Harry sputtered. He dropped his pencil.

"Something about you doesn't seem right," Beauregard insisted. "Where are you from?"

"I was a swamp rat."

"Yeah, I know. You told me. What about Tallahassee? Have you ever been to Tallahassee?"

"Nope," Harry blurted. "Don't know anything about that."

"Don't know anything about what?"

"Nothing," Harry stammered, "just an expression."

"Could be, but let me think on it."

As the interview was obviously over, Harry got out the door and left the fort. He had to avoid Bemrose. He went back to his shop, printed the story, and assured the residents of Tampa Town that there wasn't going to be a war. Most of the Tampa residents accepted the story as fact, breathed a sigh of relief, and went back to business as usual.

Jake Sutherlin continued catching cows and shipping them out of Charlotte Harbor. Captain McRae made regular runs between Tampa, Key West, and Havana. As Sarah was expecting a child, Isobel hovered over her daughter, kept track of her son-in-law, and ran the hotel. Harry avoided Bemrose and continued putting out the newspaper.

Beauregard unfurled the bonny blue flag of West Florida, now the banner of secession, and drilled his Tampa Bay City Home Guards for an uncertain future that might someday come. Then he sent out his boys to secure the base. "Track 'em down," Beauregard asserted. "They're out there," Beauregard claimed, "harboring thoughts about the Union. Bring them in."

The guards scoured the town looking for those who might be harboring a few good thoughts about the old Union. These misguided souls were confronted about the error of their ways and chastised to correct the errors in their thinking. There were a few scuffles and a couple of fires.

Mayor Dunigan viewed Beauregard's overt rise to power with some anxiety and concern. Although a few of Beauregard's boys seemed a little excessive, Beauregard hadn't done anything to spark alarm. Some feared that Beauregard might use his self-proclaimed authority to settle old scores. He still harbored a grudge about being thrown in the hoosegow, was upset with Captain McRae for making a fuss about hanging the slave, and continued nurturing a long standing animosity toward those who had destroyed his life over a few issues pertaining to the dog business.

That being the case, Diggory gathered up a few documents, slipped off one morning, and rode to Tallahassee to check on Beauregard and determine his official standing. But the mission fell through when Diggory got to Tallahassee. The militia adjutant had gone to Pensacola to deal with a standoff at Fort Pickens. Union troops held the fort and wouldn't give it up.

Diggory tried the governor's office but nobody knew much about anything. They were more concerned about the meeting taking place in Montgomery. Delegates from South Carolina, Florida, Mississippi, Alabama, Georgia, Louisiana, and Texas were determining the future of secession. They organized a provisional government for a new confederation called the Confederate States of America. Jefferson Davis was sworn in as president.

Northern Florida welcomed the news, but Key West had a different reaction. The Stars and Stripes of the United States waved over Fort Taylor and the rest of the island. The United States navy sailed in and out of the harbor bringing reinforcements, military equipment, and supplies. Major French brought a Pennsylvania infantry regiment to reinforce Fort Taylor. Union money, Union men, Union material, and Union supplies flowed to the city on the island.

Key West residents didn't have much interest in the matters dominating the discourse of power in far off Washington and Tallahassee. Most residents considered themselves a separate entity. They were set off by tradition and location from the continent to the north. That was the way it had always been and that was the way they wanted it. Key West was a city of passion but few loyalties.

Diego and Sidney checked their cash flow and determined they were loyal to the Union. Diego ran over to the fort, purchased an American flag, and ran it up over the office. A few misguided souls around town tried running up the bonny blue flag of secession, but their neighbors ripped down the flags and threw them away.

Island residents demonstrated their commitment to the Union by raising a loyal Union Militia Company. The Militia Company rounded up all the men on the island between fifteen and fifty and marched them to Tift's wharf. Everyone had to swear an oath of allegiance to the Union.

Captain McRae stood next to Sidney and Diego while he pledged his sacred honor to protect and defend the Constitution of the United States while abiding by the laws and regulations thereof. After all, Captain McRea had to get his boat in and out of the Key West harbor before he could sell his cows to the army.

A few men refused to swear the oath. They were kicked off the island. Some went to Tampa.

CHAPTER THIRTY TWO

April Fool's Day

Washington City
April 1 through April 12, 1861

The State Department was created by congress in 1789 to conduct foreign relations with England and France. It increased in size over the next seventy years until it conducted diplomatic relations with over twenty nations and principalities. Thirty-seven men worked in the department's archives office and three bureaus housed in a nondescript row of red brick buildings on Pennsylvania Avenue.

The Archives Office stored the national seal, the nation's records, and original copy of the constitution. The Diplomatic Bureau conducted the nation's foreign affairs. The Consular Bureau assisted American nationals who happened to be doing business in foreign countries, and the Home Bureau managed the nation's espionage and security operations while running an off-the-books banknote brokerage operation.

Banknotes issued by sixteen hundred state chartered banks constituted the bulk of the nation's currency. The banknotes were noninterest-bearing promissory notes payable on demand at par at the issuing bank. These were used by the general population to purchase items and services. But there was a problem with the banknotes. Although the nation's specie redemption clause stipulated that banknotes had to be traded at face value in the immediate vicinity of the issuing bank, they traded at different values at different places in the country because of the difficulties involved in getting the notes to the bank.

The notes generally traded at ninety cents on a dollar and at other times they traded for as little as twenty cents on a dollar, depending upon the distance to the issuing bank. Caleb was able to collect banknotes at his assets scattered around the country, and bring them to Washington using the dispatch services. He redeemed these notes at face value at his New York bank, generating a substantial source of off-the-record income.

Most of the gentlemen who served as Secretary of State were unaware of Caleb's banknote business. Thirteen gentlemen had come and gone. Caleb had never felt any special urgency to share the details of his banknote redemption operation with any of them. Most weren't around that long, and most spent most of their time in their office on the second floor of the corner building.

William Seward became the twenty-fourth Secretary of State on March 5, 1861. Secretary Seward, a former New York senator, was an energetic fellow and early riser. He bounded into the building at sunrise on most days, wandered through the offices and corridors, and engaged in spirited conversations along the way. Many found his behavior disconcerting but most believed it would dissipate over time.

Even so, the new secretary strolled into the building before daybreak on the first day of April. Secretary Seward nodded at Ephraim Hardy, the night watchman who had held the job since the Harrison administration, and bounded up the stairway to the second floor. As Secretary Seward strolled down the hall, he noticed Caleb's open door. Caleb was in his office.

Caleb was always there. Martin Van Buren brought Caleb to Washington in the 1820's to manage some of the more unsavory aspects of General Jackson's presidential campaign. Caleb stayed on to become Martin's special assistant when Martin served as secretary of state.

Secretary Seward knew Caleb. Both were from Auburn. Caleb spent a year sweeping Mr. Seward's law office when Caleb was fourteen. Then Attorney Seward helped Caleb get into Union College, a nondenominational college in

Schenectady. They lost track of each other for a time but caught up with each other in Washington.

Secretary Seward stepped into Caleb's cluttered office. "Morning, Caleb. See you're still an early riser."

"Got the habit from an old boss, haven't been able to shake it."

"That's a pity," Secretary Seward replied. "If you've got a few minutes, I'd like to talk."

"Certainly, come in. I've got coffee and cinnamon rolls."

Secretary Seward smelled the coffee. "Where'd you get rolls at this hour?"

"I've got my sources." Caleb jumped up and reached over to lift the pot off the caboose stove. Caleb poured a mug of brew.

"Expect you do." Secretary Seward chuckled as he settled into a battered captain's chair. Although the budget for the Home Bureau had grown from a few hundred to several million a year, Caleb didn't spend much on his office.

Caleb handed the mug to the secretary. Then Caleb rustled around in his bottom drawer to yank out a bag of cinnamon rolls. Secretary Seward selected a roll.

Caleb asked, "What's up."

Secretary Seward didn't know where to start. The administration had been in office for almost a month and President Lincoln hadn't done anything of significance. Seven states had left the union, more were leaving, and rebels were seizing federal forts and property. The Union still held Fort Sumter in Charleston Harbor, Fort Picket at Pensacola, and Fort Taylor on Key West. Almost everything else was gone.

President Lincoln seemed overwhelmed. He appeared obsessed with picking postmasters and assistant postmasters for small towns in Illinois, Indiana, and Ohio. He wasn't dealing with anything of substance. The man had never held an executive position in his life, and it showed.

"Sugar," Secretary Seward asked. "Do you have any?"

"Cuban sugar," Caleb replied as he rummaged around the papers on his desk. He found a packet and tossed it to Secretary Seward. "That was a priority."

Secretary Seward smiled.

Caleb asked, "What did you want to talk about?"

Secretary Seward opened the packet and poured the sugar into his mug. Caleb handed the secretary a spoon and watched as the secretary stirred the sugar into his coffee. Secretary Seward asked Caleb, "What's happening down south."

"Governor Pickens is spoiling for a fight. He's bringing another regiment to Charleston."

"Know that," Secretary Seward replied. "I mean farther south, the Caribbean."

"It's going to hell in a hand basket. Spain's making a move on the Dominican Republic using their debt as their excuse to move in and take over the island. Spain and France are getting ready to move on Mexico as soon as Spain wraps up their Dominican adventure."

"Damn," Secretary Sward sputtered. "They know we've got a mess on our hands and taking advantage of the situation."

"It's going to get more complicated. The English seem to be going along with Spain and France."

"Do we have anything down there?"

"Not much," Caleb answered. "Key West, but it's something."

"Got any assets on the island?"

"A club and import/export business," Caleb replied. "The import/export operation is running a couple of steamboats. That gives us some access to Havana."

"This club," Secretary Seward asked. "Is it a sporting house?"

"Sort of, but not really," Caleb claimed. "More of an intelligence operation, they've never turned a profit on their other endeavors."

"Nevertheless, we have to be concerned about the perception of morality," Secretary Seward insisted. "We campaigned on decency, morality, and abolition. We can't be caught supporting anything even suggesting licentious behavior."

"Nobody can trace anything."

"Cut them lose. We can't risk the chance that somebody might find out."

"No problem," Caleb acquiesced. "I'll shift my funding to the import/export business. One of Thurlow Weed's old stringers runs the business with a Spanish agent who's playing both ends against the middle. He's been useful so long as we're the middle."

"Interesting," Secretary Seward replied.

"But valuable," Caleb insisted. "We feed him the information that we want to get to Havana and it gets there."

"How about setting him up for a few schemes?"

"Got anything in mind?"

"Nothing now," Secretary Seward deferred. He chewed on his roll and took a sip of coffee. "Let me think on it." Secretary Seward got up, left the office, and walked down the hallway to his office. He needed to get the president's attention, so he sat at his desk, pulled out a sheet of paper, and started scribbling.

Secretary Seward's short memo entitled *Some Thoughts for the President's Consideration* arrived on President Lincoln's desk that afternoon. The memo started out by asserting that the administration had been in office for about a month and formulated no policies either domestic or foreign. Seward went on to say that the issue separating the North and South should be redefined and changed from a disagreement over slavery to an emphasis on union and national unity. The Union forts on the gulf should be held and supported. The navy should be brought back from foreign ports and the nation should confront the Spanish and French inroads in the Caribbean, declare the western hemisphere off bounds for exploitation, and if necessary, call congress into session for a declaration of war against Spain and France.

201

President Lincoln took note of the memo and summoned Secretary Seward to the Executive Mansion. The president said, "My dear sir, it seems you have decided to make the most of the opportunity provided by this day to write a persuasive memo."

Not catching the president's allusion to the date, Secretary Seward insisted, "We need to talk."

"Talking is probably better than doing given our situation," President Lincoln replied. "I like your idea about emphasizing national unity and we'll do that while we wait for our navy to come home. They tell me that we've only got about forty ships in the whole navy and old Buck left them scattered around the globe. It's gonna take us a good six months get them back."

"What about Spain and France?"

"You seem to be pretty adept at writing letters. Perhaps you should send them a letter expressing our displeasure but don't rile them up too much. We're not in a position to do much of anything about it right now," President Lincoln insisted. "It's not a good idea to run pick a fight with the neighbors when you got problems at home."

Secretary Seward nodded. There were only sixteen thousand poorly trained men in the army, and they were scattered along the frontier. Several key officers had already resigned their commissions and shifted over to the Confederacy. Secretary Seward insisted, "We're still holding some of our southern forts."

"For the time being," President Lincoln cautioned. "Getting reinforcements and supplies down there is gonna be a hard row to hoe. If you got any clout in those parts, you'd better start using it."

"We've got a few assets on Key West," Secretary Seward suggested.

"That's good," President Lincoln replied. "We'll probably need them before we get through this business." Then the president picked up Secretary Seward's April fool's day memo. The president said, "I like the national unity idea. It's got a nice ring to it"

Secretary Seward nodded. The president folded the memo, opened the drawer in his desk, and put the memo in the drawer. He closed the drawer and glanced at his secretary of state as he asked, "What about Mr. Merryman?"

"Who's he?" Secretary Seward blurted.

"A member of the Maryland legislature and he's trying to get the Maryland legislature to pass an ordinance of secession. It's a little closer to home. I figured you'd be keeping track of it."

Being embarrassed and alarmed by the revelation of unanticipated danger, Secretary Seward mumbled, "I'll check on it."

"Better do that," President Lincoln urged. Then he asked, "Anything else we need to talk about?"

Seward shook his head. President Lincoln smiled as he said, "Nice of you to stop over. I like some of your suggestions."

As the meeting was over, Secretary Seward excused himself and left the office. He rushed back to Caleb's office, walked in, and shut the door. "What are you doing about John Merryman and the Maryland Legislature?"

Caleb said, "Keeping track of them."

Seward blurted, "We're in trouble if they take Maryland out of the Union."

"Guess so," Caleb replied. "Some of our southern neighbors have been trying to get the Maryland legislature to go along them but the governor of Maryland got his dander up and sent them home. Now they're trying to hold a session in Fredrick but our boys will pick them up as soon as you give the word."

"For God's sake, pick them up," Seward ordered. "Why didn't you tell me about this?"

"Never asked," Caleb replied, "figured you knew."

"How would I know," Secretary Seward sputtered.

"Pretty close to home."

Secretary of State Seward nodded. He walked off and was halfway to his office before realizing the full significance of the president's warning about not picking fights with the neighbors when you've got problems at home. Nevertheless, President Lincoln decided to resupply Fort Sumter.

The war started on April 12th.

CHAPTER THIRTY THREE

Isle of Dreams

Washington City and Key West
July 1861

Caleb didn't like traveling, but there are times when things are better off not being written. This was such an occasion. Caleb took passage on the *Harriet Lane*, the new revenue cutter named after President Buchanan's niece. The warship was the prototype for a new class of high speed, steam powered, vessels authorized and constructed during the Buchanan administration. She was being operated by the United States Maritime Service for the Treasury Department and being used as a diplomatic carrier by the State Department.

Although rigged as a schooner, the cutter was powered by a high pressure steam engine and two huge paddle wheels. The *Harriet Lane* was armed with two massive thirty-two pound rifled cannons, one at the front and the other at the rear of the ship. Smaller cannon protruded from gun ports along the hull. She was not to be trifled with.

Caleb went aboard, retired to his cabin, and remained there for most of the cruise to Key West. Key West was the largest city in Florida with a population of about three thousand people, but Caleb had never been there. He emerged from his cabin when the revenue cutter docked and strolled across the deck to warn the ship's master, "Don't leave without me."

Master Perry said, "I'll be going out with the morning tide so don't delay."

"Don't despair! I'll be there." Caleb turned and left the ship.

It was hot and humid. Caleb loosened his cravat as he stepped ashore. Then he removed his coat and draped it over his arm as he made his way through the crowd on the pier and stepped out onto Front Street. Shops, taverns, and bawdy houses lined the street.

Caleb ventured into side streets to get his bearings before making his calls. He ventured down crushed shell, tree shaded streets. Brightly colored houses with broad verandas were obscured by tropical foliage. Key West was an isle of dreams far removed from the drama, dissension, and conflict ravaging the rest of the nation.

Gaining a general perception of the layout of the city, Caleb walked back to Front Street. He made his way through mobs and swarms of sailors, Latin merchants, British smugglers, Bahaman sponge divers, and transplanted Yankees as he walked to Fort Taylor.

The great stone structure was almost finished. Carpenters, stone masons, and blacksmiths were still working on it even though the whole thing could be reduced to rubble in an hour or so by the rifled cannon being carried on modern gunboats. Such are the dictates of bureaucracy. Once started, projects persist.

Even so, the fort provided shelter and housing for the Union troops on the island. Detachments had been rushed to the island as the War Department feared that there might be a rebel uprising. That had never happened. The better part of the good citizens of Key West supported the Union, or at least, they welcomed the trade, wealth, and commerce provided by the Union.

Two sentinels roused themselves to greet Caleb at the drawbridge that served as the gate. They checked his credentials, noted he was a state department official, and admitted him to the fort. A sergeant took him to Major French's office.

Major French didn't hold state department officials in high regard but took notice when Caleb said, "Good afternoon, Major French. I believe you were born in Baltimore in 1815, graduated first in your class from the academy in '37, were stationed at Fort King during the Seminole War, and served under General Pierce during the Mexican War where you were honored for gallant and meritorious service."

"Who are you?"

"Not significant or important," Caleb replied. "Let's say that I'm here at the bidding of significant gentlemen."

"You're carrying state department credentials, but they don't tell me much. Why are you here?"

"Not your concern," Caleb suggested. "It's not important."

"So, what's important?"

"You've secured the island for the Union and are holding the fort. That's important. You'll be receiving a congressional commendation for your effort and foresight. That's important."

Major French nodded but didn't say anything. Promotions and commendations had been rare since the Mexican War. Caleb said, "Continue holding this fort until you are properly relieved. Then you'll be given a promotion and assigned to McClellan's staff. Of course, this depends on a few circumstances and several factors. Hold the fort."

Major French said, "Will do."

Caleb said, "I'm here to negotiate the details of an arrangement with some gentlemen on the island. They'll be conducting various activities and I trust you'll provide them with adequate and suitable support."

"Who are they?"

"Sidney Benson is one of the gentlemen. Perhaps you have met him."

"Jacaranda Import/Export fellow," Major French replied. "I know who he is."

"Mr. Benson and his associates will be carrying out special assignments related to the conduct of the war. I could be more specific, but it's best to leave matters as they are."

Major French nodded. "I'll do what I can."

Caleb said, "Good! I'll send you a verifying dispatch with appropriate details when I get back to Washington."

"What do I do in the meantime?"

"Tell your disbursing officer I'll be in touch. If things work out, Benson will be bringing in dispatches to be forwarded to my office and I'll be providing him with vouchers to be drawn upon a special account."

Major French asked, "Do you want to talk with Lieutenant Reynolds? He's my disbursing officer."

"You do the talking," Caleb insisted. "I've got better things to do."

Caleb shook hands with the major, walked out the door, and left the fort. He was ready for his second task. Caleb walked down Front Street, stopped at the office of the Jacaranda Import/Export Company, and walked in the door.

Sidney was seated behind his pedestal desk reading a copy of the *Key of the Gulf*, an underground, secessionist newspaper. Sidney looked up at the intruder, didn't recognize him, folded his paper, and put it aside. "How can I help you?"

"You're Sidney Benson."

"Sure am," Sidney replied. "What's up?"

"You were born in Geneva on January 5, 1810. You spent a term at Union college before being dismissed for rowdy behavior involving a mule. Then you went to work for Thurlow Weed espousing his anti-mason causes and moved on to generate some lurid fantasies of dissolution and life in the tropics."

Sidney jumped up. "It was a goat, not a mule! Who are you?"

"Stand corrected," Caleb conceded. "You stole the mule from the *Daniel Garney*, an old canal boat, and the goat from Farmer Howard on your way back to the college. You released the mule before you put the goat in the president's office. Let's just say that I'm here today to talk about a business opportunity."

Smarting from the unexpected but essentially accurate revelations, Sidney slid into his chair. "What you got in mind?"

"Actually, it's more of an enhancement of your existing state of affairs than an offer," Caleb explained. "I represent some people of significance and have established arrangements with various commercial enterprises in the past."

"Such as," Sidney countered.

"Jacaranda Club," Caleb revealed. "There are others."

"You're the man with the money," Sidney surmised. "It's good to meet you. What can I do for you?"

"Offer me a chair." Caleb grabbed a Chippendale chair and sat down. "I'm redirecting my funding."

"How so," Sidney asked.

"There've been a few changes in the political make-up," Caleb stated in a matter-of-fact voice. "As you've been a long time accomplice in many of Mr. Weed's endeavors, I'm certain you understand the tenor of the alterations."

"Republicans," Sidney suggested.

"They appear to operate under certain perceptions of moral rectitude. As I'm redirecting my arrangements, I wish to ascertain your interest regarding the opportunity to function on a contractual basis with the Army regarding various import and export activities of a sometimes clandestine nature."

"What about the club?" Sidney asked. "Nicole's not going to like this."

"As they can facilitate some aspects of our operation, I'm certain you'll make the arrangements to continue to provide them with an adequate level of financial support. This need not be a matter of record and should exist as a personal arrangement between you and the people involved."

"What's the problem with the club?"

"Now, I find that an unusual question coming from a long time associate of the champion of public morality. I believe the *Albany Evening Journal* has vociferously condemned the strident evils of slavery, spirits, and concupiscence. Perhaps you adhere to certain perceptions of their peculiar obsessions."

"Just business," Sidney protested, "doesn't mean anything."

"So I've noticed," Caleb replied. "Your long time mentor and erstwhile employer Mr. Weed suggested I talk with you."

"I'm not working for Thurlow anymore."

"A matter of debate," Caleb suggested, "but not my concern."

"So what's the deal?"

"We've taken on an unfortunate and perhaps unnecessary war, but we're having it. A number of people believe it's going to be a short, little thing, maybe thirty days or so in duration. It would be fortunate if that were the case but I believe that it's going to be a risky venture that may persist for some time with an uncertain outcome."

Sidney said, "Doesn't sound good."

"Not especially," Caleb asserted. "Nevertheless, it's happening. Our government will take certain positions during the course of the war when in reality we'll be conducting other necessary activities to ensure the outcome of long and short term interests."

"What are you talking about?"

"Let me provide you with a significant concern and ramifications," Caleb answered. "We need to remain at peace with the European powers while we take on the war. Our adversary, the Confederacy will be fighting a defensive war so they'll probably prevail during the initial engagements. This may encourage some of the European powers to intervene in our domestic matters. We must keep this from happening."

"So how are we involved?"

"There's a Cuban working for you or perhaps you're working for him," Caleb replied. "The arrangement appears uncertain. Nevertheless, Mr. Diego is a long term Spanish agent who was planted in this country as part of an old dog caper."

"So I've heard," Sidney conceded.

Caleb placed a packet on the desk. "There's such a thing as a back door emissary to foreign powers. Your friend Diego

210

is uniquely suited for such a mission. Please tell him to deliver this to his Havana contact and assure his contact that we won't intervene in their Hispaniola intervention contrary to the official protest they'll be receiving. Moreover, we won't resist the efforts being undertaken by Spain, England, and France for an armed intervention to collect their Mexican debts."

"How does that strengthen our interests?"

"Long and short term," Caleb asserted. "A little Spanish, French, and English activity along the southern border of the states in rebellion may keep some of their people somewhat uncertain about incursions."

"What else?"

Caleb continued, "The cotton supply. Several English and French merchants are expressing concern about the adequacy of their cotton supply. As the president has authorized a blockade of the Confederate coastline, foreign registered ships will soon be reluctant to traverse the southern waters. That being the case, I want you to get into the cotton business and haul as much cotton to Havana as you can. This will help allay the merchant's fears until we work our way through the initial disappointments of this war."

"How do we do that?"

"You've got boats," Caleb replied. "Use them and you'll get more."

"What else?"

"We'll be running a few direct campaigns down here after the war gets going. Guerilla action, that sort of thing," Caleb added. "We'll need logistical support."

"How are we funding this?"

"I told you," Caleb insisted. "You'll be getting a substantial cow contract from the army. They'll pay for everything."

"How do I get my hands on the money?"

"You'll be paid upon delivery. We'll also cover your operational and related expenses as they occur. You'll have to submit a monthly voucher. The officer will send your voucher to my office and I'll review your requests. If they're in order, you'll be reimbursed. Do you have any more questions?"

"Do you want to talk with Diego?"

"You talk with Diego. Give him the packet to authenticate his message. You can mention your contract with the army but it would probably be best if you omitted the details of our discussion today. He doesn't really need to know the content of the envelope although I expect he'll find out soon enough. Do we have a deal?"

"What about the club?"

"I've already suggested that their operation might be of value so I'll expect you'll find a way to assist them. That's your problem."

Sidney said, "I see but I haven't seen any contract."

"I've found little need to put things in writing," Caleb asserted. "That's the way I do business."

"But how do I know you're on the up and up?"

"You'll be hearing from Lieutenant Reynolds, the disbursing officer at the fort. He'll confirm our arrangement and give you a contract. You'll generate enough money to make it worthwhile and I'm not counting the loose change you'll pick up running your contraband through Mr. Lincoln's blockade."

"What happens if we get caught?"

"Make the runs after dark so you don't embarrass the navy. If you get caught, you'll go to jail. It'll take a month or so to get you out."

"Is there anything else?"

"Nothing," Caleb insisted. "Do the job."

Caleb got up, took a watch out his pocket, opened the cover, and checked the time. Caleb said, "Got another meeting. We'll be in touch."

Caleb departed. Sidney sat at his desk for a few minutes before writing up a brief report of the meeting and sending it off to Thurlow Weed. Caleb strolled down Front Street, turned on Whitehead, and turned again on Petronia. He walked along down Petronia Street until he came to a Voodoo shop.

Nicole got up from a bench by the door. "What took so long?"

"Anticipation is essential for the fulfillment of expectation."

"Balderdash," Nicole replied. "You're the one who wanted secrecy."

"A precaution, there've been some changes in our operational mode."

"So I gather." Nicole took Caleb's hand, led him down the street, through the cemetery, onto the beach, and to an old mahogany log.

CHAPTER THIRTY FOUR

Contracts and Confessions

From Key West to Havana
June through July 1861

The Jacaranda Import/Export Company received its cow contract a few days later when Sidney Benson was summoned to Fort Taylor to meet with Lieutenant Reynolds. Lieutenant Reynolds told Sidney, "Don't know how this happened but we're buying cows from you guys."

"Commissary department," Sidney suggested, "gotta feed your troops."

"We do, but there are some irregularities."

"Such as," Sidney asked.

"We're required to purchase at least thirty a month."

"Reasonable," Sidney replied. "How much are you paying?"

"Thirty dollars a head, cash on delivery."

"There's nothing irregular about that."

"But there's an unusual provision," Lieutenant Reynolds insisted. "We're supposed to cover your operational expenses, whatever that means."

"Our cost of doing business," Sidney insisted. "We've got expenses. How do we get reimbursed?"

"Submit a monthly voucher. I'll send it to Washington. They're covering your expenses, whatever they are."

"Sounds reasonable," Sidney said. "Where do I sign?"

The contract being finalized, Sidney went back to his office. Captain McRae was already bringing in a load of cows about once a month and trying to sell a few on the island before going on to Havana. Now they had a guaranteed Key West market and would be able to generate a substantial profit. Captain McRea was paying three dollars a head for the cows.

They were going to make money. Sidney wanted to get started so he sent Diego to round up Captains McRae and Simon. The gentlemen gathered in the office later that day. Sidney said, "We gotta talk."

"Better be good," Captain McRae grumbled. "Willy's getting up steam."

Sidney said, "It is. We've got a contract to supply the Union Army with beef."

Captain Simon asked, "How much they paying?"

Sidney said, "Twenty dollars a head for thirty head a month"

Captain McRae whistled. "Damn! That's a good six hundred, maybe thousand a month."

Captain Simon said, "Sounds good, but there's gotta be something else."

"Good news," Sidney insisted. "We got the go-ahead to haul cotton to Havana. We can sell it on the market and make another bundle."

Diego came in. "How official? They're setting up a blockade."

"For everybody else, not us," Sidney replied. "We've got clearance but gotta be careful about using it."

Captain Simon asked, "Where do we get cotton?"

Captain McRae said, "Isobel's gotta bunch in the warehouse."

"We'll start with that," Sidney insisted, "and Diego's got Cedar Key and Jacksonville contacts. We'll get more there."

Diego nodded. Captain Simon said, "You say we got the go-ahead, but how do we get around or through the blockade?"

"Be careful," Sidney insisted. "You can't get around it. You gotta go through it, preferably after dark. Our clearance is unofficial but it's good."

Captain Simon asked, "What happens if I get caught?"

"You'll spend a few days in jail," Sidney said. "It'll take a week or so to get you out, but we'll get you out and get your boat back."

"No shit!" Captain McRae mumbled. "Does that go for me if I keep bringing my stuff from Havana?"

"I expect," Sidney assured Captain McRae.

"Then what are we sitting around here for," Captain McRae growled. "Time's a wastin, let's get going."

"As the gentlemen got up to leave, Captain Simon asked Diego, "You'll be making arrangements for cotton?"

"I guess."

"And another thing," Sidney suggested. "You'll avoid trouble if you hoist the Union flag in the open waters and the Confederate flag when you're in the Confederate harbors."

Captain McRae said, "I'm flying my Union Jack when I don't know what else to fly."

Sidney asked, "How'd you get a Jack?"

"Highlander by birth," Captain McRae explained. "I'm a loyal subject of the Queen, bless her soul."

"Be whatever you want," Sidney conceded, "but remember, you're steaming in troubled waters."

The seafarers acknowledged the warning with a grunt and left the office. Diego waited before asking, "What's going on?"

"Making money," Sidney replied. "By the way, another topic has come up."

"What's that?"

"Know anybody in Havana?"

"Lots of people," Diego replied. "Why are you asking?"

"What about government people? Know anybody in the government?"

"I know a few."

"Such as," Sidney asked.

"Don Dulce," Diego suggested. "He's a nice man."

"Who's he?" Sidney asked.

"He's the Captain General. He runs the place."

"How'd you meet the Captain General?"

"Wasn't Captain General when I met him," Diego replied. "He was my captain when the gringos came for the dogs."

"You were in the Spanish army!"

"For a time," Diego admitted.

Sidney pondered the item of information. Diego had never told much about his past, but he had never asked. "Well, so be it. I've got an offer for you."

"What's the offer?"

"Some Washington people believe you can get a message to this friend of yours. How about it? Can you do it?"

"Of course," Diego replied. "I can so long as your people make it worth my while."

"They will." Sidney gave Diego the packet.

"What's this?"

"Don't know," Sidney relied, "but you're supposed to give it to your contact to authenticate your mission."

"What's in it?" Diego concluded, "Guess we're assets."

"We are."

"Guess you met the big man?"

"Not that big, really," Sidney said, "sort of nondescript fellow. He walked in without warning, talked, and left. He said something about another meeting."

"Nicole knows him," Diego suggested, "I never met him. Nicole won't be happy if she finds out we're calling the shots."

"I'll talk with her."

"Better you than me," Diego insisted. "I'm going to Havana."

CHAPTER THIRTY FIVE

Retribution and Complications

Tampa Bay
August, 1861

Captain McRae dropped Diego off in Havana, unloaded his freight, purchased merchandise, and continued on to Tampa Bay. Colonel Beauregard Bemrose was waiting for the *Salvor* with a detachment of Tampa Bay City Home Guards. Beauregard waited until Willy dropped the gangway. Then Beauregard's guards rushed aboard the steamboat and grabbed Captain McRae as he came out of the wheelhouse.

Captain McRae shouted, "What's the meaning of this!"

Willy asked, "What's going on?"

Colonel Bemrose limped across the deck, "It's a simple situation. You defied the authority of the sovereign state of Florida and I'm the authority."

Willy said, "Appears to be the case."

Captain McRae bellowed, "What did I do!"

"You're working under a contract with the Union army on Key West and I've got witnesses telling me that you swore an oath of allegiance to the Union. That makes you a traitor and pretty much guilty of treason in my book so I'm going to have to hang you."

Willy asked, "When you doing the hanging?"

"When I'm good and ready," Beauregard shouted. Then he dragged Captain McRae up to the old lockup at Fort Brooke, chained him to the wall, and slammed the door.

Willy sauntered off to the Tampa Bay City Hotel to tell Isobel what had happened. Isobel listened with dismay. Then she rushed off to find Carey and Jake. They rushed up to the fort to intervene on Captain McRae's behalf.

Beauregard received the delegation and heard them out before claiming, "The law's the law and a traitor's a traitor. That's the way it is!"

Isobel pleaded with Mayor Dunigan for help. Diggory responded by sending a letter to Governor Perry, but the letter took a couple of weeks to get to Tallahassee. The governor was reluctant to get involved in such a matter so he sent a report of the incident on to the new Confederate government in Montgomery. President Davis assigned the matter to Leroy Walker, his secretary of war, and Leroy turned the matter over to his aide, General Haines Cotesworth, decorated hero of the battle at Buena Vista.

As General Cotesworth had survived the Dallam's Store massacre, he accepted the assignment with interest. He traveled to Tallahassee, conferred with Governor Perry, and took passage on a packet sailing out of St. Marks. It took a couple of days for the steamboat to get to Tampa Town.

General Cotesworth had been away for over ten years. The layout of Tampa Town had changed, but it was still a collection of roughshod, run-down, wooden buildings clinging to the edge of a semi-tropical wilderness. Nevertheless, General Cotesworth went ashore and walked up to the dusty street to nearest and most prominent roughhewn structure he could see, the Tampa Bay City Hotel.

The two story building stood on the site of the old Groggery but was larger and appeared to be in better shape. Haines walked across the porch, opened the door, and entered the taproom. A stern woman was at the bar.

General Cotesworth asked, "Any chance of getting a drink?"

"That's what I sell," Isobel replied. "What do ya want?"

"Tonic, if you still serve them."

"Still do," Isobel grumbled as she prepared the drink.

"Is there any chance of getting a room for a week or so?"

"Expect so," Isobel replied as she slid the drink to the Confederate officer. "Expect you'll wanta use cotton money, so I'll need ten dollars and money up front."

219

The price seemed steep but as he had few other choices, Haines acquiesced. He pulled out a roll of bills, peeled off a couple of fives, and handed them to Isobel. She glanced at the bills before announcing, "Dinner's at 6:00 or thereabouts. It's probably none of my business but what are ya doing here?"

"It's a fact-finding mission."

"Aren't many facts to find," Isobel insisted, "figured you might be here to get my husband out of the stockade."

"You've got to be Mrs. McRae," General Cotesworth surmised. "I didn't know he was married."

"Sure enough," Isobel snorted. "I figured that was what you were here for. Bemrose locked him up on a trumped-up charge and says he's going to hang him! What do you think about that?"

General Cotesworth didn't know. He didn't know the particulars and didn't know that McRea was married. He didn't say anything.

Isobel demanded, "Cat got your tongue or something?" She continued, "You might as well get it out. There's not much I don't know around here."

General Cotesworth reflected on his situation for a moment before revealing, "I got sent down on fact-finding mission regarding a security violation. I don't know the particulars on this case and didn't know that your husband was married."

"There aren't many particulars! Husband's been minding his own business and running the *Salvor* in and out of the harbor here for a dozen years or so while I'm trying to run this hotel. Then this war came along and messed up everything. Now Beauregard's locked up my husband and we're running out of merchandise."

"I didn't mean anything. I just meant I got to talk with Captain McRae and work this out."

"You know James?"

"Sure, I do," General Cotesworth insisted. "I met him during the Seminole Wars. Never knew he was married."

"You know he's not a traitor," Isobel insisted.

"No reason to believe he is," General Cotesworth admitted.

"Then you can have your money back." Isobel reached into the drawer, pulled out the bills, and slapped them on the counter. General Cotesworth kept a five and left the other.

"We've got to keep this on the up and up. Five should cover my lodging for the week."

Isobel took a five as she said, "Get my husband out of jail and put him back to work. We'll call it even."

Haines didn't respond. He excused himself, walked upstairs, found his room, and unpacked his bag. Then he sauntered back to the taproom. Four or five men were at the bar. He recognized Carey Hayes, the cart man. General Cotesworth walked over, took the stool next to Carey, and ordered a tonic. He asked Carey, "How's it going?"

Carey took a look at the Confederate officer before blurting, "Hot damn, I know you! You were here during the old Injun war."

"I was," General Cotesworth replied. "But that was a while back."

"See you changed uniforms and got promoted."

"Difficult choice," General Cotesworth conceded. "But I had to go along with South Carolina and the South."

"What are you doing? How come you're here?"

General Cotesworth said, "I'm working on Walker's staff in Montgomery and got sent down to help straighten out a few things."

"Figured Beauregard's already done that," Carey suggested. "He's got his boys all gussied up as the Tampa Bay City Home Guards. That's what he's callin' them."

"So I gather," General Cotesworth replied. "That's why I'm here. I've got to straighten out a few things and get everybody back to work. We got a war going on up north and don't need distractions down here."

"I guess." Carey lifted his glass and drank to the success of the Confederacy.

General Cotesworth strolled up the road to the fort the next morning and spent an hour or so with Colonel Bemrose. Beauregard didn't say much. General Cotesworth told him, "We've got to go over a few matters."

"What do you want?"

"Checked out in a few things in Tallahassee but I didn't find anything on record pertaining to your status down here."

"Just a minute," Beauregard growled. "I held this place for you boys. You didn't give me any help or nothing, but I did it."

"Glad you did," General Cotesworth replied. "I just need to work out a few details regarding your status and commission."

"Governor Eaton gave it to me. It's good!"

"Expect it is," General Cotesworth conceded. "I'll have to straighten out a few things when I get back to Tallahassee."

"Better do that," Beauregard grumbled. "I been busting my hump fer you people fer a long time now and aint got nothing to show fer it."

It was quiet. General Cotesworth glanced around the remnants of the room that had once been his office before Beauregard suggested, "Something about you seems familiar. Aint we run across each other before?"

"Don't believe so," General Hanes insisted. "Tell me about your prisoner."

"He's been stirring up a bunch of trouble with his wife."

"Not concerned about his family life," General Cotesworth replied. "You're claiming he's been aiding and abetting the enemy. What's he done?"

"Wife's helping him. That's what I meant to say. Besides, they never helped me clean up this place. Now, he's shipping cows to Key West and selling them to the Yankees. That's aiding and abetting in my book."

"I'll be the one to determine that," General Cotesworth insisted. "Where's the prisoner?"

"I got him locked up in the old brig. I even went to the trouble of bringing up some of the chains and shackles from the business. They'll hold him."

"Probably so," Haines agreed. "I'm holding a hearing on the charges tomorrow morning. He can bring witnesses or others who can vouch for him. Look them up and get them here."

His business being completed, General Cotesworth went back to the hotel.

When word of the proceeding leaked out, Beauregard's boys brought along a coil of rope and waited outside the office. Carey and his bullwhackers arrived to counter the exuberance of Beauregard's boys. Isobel McRea stomped up to the commandant's office with her daughter and son-in-law in tow.

When General Cotesworth entered the office to start the proceedings, he glanced at Isobel and recognized Harry. Harry nodded. General Cotesworth returned the nod. Neither man said anything as it would not have been appropriate. Beauregard limped in and took his seat at the prosecutor's table.

Once General Cotesworth got situated, he rapped the table with his knuckles. "I'm hereby proclaiming this court of inquiry in session. Bring in the prisoner."

Beauregard nodded to one of his boys waiting inside the door, and a couple of the Tampa Bay City Home Guards dragged Captain McRea into the room. Captain McRea was not in good spirits. He had been chained to the wall in an old holding cell for the last three weeks, been denied the comfort of his usual meals, and resented this intrusion on his life.

Isobel reacted with a start. "Doesn't look like you've been treating him very good."

"About as good as can be expected for a traitor," Beauregard shouted.

Isobel snapped, "Beauregard Bemrose, you got to get your facts straight before you go mouthing off. James and I are not traitors. We're loyal subjects of the Queen of England and aint done nothing to hurt Scotland or Great Britain either, for that matter."

223

General Cotesworth said, "Take it you're not citizens of the Confederacy."

"Got that right," Captain McRae grumbled. "I've been doing you folks a favor by selling your cows, hauling in your merchandise, and keeping you alive."

Beauregard said, "But you're working fer the Yankees."

Isobel shouted, "To hell too! We're not working for anybody. We run our own business and do what we do to make a living. We sell the Yankees your worthless cows and use their money to haul in your gunpowder, firearms, cloth, medicine, and all the other stuff you have to have to keep this place alive. This is what we get fer it."

Harry said, "I can attest to that."

General Haines Cotesworth was on the spot. Nobody told him that he was dealing with British subjects. The Confederacy did not want to jeopardize its relationship with Great Britain as the Confederacy was seeking diplomatic recognition from England. Besides, these people were using their trading relationship to bring needed supplies, equipment, and hardware to south Florida.

General Cotesworth said, "It appears there's been a misunderstanding in this matter."

Beauregard said, "I can't hang 'em."

"Not today," General Cotesworth replied. "It appears he's a subject of the crown. As we're in no position to jeopardize our relationship with Great Britain, you'll have to release him."

"Damn!" Beauregard shouted. "I can't do that."

Harry jumped to his feet. "You heard the man. Turn him loose. You had no business holding him anyway."

Beauregard started to say something but stopped. A number of things about the situation troubled him. General Cotesworth was now trying to smooth things over by telling Captain McRae, "I do however need your assurance that you won't do anything to jeopardize the security of the Confederacy while you continue serving our mercantile interests."

Captain McRae asked, "What do you want?"

"Swear an oath to support the Confederate States of America and promise to continue assisting us in our lawful endeavors."

"Sounds about right to me," the Captain McRae replied. "Turn me loose.

Then Beauregard Bemrose suddenly remembered where he had seen the smug, officer who was now wearing a Confederate uniform. He was a little older, put on a little weight, and picked up a few gray hairs, but he was just an older version of the smug, city boy from Charleston who bought the dogs, shot off his mouth to the big shots in Washington, sent him into the swamps, and ruined his life.

Harry, the local printer and former swamp rat who had lied to him on so many occasions, was the city boy's accomplice! Beauregard bit his lip. He couldn't do anything about the smug city boy sitting behind the desk flaunting the gold wreath and three star insignia of a general officer of the Confederacy. The city boy's low country accent, slurred speech, and mannerisms gave him away.

"Sumabitch," Beauregard grumbled.

"What's that?" General Cotesworth demanded.

"Nothing," Beauregard mumbled. He was powerless against a general and couldn't do anything about Harry while the general was in town.

Beauregard decided to wait.

CHAPTER THIRTY SIX

Reprieve with Reprisals

Tampa to Key West and Havana
August through September 1861

The victors celebrated into the evening at the Tampa Bay City Hotel. Captain McRea was gloomy and didn't have much to say. Isobel was upbeat and served flask after flask of tonic. General Cotesworth was the hero of the occasion. As the evening progressed, Harry asked, "How'd you ever get to be a general?"

"Being in the wrong place at the right time," General Cotesworth replied. "I was marching south with General Taylor when we ran up against Santa Anna and about twenty thousand Mexicans."

Jake said, "Sounds like a wrong place. How many did you have?"

"We had five thousand more or less."

Jake whistled. "What was right about that situation?"

"We kicked their butts.

Harry asked, "How'd you do that?"

"Taylor pulled us back into a mountain pass and we waited for them to come through," General Cotesworth explained. "Santa Anna lined them up like they were on a parade and marched them into the pass a unit at a time. We mowed them down."

Jake said, "Like fish in a barrel."

"Sort of like fish in a barrel, but the barrel was pretty big. It got hairy but Jeff Davis saved the day by running a cavalry charge through the pass while it was filled with Mexicans. Some of our boys took off after the cavalry, and I took off after the boys to get them back. I happened to be in the right place to pick up Davis after the Mexicans shot his horse out from under him, and we held off the Mexicans until they gave up and backed off. It was some day."

Harry said, "So that's how you got to be a general."

"Indirectly, the Union kept me on as a colonel after the war and sent me to California. I resigned from the Union and shifted over to the Confederacy after Sumter. I ran into Jeff Davis when I got to Montgomery. He remembered me and signed me up as a general."

"Made out pretty good," Jake said. "How's this war going to end?"

"Not much of a war," General Cotesworth replied. "We've got the Yankees on the run."

"Sounds like it," Jake agreed.

General Cotesworth asked, "Still catching cows?"

Jake said, "Sure am".

"How's it going?"

"Not too bad. Got thousands of them running lose out there. Just gotta catch 'em. Then we can ship 'em."

"I do the shipping," Captain McRae insisted.

"Key West," General Cotesworth suggested, "for the Yankees."

"The scrawny ones," Captain McRae replied. "Then it's on to Havana, but the Yankees are putting up a blockade. Don't know how many more Havana runs I can make."

"Gotta make 'em," Isobel insisted, "if we're gonna stay in business."

"I'll see what I can do," Captain McRae concluded.

Captain McRae was up early the next morning, loaded a bunch of cows on the *Salvor,* and steamed out of the harbor. He flew the Stars and Bars of the Confederacy on the way out, shifted over to the Union Jack of Great Britain while at sea, and ran up the Star and Stripes as he approached Key West. Then he unloaded most of his cows and sauntered up to the Jacaranda office to collect payment.

Sidney said. "Heard they was gonna hang you."

"How'd you hear that?"

"Cuban fishermen, they were looking for Diego."

"Where's Diego?"

"In Havana, where you left him," Sidney replied. "Take a few dispatches, pick him up, and bring him back."

"I'll do that," Captain McRae replied. The crew loaded the *Salvor* with hides and other products to be sold in Havana. Once loaded, the steamboat left Key West harbor and chugged across the channel toward Havana. Captain McRae flew the Stars and Stripes on the way out the harbor then flew the Union Jack.

It took two days to get to Havana. As Captain McRae was a regular caller, the Spanish gunboat cleared him for entry and waved him through. The *Salvor* steamed into the harbor passing between El Morro castle and Castillo de Real Fuerza. Dozens of vessels were flying the flags and banners of various nations.

Captain McRae tied the *Salvor* at the commercial wharf and put his deckhands to work. Then he went ashore to deliver the dispatches. The old city was laid out in a grid. Massive stone buildings were crowned with ornate facades. People packed the streets and congregated in the alleyways. A throng celebrating some sort of festival was gathered on Plaza de San Francisco.

Something was always happening in Havana. The world's trade routes converged on the city. Silver, spices, cotton, and gold were exchanged on the streets and in the counting houses around the harbor. Captain McRae took note of the Spanish soldiers stationed along the way as he made his way to the Jacaranda office.

The office consisted of a couple of rooms on the far corner of the second floor of a building about a block from the harbor. An outer office opened off a hallway and an inner office looked over an alley. As the outer office was empty, Captain McRae made himself at home. Diego was ensconced in imperial splendor seated behind a huge desk in the inner office, talking with two well-dressed gentlemen.

When Diego noticed Captain McRae, he jumped up and rushed out to greet him. "Where you been?"

"Had a few problems in Tampa," Captain McRae replied.

"So I heard, guess they didn't hang you.

"Not this time."

"Maybe next time, eh."

"Maybe," Captain McRae replied. "I got the boys unloading cargo and loading merchandise. Willy's keeping up steam. I'd like to go out with the tide."

"I got a few more details that I got to work out with the French, and I'll be ready."

"What are you doing with them?"

"Business," Diego answered. "I'm taking cargo with me, so I'll have the boys put it on the boat. Did you bring dispatches?"

Captain McRae gave Diego the envelope and went back to the *Salvor*. Cart men on the pier were lugging heavy crates aboard the *Salvor*. McRae asked one of them, "What you got?"

"Souvenirs," the man said, "for Diego."

Diego came aboard and they left with the tide. Captain McRae flew the Jack on the way out and shifted over to the Stars and Bars as they approached Tampa. All seemed to be going well until the *USS Keystone State* spotted them and gave chase. "Dammit," Captain McRae yelled. "Change the flag."

Crew members yanked down the Stars and Bars and started hoisting the Stars and Stripes. The *Keystone State* pulled alongside and fired a blast across the bow. Captain McRae yelled, "Stop the engine!"

Willy stopped the engine and the steamboat came to a halt, bobbing up and down on the waves. A marine detachment rowed over and boarded the *Salvor*. Captain McRae asked the sergeant, "What's the problem?"

"No problem, sir," the marine sergeant replied, "where you headed?"

"Key West!" Diego shouted. "We're going to Key West."

The sergeant said, "You're a bit north for Key West. Let's check the cargo."

Marines spread out over the ship. They checked the wheel house, cargo lockers, and hold. A few minutes later a marine came back carrying a Union Jack and the Stars and Bars. The marine said, "Seems to be some confusion about nationality."

"Souvenirs," Diego shouted. "I got 'em in Havana."

Other marines came out of the hold lugging a crate of European percussion cap revolvers. One said, "Got about five hundred of these and a million caps."

"Not that many," Diego argued. "You're exaggerating."

The sergeant asked Diego, "What do you know about this?"

"Nothing," Diego insisted. "I'm a passenger. I'm going to Key West."

"In that case, you'll have no objections if we escort you there."

Diego said, "Nope, no objection."

Captain McRae started to say something but changed his mind. Isobel was going to be upset, but he couldn't do anything about it. He told the sergeant, "We'll follow you back."

"We'll ride along," the sergeant said, "to make sure you get there."

CHAPTER THIRTY SEVEN

Contraband

Key West
October 1861 through December 1861

As much of the country was in rebellion against the United States, President Lincoln proclaimed a new policy: *Henceforth, all items of private property used by those engaged in acts of rebellion against the authority of the United States will be considered as contraband subject to seizure by the armed forces of the United States and sold at public auction.* Ships, slaves, arms, and items of merchandise were included in the sweeping edict. Slaves would be held in government encampments for the duration of the conflict and provided with food and lodging.

But Gideon Welles, Secretary of Navy, decided it was not in the nation's best interest to let these able-bodied black men sit on the sidelines. He needed manpower for his blockade so he authorized their enlistment as "ship's boys." Able-bodied black men were signed up and assigned to serve on the nation's warships. They were paid ten dollars a month and given a daily ration. Commodore Farley, the Key West Squadron Commander, was the first to implement the policy.

Black men who got to the navy yard or appeared on the shores of the command were enlisted. Then the commodore ordered his officers to seek out and seize vessels carrying contraband cargo. The ships were taken into custody and added to the blockade.

Commodore Farley was working in his office on the morning the *Keystone State* brought the old cattle boat into the harbor. A few hours transpired before Lieutenant Simms, commanding officer of the *Keystone State*, brought his captives to the office.

231

Four marine guards, Captain McRae, and Diego marched behind Lieutenant Simms as the lieutenant led his entourage into the office. Commodore Farley looked up. "What's this?"

"Blockade runners," Lieutenant Simms announced, "caught 'em red-handed hauling contraband to the rebels."

"What'd you get?"

"Rifles, pistols, and percussion caps, they were also carrying pharmaceuticals, coffee, dry goods, and cigars."

"Cigars," Commodore Farley demanded, "what kind?"

"Havana Cabanas, about as good as it gets."

"Sure are," Commodore Farley agreed. "Bring any?"

"Left them on the boat but I'll send over a crate if you wish."

"Gotta keep some for evidence, but I could use a few."

"I can get more if you want," Diego offered. "I got connections."

"Expect you do," Commodore Farley grumbled. "I've had a few run-ins with you in the past. First, it was dogs. Then it was Narisco and that bunch. Now, we've caught you hauling arms, ammunition, and cigars."

Lieutenant Simms asked, "You know these people?"

"Unfortunately, I do," Commodore Farley admitted. "We've been giving them coal under some kind of a cockamamie arrangement with somebody in Washington. I didn't know they were using this coal to smuggle stuff for the rebels."

"Not me!" Diego claimed. "I'm not doing that. I wouldn't do such a thing!"

"Headed toward Tampa," Lieutenant Simms insisted. "There's no doubt about it. We're holding the steamship and contents as contraband."

"I don't know anything about it," Diego insisted. "I was a passenger."

Commodore Farley said, "I thought you owned the boat."

"Not that one," Diego sputtered. "It was a different boat. I'm an honest merchant just trying to make a living. I've got business to do and gotta be going. I'll get you cigars if you want, but you gotta let me go."

Commodore Farley asked Lieutenant Simms, "Do you have anything on him."

"Not really, it's McRae's boat."

Commodore Farley said, "That'll do. Hold the boat and throw McRea in the brig until we sort this out."

Captain McRae sputtered, "But I'm hauling cows."

"Not anymore," Commodore Farley insisted. "You're not going anyplace."

"What about me," Diego pleaded.

"Believe you're a Spanish national," Commodore Farley replied. "As you've already given us more than enough trouble and I don't want to stir up an international incident, I'd be most appreciative if you got out that door as fast as you can get."

Diego did. He dashed out the door and hustled down Front Street to the Jacaranda office. Willy Fairchild was in the office talking with Sidney. Diego dashed in and slammed the door.

Sidney asked, "What's up?"

"Someone put wrong stuff on the boat."

"I guess," Sidney replied. "Where's McRae?"

"He's in the slammer!"

"Damn!" Sidney blurted. This was a complication. Sidney fired off a dispatch to Caleb but nothing happened.

The navy cleaned up the *Salvor,* gave it a new name, and put it on the blockade. Captain McRae sat in the brig. Commodore Farley wasn't much concerned. He had other concerns. September in the tropics is marked by severe gales and storms. These delay ship arrivals and departures.

Caleb came to Key West on the *Harriet Lane* and arrived in the middle of such a storm. The cutter rode out the heavy water at sea for awhile and slipped into the harbor during a lull. Caleb got off the boat and made his way against a headwind, sloshing up Front Street in ankle deep water. He yanked the door to Sidney's office open and stumbled in, wet and disheveled. Sidney barked, "Who's that?"

"Oughta know," Caleb answered as he plopped into the nearest chair chair. "You gotta mess."

"Just a squall," Sidney replied.

"Not talking about the weather," Caleb insisted. "I'm talking about Diego and the boat."

"Boat's gone." Sidney replied. "Diego's at the club."

"Let's go." Caleb jumped to his feet.

"Go where?"

"The club," Caleb demanded. "Come on! Let's go."

"Go outside, in this storm. You can't be serious."

"Right now, let's go." Caleb started for the door.

Sidney ran behind Caleb as they dashed down the street dodging palm fronds and branches. Water filled the air. Nevertheless, they reached the club. Stumbling up the steps, they dashed across the porch as the water laden wind rattled the shutters.

Sidney shoved the door open. They tumbled inside. Caleb slammed the door. Hector came out to say, "Sorry, we're closed."

"Damn it, Hector," Sidney shouted. "It's me."

"Mr. Sidney, I didn't recognize you," Hector mumbled. "Nicole's in the dining room with Diego."

Sidney said, "Thank you, Hector."

Sidney led the way through the parlor and into the dining room. Nicole said, "We got company."

Caleb pointed his finger at Diego. "We gotta talk."

"Who's we," Diego demanded.

"You, I've got questions."

"I don't know anything."

"That's why we're talking."

Diego said, "I don't know this man."

"That's why I'm here," Caleb suggested. "We're getting acquainted."

"Here, now," Diego blustered. "This isn't a good day."

"Not talking about the weather," Caleb insisted. He asked Nicole, "Where can we talk?"

"The library, close the door."

"Is it secure?"

Nicole said, "Secure as we got."

"Don't know this man," Diego mumbled. He got up from the table.

"Not many do," Caleb replied. "That's how I like it."

"Your lucky day," Nicole told Diego. "You're meeting the man!"

Diego looked perplexed. Roslyn said, "Go ahead. It's dry in there."

The library had chairs and a small conference table. Leather bound books filled the shelves. Wind gusts rattled the sashes. The gentlemen sat around the table.

Caleb asked Diego. "What's the story with the French?"

Diego asked Sidney, "Who is this guy?"

"The man," Sidney insisted. "He pays our bills."

"Then you're the big little man from Washington," Diego suggested. "I've heard about you. Pleased to finally meet you. What do you want?"

"Tell me about the French."

"They're my friends."

"So I heard," Caleb replied. "England's on the verge of granting belligerency status to the Confederacy. If they do, Confederate ships will have access to English ports and the Confederacy will be on its way to gaining recognition. Your French friends are part of this."

"Not really," Diego replied. "They've got their own plans. Individual Confederate states are cutting their own deals. The Virginia guys will go along with everything to get what they want. Texas guys are different. They back Spain on the Dominican thing but don't want Frenchmen at their back door. Louisiana doesn't much care. They're French at heart are going along with the French on the Mexican scheme."

"What's the scheme?"

"I know about it," Diego boasted. "Juarez, the Mexico president, hasn't been paying his loans and the French are going after him. He owes them a lot. Spain and England are going along with France. They're going in January."

"Tripartite Agreement," Caleb suggested.

"How did you hear about it?"

"I've got my sources. Your Captain General, what's he doing?"

"Getting ready," Caleb answered, "if you know so much."

"Only so much, what's he doing?"

"What he's supposed to be doing."

"Which is?"

"Supporting Spanish, French, and English naval forces and organizing troops for Tampico. The French are going ashore at Vera Cruz."

"Then it's decided," Caleb suggested.

"French are sending thirty thousand."

"You're part of it?"

"I'm on the payroll."

Sidney let out a groan.

Caleb asked, "Doing what?"

"Things," Diego admitted, "making arrangements."

"What arrangements?"

"Helping them get Key West if things go bad for the Union. The Confederates want recognition, but England's waiting until they launch their big invasion of Maryland and Pennsylvania to cut off Washington. Lee's gettin' ready. It's a done deal."

"You're involved."

"Backing all the dogs in the race, that's all."

"They're paying you."

"I fish while they bite."

"Probably," Caleb concluded. "Keep us informed but I don't want anything in writing."

"How do I keep you informed if I can't write?"

"Tell Nicole. She'll get it to me. Otherwise, we don't know each other."

Diego asked, "Do I get paid?"

"You'll get paid what Nicole thinks you're worth."

A gust rattled the windows. Sidney blurted, "What's going on?"

"Not your concern," Caleb snapped, "anything else?"

Sidney said, "McRae."

"I'm taking him to Washington," Caleb replied. "The British have filed a protest, claiming he's a subject of the crown."

"Our boat," Sidney insisted, "we can't run our company without our boat."

"You've got others," Caleb replied. "What are you doing with them?"

"Simon's making runs," Sidney replied. "He's hauling cotton. Angus, the captain's kid, has been making a few coastal runs with the old *Highland Princess* but that's it."

Caleb said, "Pick up a couple of boats and run them under the Spanish or French flag." He nodded at Diego. "You're working for the French."

"I'll need more money."

Caleb said, "Use your French money."

"That's my retirement fund."

"Think you'll live long enough to retire."

"What do you mean?"

"You're on the Captain General's payroll. I expect he's big on loyalty."

Diego said, "He's my friend."

"What about the Confederacy?" Caleb asked. "I thought they were paying you."

"A small retainer," Diego claimed, "not much."

Sidney groaned. Caleb said, "Maybe you're just slippery enough to survive this thing. Keep me posted."

Diego suggested, "So long as you keep paying."

Caleb said, "So long as you keep talking."

"You're a true gentleman," Diego claimed.

"Don't take it to heart." Caleb took a watch from his pocket. "I've gotta be going." Caleb jumped up, opened the door, and found Nicole waiting for him. She said. "We gotta talk."

"Not now," Caleb replied, "maybe later."

"Not much later," Nicole snapped. "Get back here before you go high-tailing to Washington."

Caleb assured her, "I'll be back." Nicole walked off.

Diego asked Caleb, "You the man?"

Sidney said, "Sure is."

"Then Nicole's the woman," Diego blurted. "I'm going with her."

Caleb and Sidney left the club to find the storm had blown over. Caleb took Sidney to his office and continued on his way to the navy yard. Commodore Farley greeted the state department representative with reservation as he had made it a practice to avoid all contact with these people at all times if at all possible. But when Commodore Farley learned that Captain McRae was a subject of the crown, he was glad to hand off the problem.

Caleb had a short conference with the commodore. Then he went back to the club and was on the deck of the *Harriet Lane* when the marines brought Captain McRae to the revenue cutter.

CHAPTER THIRTY EIGHT

Soothing Troubled Waters

Washington City
January through February 1862

After the marines departed, Captain McRae rubbed his wrists while glancing around the deck of the unfamiliar vessel. He didn't know Caleb, but Caleb seemed to be in charge. Captain McRae asked, "What's going on?"

"Taking you to Washington," Caleb explained. "We're defusing an international incident."

"What are you talking about?"

"You," Caleb replied. "You've stirred up a mess."

"Aint done nothing wrong," Captain McRae protested. "Just minding my own business and hauling a little cargo. That's all."

"The navy caught you running the blockade," Caleb replied. "That wasn't part of our plan."

"Running the blockade?"

"No, getting caught," Caleb insisted. "You should have made your run after dark."

"Damn fool thing to do," Captain McRae claimed. "You can't run up the bay after dark. You'll run aground. You can't do that."

"Let's make something perfectly clear," Caleb asserted. "You're in trouble. I'm trying to get you out. Things will go better if you keep your mouth shut and keep your opinions to yourself. I ask questions and you provide answers. That's it."

Captain McRae nodded agreement as he followed Caleb across the deck and below to the cabins. It took a week to reach the Potomac and make the short up river run to the navy yard.

The navy yard had become a massive industrial complex with foundries, iron works, and rolling mills. The rolling mills produced the copper sheets to sheath wooden hulls, the iron works manufactured the iron plates for ironclads, and the foundries cast the cannon for the navy's ships.

Captain McRae didn't pay much attention to the noise, confusion, and commotion. Ash, soot, and smoke billowed around them as they made their way to the main gate. The nation was at war.

They emerged at the foot of 8th Street. Caleb strolled over to the driver of a carriage, got his attention, and shouted out a destination. The driver tipped his hat. They boarded the phaeton and were off, trotting down 8th Street, dodging and weaving through the traffic to M Street.

Captain McRae looked around but didn't say anything. The street was crowded and traffic confusing. The driver stopped in front of a row of red brick buildings and dropped them off. Captain McRae followed Caleb as they went inside and upstairs to Caleb's office.

Caleb took off his jacket, glanced at the dispatches piled on his desk, and ignored them. He told Captain McRae, "Wait here. I'll be back."

Captain McRea sat on a sofa inside the door. Caleb left, closing the door behind him. Captain McRea was alone. He waited for a time but nothing happened.

Then he got up, walked over to the door, and opened it to find a uniformed guard on the other side. The guard asked, "May I help you?"

"Thanks, just checking." Captain McRae closed the door.

Caleb returned an hour or so later with a little man with a big nose and great mop of white hair. The man stared at Captain McRae. "So you're the old Scotsman who caused the big fuss."

"Not that old," Captain McRae grumbled.

"In a manner of speaking," the man replied. "I'm Bill Seward, Secretary of State."

"I'm James McRae. So what's that got to do with anything?"

"Quite a bit, it appears," Secretary Seward insisted. "Lord Lyons, the British ambassador, has filed a protest concerning your seizure. He's claiming one of our navy vessels fired on your vessel while it was flying the flag of Great Britain in international waters. Then they seized the boat and detained you."

"Not true," Captain McRae argued, "We were flying your flag when they stopped us."

"Had a collection of flags, I understand," Secretary Seward insisted. "The log claims you took down your Jack before you hauled up the Stars and Stripes, and you were carrying a Stars and Bars of the Confederacy."

"I'm a loyal subject of the Queen, bless her soul. I'm trying to help you folks, doing you a favor when I got stopped for no reason. Then you took my boat and hauled me up here. My missus is gonna get real mad. I don't even know what it's about."

"You violated our blockade and compounded your felony by carrying multiple banners. Your ship and its cargo are contraband of war, and you've placed our relationship with Great Britain at risk. Now, we've got to figure out what to do with you."

"Haven't done anything wrong, so drop it and let me go."

"That's because we seized the arms and ammunition you were hauling to the rebels," Secretary Seward insisted. "Perhaps I should have Caleb put you away for the duration but that might jeopardize our relationship with other individuals."

Captain McRae didn't like where the conversation seemed to be heading but Secretary Seward eased off a bit, "That could solve certain natters but might complicate others. Come along. We'll see the president."

"Who's that?"

"Abraham Lincoln, you know, the president."

"I haven't met the man."

241

"Probably not, he hasn't traveled that much."

Secretary Seward and Captain McRae found President Lincoln in his telegraph office on the second floor of the old War Department Building. The room had been a library before the war. Shelves along the wall were crammed and cluttered with books and ledgers. The room was filled with tables, telegraph machines, and operators who spent their time clicking out and receiving messages. Scraps of paper were tacked to the message boards leaning against the shelving. Lines and circles were drawn on maps stapled to the walls. The place was a mess.

Abraham Lincoln, president and chief magistrate of the United States, was glancing through messages while he rocked back and forth in an old ladder back rocking chair. He looked a little bit like the newspaper caricatures.

Secretary Seward said, "Figured I'd find you here."

"Getting good news about Donelson," President Lincoln claimed. "Aint been getting much of that."

"Not much," Secretary Seward agreed. "Brought over the fellow the *Keystone State* picked up. Probably recall the incident."

President Lincoln said, "You're the fellow hauling guns and cigars."

"How'd you hear about the cigars?"

"Havana Cabanas, I heard," President Lincoln suggested. "Did you by any chance bring any?"

"They weren't mine. They were Diego's."

"Be that as it may," President Lincoln conceded. He rocked back and forth a few times before asking Secretary Seward, "What are you going to do with this fellow?"

"That's the problem," Secretary Seward replied. "Great Britain's filed a diplomatic protest and we're trying to deal with that issue as best we can while we try to maintain the blockade."

"Gotta get more ships down there," President Lincoln insisted. "We're a little short on ships, so the Brits probably think our blockade's more of a bit of fiction than a reality."

That being said, President Lincoln leaned forward to examine the culprit. He said, "So, you've become the subject of a diplomatic protest. How'd you manage that?"

"Trying a make a living," Captain McRea replied. "Don't know anything about blockades and haven't done anything to hurt anybody."

President Lincoln rocked a few times as the telegraph machines clattered. The president finally said, "So, why don't you tell me what's going on?"

Captain McRea said, "I've got a store in Tampa and the wife runs it. She's gonna be really mad at me if I don't get back to work and start tending to business."

"I can sympathize with that," President Lincoln suggested. "It appears we bear a common affliction. So, what does this store have to do with our problem?"

"That's how I stock the store," Captain McRae explained. "I buy cows in Tampa and haul them to Key West. Then I take hides to Havana and bring back merchandise for the store. I've been doing this for a long time and nobody ever paid attention. Then the war started and everybody went crazy. I've been trying to get along with you guys and get along the other fellows to keep the wife happy but it aint working."

President Lincoln said, "Heard you were in Havana."

"That's where I get the stuff for the store."

"And sell this stuff to the other fellows, I presume."

"Some of the time," Captain McRea suggested. "I gotta sell it to somebody."

"Making any money?"

"Some but not enough," Captain McRae replied. "Wife's been on my back about it, but I don't want any trouble."

"That the Key West wife or Tampa wife?"

"Only got one wife," Captain McRae insisted.

President Lincoln rocked while he considered the matter. Coming to a conclusion, the president said, "Mr. McRae, you sort of remind me of the old Mormon fellow with a couple of bossy wives who's chatting up a new lady friend."

"What do you mean?"

243

"You're trying to get a little piece in between!" President Lincoln guffawed as he slapped his leg. Captain McRea looked confused.

A telegraph operator laughed, but Secretary Seward didn't laugh or say much of anything. Secretary Seward asked the president, "So, what do you want me to do with him?"

President Lincoln said, "We don't really need Mr. McRae around here. Why don't we have him sign an oath of loyalty and send him home?"

Secretary Seward said, "I'll do that."

"And make certain Lord Lyons knows about our decision," President Lincoln added. "Perhaps you should invite the Lord over and give him a chance to meet his subject."

"I'll do that," Secretary Seward agreed as he ushered Captain McRae out of the telegraph office. Captain McRae had lunch with the secretary of state and British ambassador the next day. The ambassador didn't seem to show much interest in the lunch or his subject.

Captain McRae signed an oath of loyalty promising to not to interfere with or otherwise hamper the lawful pursuits of the United States. Then Secretary Seward took him to the navy yard, put him on the dispatch boat, and sent him back to Key West.

CHAPTER THIRTY NINE

Peace River Exile

Tampa to Fort Meade
March through August 1862

Rumors of battles being won and lost in far off Virginia and the west started seeping home to Florida and Tampa Town. The *Salvor* got a new name and joined the blockade. Union vessels prowled the coast imposing an absolute blockade on all commerce. Captain Simon scrounged up a little coal from time to time and took the *Scottish Princess* out after dark on the darkest of evenings. Otherwise, he kept the blockade runner tied up next to the old *Highland Princess* far up the Hillsborough River.

General Haines Cotesworth left Tampa. Colonel Bemrose was left to his own devices. Isobel didn't have much to do as the Tampa Bay City Hotel sat empty and the store was running out of merchandise. Sarah took care of baby Emma while Harry printed occasional editions of the paper and did his best to avoid Colonel Bemrose.

As the war continued, the difference in available manpower between the Union and the Confederacy became more significant. Over twenty-two million people lived in the North but only nine million lived in the South. Over three million of the people in the South were slaves. Being besieged by Union armies advancing from all sides, President Davis announced that the army had to have more men.

The Confederate Congress met the need by passing the Confederate Conscription Act of 1862. The act ordered the immediate, mandatory, and involuntary call-up of all white males between the ages of eighteen and thirty-five residing in the South for three years of Confederate army service. When

Colonel Bemrose got word of the policy, he put his boys to work.

Harry received his summons a few days later. Sarah was flabbergasted, Isobel was resigned, and Harry reported to the fort for a physical exam and processing. Doc Dunfield, Beauregard's old neighbor, conducted the physical exams by making certain that each conscript had at least one good eye to sight the gun, a tooth to tear the powder cartridge open, and a finger to pull the trigger.

The medical exam didn't take long and Doc sent the conscripts out to the porch to get sworn in by Colonel Bemrose. It was a little bit like the old Groggery swearing-in only this time Colonel Bemrose was wearing a gray uniform. He had given up his gold eagle collar devices for the gold stars of the Confederacy, but a colonel was still a colonel. Colonel Beauregard Bemrose, C.S.A. Home Guard, limped down the line of twenty-five reluctant recruits and halted in front of Harry.

Colonel Bemrose said, "Sumabitch boy, I know you from someplace."

Harry mumbled, "Your boat crew in the last war."

Beauregard shouted, "Speak up, boy! Say what you got to say. I want to hear you."

"I was on your boat crew," Harry shouted.

"So you were," Beauregard replied. "But we ran into each other before. It took me awhile to figure out where that was, but I figured it out. You were with that smug, highfalutin, Charleston society boy who came up to Tallahassee and screwed up my life, my career, and dog business. If I remember right, you told me you were a Yankee. New Yorker, I believe you said."

The recruits turned enmasse to confront the interloper. There were gasps of amazement and a few curses.

"Dogs were no good," Harry protested. "They didn't do anything!"

"Now, is that so?" Beauregard countered. "I tried to tell you that a man's got to be at least half as smart as a dog if he's going to run the dog. I never knew a Yankee who was smart enough to do that."

The conscripts erupted with laughter. This was becoming confusing. Harry had been a local, a Florida resident, for several years. The distant past was coming back to complicate his life.

Colonel Bemrose glanced around at the troops and conscripts before shouting, "Hey, boys! We got ourselves a Yankee spy here. What do you want to do with him?"

Someone shouted, "Hang him!"

A more lenient soul called out, "Run him out of town."

Beauregard considered the suggestions for a moment before saying, "That ought to work. Tell you what, Yankee. I'm a sporting man so I'm gonna give you a head start. You got twenty-four hours to get out of town, and if we catch you, we'll hang you from the nearest tree."

A voice grumbled, "Come on, let's hang him now and get it over with."

"Hold your horses," Colonel Bemrose insisted. "Let's give the poor sumabitch a sporting chance. It'll be a lot more fun to run him down, drag him back, and then hang him."

The entourage of Harry's former neighbors, friends, and acquaintances laughed, whooped, and hollered as Harry backed away, made his way out the front gate, and dashed down the road. It was becoming downright exasperating.

"Get out of town," Sarah screamed. "They'll hang you."

"Where do I go?"

Isobel rushed in, shouting, "Get out. Go with Wiley. He's taking a load to Fort Meade."

"Where do I go?"

"Down the Peace River," Isobel suggested, "back to your own kind, the Union Navy's patrolling the river. They'll pick you up and take you to Key West or someplace. We'll catch up with you later."

"What about Sarah and Emma, I can't leave them," Harry protested.

"Can't take 'em," Isobel insisted. "Get out while you've got a chance."

Harry took Isobel's advice, kissed Sarah, grabbed his hat, dashed out, and jumped on Carey's freight wagon. Cary hid him under a tarp and they rolled out of town as part of a wagon train headed for Fort Meade. The oxen spent three days plodding along the wagon road through tall grass and oak clusters to get to Fort Meade.

Harry slipped off the wagon a couple of miles out of Fort Meade. He thanked Carey for the ride and dashed off trying to find a hiding place in the thickets along the Peace River. The river was running high. Harry didn't have a way to get across the river or down the river. He'd have to find a boat or make a raft.

Harry crashed through a thicket, emerged in an open section, dashed across the clearing, and plunged into another thicket. He rested, checked for snakes and alligators, took a chance, and took a drink from the river.

He continued on his way, pushing through more thickets, and almost bumped into a black man hacking away on a cypress log. The black man dropped his axe. Harry backed off. "Sorry, I didn't see you."

"Looks like you're in a powerful hurry to get someplace. That don't make no sense. No place to go around here."

Something was familiar. It wasn't just the man's arrogance. It was his presence. It was Floyd. Harry caught his breath. "I know you! You're Floyd. What are you doing here?"

"Digging a dugout, I live here. What are you doing?"

Harry looked around. There was a thatched hut, cooking fire, and kettle of something over a low fire. "What's in the kettle?"

"Sofkee," Floyd said. "Have some."

Floyd went back to hacking out his canoe. Harry scrambled to the kettle, picked up the wooden spoon, and tasted the soup. It was good. He hadn't had anything to eat for a long time. After he satisfied his hunger, he asked, "What you got in this soup?"

"Told you," Floyd replied. "It's sofkee."

"What's sofkee?"

"Soup," Floyd answered.

"I know that. What's in it?"

"Corn, turtle, beans, pepper, and a bunch of other things," Floyd answered. "Aint you had it before?"

"Nope," Harry replied.

"Where you been? Everybody eats sofkee."

"Tampa," Harry answered.

"You never spent time with the people."

"What people?"

"Seminole," Floyd explained. "Seminole eat sofkee."

Floyd was silent as he hacked away. Harry walked over to ask, "What are you doing?"

"Already told you," Floyd replied, "digging a canoe. Not sitting around waitin' fer your cracker army to round up us poor black folk and put us to work. I'm gettin free, going down the river."

"Seem to be pretty free to me," Harry observed as he looked around. "What are you going to gain by going down the river?"

"Decent living, maybe," Floyd asserted. "Camping has its disadvantages."

"I expect," Harry conceded.

Floyd looked up. "Probably aint none of my business but appears you got yourself into a bunch of trouble. White folk don't go running through the brush like they got dogs after 'em. As it seems you aint doing much, I would surely appreciate a little help on digging out my dugout. I'd like to get it finished and am going to need some help getting it into the river."

Harry considered his options before saying, "I'll help."

"Figured as much," Floyd replied. "You surely must have got yourself into a bunch of trouble."

They worked on Floyd's dugout for several days. Harry was not accustomed to working with tools, but Floyd coached him along. "You gotta make do with what you got. I was a carpenter in Georgia, ran off, got caught by the Seminole, got rescued by the army, got captured by the Indians got rescued again, almost got hanged, and now, I'm gonna be a sailor."

"Sort of a sailor," Harry insisted.

"Don't you get uppity with me," Floyd warned. "I took you in so I gotta take care of you. Maybe you'll learn to take care of yourself someday but you sure got a bunch of learning to do before you can get to be a halfway decent wood worker."

"Or ship fitter," Harry agreed. They scraped away.

They launched the dug out and abandoned the camp a few days later. The Peace River took a long meandering route, flowing around hammocks, through pine groves, and open grasslands as it made its leisurely journey to Charlotte Harbor and the Gulf of Mexico. Alligators lounged in the mud and sometimes swam beside them. Harry was concerned but Floyd didn't seem to care. "Ever eat gator?"

"Haven't tried it," Harry replied.

"Have to get one," Floyd suggested. "Not a big one though, they're too tough."

Multi-colored birds flew through the air, plunged into the river, and sometimes pulled up fish and other things. Occasional water moccasins glided by. As they talked and floated, Harry asked Floyd, "What's your real name?"

"Floyd, I guess."

"But that wasn't your real name," Harry insisted. "You've gotta have a name."

"Mother called me Kwadwo. It's African."

"What's it mean?"

Floyd said, "Born on Monday."

"But the name, what does it mean?"

"Name means I was born on Monday."

Harry considered the explanation. "Guess that's a good reason for a name. Makes sense, in a way."

"This name you call me, Floyd. What does it mean?"

"No idea," Harry answered. "Think they called you Lloyd or something like that, means black in Welsh."

"What's that?"

250

"What do you mean?"

"Welsh, what is it?"

"A different language," Harry explained.

"I never heard it."

"That's because nobody speaks it."

Floyd pondered the information for awhile before saying, "You don't seem that hairy. That's what your name means, doesn't it?"

"That's not my real name," Harry explained. "I'm Henry."

Floyd decided to drop the topic. None of the business about names made sense anyway. Floyd and Harry drifted down the river for a few days until they came upon the cluster of mangrove islands cluttering the mouth of the river.

The islands were thickets of red and black mangrove that had taken root in the shallow water to form somewhat stable masses of sand, soil, and vegetation. The knobby prop roots of the red mangrove reached into the water to grab the sand and soil brought down by the river. Mangrove plants, buttonwood, and other foliage grew a good twenty feet high. Sea birds crowded the buttonwood and perched on branches worn bare by the clutching claws of thousands of feet. Alligators loitered, waiting for tasty morsels to drop.

It was a semi-tropical setting that Harry never knew existed. Floyd seemed unperturbed as he said, "I been here before."

They were working their way through a narrow channel between encroaching islands when they heard a rolling crash. It sounded like thunder but it was a clear day. They heard another loud boom followed by a chattering, ripping sound.

Floyd asked, "What's that?"

"Heard it before," Harry replied. "It's a cannon blast, probably a twelve pounder. The other sounds are small arms."

"Better look alert," Floyd suggested as he dug his paddle into the water. They floated around the edge of an island to come upon a two-masted schooner flying the Stars and Bars

251

of the Confederacy. The schooner was being pursued by an armed sloop flying the Stars and Stripes of the Union.

Floyd took a look. "Better hunker down and wait here until those fellows get done doing what they're doing."

They edged the dugout under the overhand of the mangrove and watched the action as the Union warship fired again. The rigging on the schooner went taut and dropped in a heap on the deck. The schooner lost headway, halted, and started drifting down the river, approaching the oncoming sloop. There was another blast on the far side off the island and a rattle of small arms before things quieted down.

Floyd said, "Let's go."

They paddled into the current and around the island to find the Union vessel in possession of the Confederate blockade runner. A couple of bodies were floating in the river. As they drifted to the Union sloop, a voice called out, "Hold it! Stay where you are."

Floyd shouted, "Coming aboard."

They paddled up to the sloop and a bosun's mate tossed a rope. Floyd grabbed the rope, pulling himself to the deck. The bosun's mate shouted down to Harry, "You too, mister. Get up here."

Harry pulled himself up the rope. The petty officer helped Harry on board before announcing, "Hands in the air, mister. You're a prisoner of war."

Harry nodded toward Floyd. "What about him?"

"He's contraband. That makes him a free man," the bosun's mate replied. "You're a rebel, so you're a prisoner."

"Aint no rebel," Floyd insisted. "He's with me."

Floyd joined the navy and the sloop took Harry to Key West.

CHAPTER FORTY

Pennsylvania Volunteers

Key West
October 1862

Harry hadn't been to Key West for some time. The Union was everywhere. Navy gunboats steamed in and out of the harbor. Marine guards were on the piers. Uniformed soldiers and sailors filled the streets. Ensign Charles Clark, master of the *Rosalie,* took Harry to see Rear Admiral Farley as soon as he secured the sloop. Harry might possess valuable information that could benefit the Union.

Congress had reluctantly bowed to the persistent demands of the war by creating three admiral's ranks. Rear admirals commanded shore installations. Vice admirals commanded squadrons and full admirals commanded fleets. Rear Admiral Farley commanded the Key West Naval Ship Yard.

Admirals were entitled to an aide. Lieutenant Simms, who previously commanded the *Keystone State*, had been promoted to Commander to become Rear Admiral Farley's aide. He could select a Master at Arms. Commander Simms selected Chief O'Neil, his former bosun's mate.

Gaining access to the admiral required being cleared by the master at arms, interviewed by the aide, and perhaps, being admitted to see the admiral. This took time as Ensign Clark and Harry had to wait until the Master at Arms was able to see them and admit them to the aide's office. Commander Simms heard them out before saying, "I'll see if the admiral's busy."

They waited while Commander Simms checked with Admiral Farley. After a period of time, Commander Simms returned to say, "Admiral Farley will see you."

Harry followed Ensign Clark into Admiral Farley's office. The office had a nautical flair. Polished, waxed hardwood glistened under their feet. Signal flags hung from the walls and an American flag drooped from the wooden staff behind the admiral's immaculate desk. Ensign Clark snapped to attention although the swivel chair behind the admiral's desk was empty.

Admiral Farley was standing at the window, peering over the harbor with an extended spy glass. The spy glass and lace on his uniform added to the nautical trappings. Admiral Farley lowered the glass. "At ease, gentlemen."

Franklin Farley hadn't changed that much. He had put on a little weight but was otherwise just an older more sedate version of the young lieutenant who had once commanded the *Erie*. The admiral took a good look at the sun burned refugee before asking, "Where'd you find him this time?"

"Pulled him from the Peace River," Ensign Clark replied.

"Believe I did something like that myself," Admiral Farley insisted as he strolled over to his desk. "Only, I think it was the Caloosahatchee." Admiral Farley asked Harry, "What are you doing these days, hauling dogs, or running from Indians?"

"Neither," Harry replied. "I figured I'd stop over to see if you people needed some help."

Admiral Farley snorted, "Fine lot of help that'd be!" The admiral asked Ensign Clark, "What was he doing in the river?"

"Don't know," Ensign Clark answered. "He was coming down the river with a black man, and the black man seemed to be in charge. It was a peculiar arrangement."

"This man has a history of peculiar arrangements. What did you do with the black man?"

"I signed him up."

"We can use the manpower," Admiral Farley replied. "What about this fellow? What should we do with him?"

Harry said, "My wife and daughter are in Tampa. I gotta get 'em out."

Admiral Farley explained, "We don't have much interaction with Tampa these days."

Ensign Clark said, "Maybe he can bring us up to date on what's happening up that way."

"I can help," Harry pleaded. "I was a swamp rat in the last war and know my way around."

Admiral Farley listened and seemed to consider Harry's offer for a moment before sitting. As there were no other chairs, Harry and Ensign Clark continued standing. Admiral Farley finally said, "You don't look much like the usual red necks down here. Where'd you come from?"

"New York," Harry replied. "I'm here by mistake."

"What kind of mistake."

"A bunch of mistakes," Harry insisted. "I worked for Cambreleng at American Fur and went to Washington with him when he got elected to congress. That was a mistake. I took his job at the war department. That was a mistake. I came down with Macomb on his peace mission and that was another mistake. Once I got here, I got stuck here and couldn't get back. Now I'm married and got to stay."

"Getting married, was that a mistake?"

"Not really," Harry replied. "But the peace mission wasn't a very good idea."

"I know a bit about that," Admiral Farley said. "You came down with Joel Poinsett's nephew. That's why I had to fish you guys out of the Caloosahatchee."

"You knew that Cotesworth was Poinsett's nephew!"

"We all did," Admiral Farley replied. "Otherwise, I wouldn't have put up with you, your shenanigans, your dogs, and that Cuban."

"How did you know?"

"Jim Paulding was secretary of navy. Poinsett didn't want trouble with his sister after he sent Cotesworth down here, so he asked Paulding to keep track of the kid. I was here and got the job."

"But the army didn't know."

"Local boys didn't," Admiral Farley replied. "Poinsett didn't want to make an issue of it. Kid turned out to be an embarrassment. Now, I hear he's gone over to the rebels. Just as well, I guess. What about you? What have you been doing since the dog deal?"

"I stayed in Tampa, did some printing, and was a militia lieutenant during the Bowlegs War. That's how I got to be a swamp rat."

"See any action?"

"Some, I headed up a boat patrol. We ran missions up and down the rivers, engaged in a firefight, and brought back some renegades."

Admiral Farley glanced at Ensign Clark who was trying to follow the gist of the peculiar conversation about unknown people, places, and things. Admiral Farley finally said, "Might have a job for you."

"What's that?"

"You've told me a couple of things. You said you wanted to help and you want to get your wife and kid out of Tampa. Is that right?"

"Yes, sir," Harry replied. "It certainly is."

"You might be the guy we're looking for. We're putting together a ranger outfit to launch some operations along the coast. We've got a bunch of local boys on Useppa Island who'd like to settle a few scores on the mainland but we need someone with military experience to go out there and get them organized. You interested?"

"I'll do what I can."

"That's good. I'll have to work out the details with General Woodbury but this might work. Run along but stop over tomorrow and we'll see how things go."

Ensign Clark said, "Thank you, Admiral." They left the office. On the way out, Ensign Clark said, "Sounds like you got a job."

"Sounds like it, but I didn't know there were people on those islands. Who are they?"

"South Florida people," Ensign Clark replied. "They had farms on the mainland but left everything behind and moved to the islands to get away from the Confederate conscription agents and tax collectors. Slavery wasn't a big issue."

"How many are there?"

"Couple of hundred, I believe," Ensign Clark suggested. "Some are rebel army deserters."

"How do they survive?"

"We feed them."

"So they support the Union."

"Guess so," Ensign Clark answered. "I don't think they cared much about the Union or anything else for that matter before the war started. They got fed up with the Confederacy when the conscription agents started showing up on their doorsteps and dragging them off to serve in the Confederate army. We're taking care of them and protecting them. They like that."

"Probably so," Harry replied, "and they've got a few scores to settle."

"So they say, I don't know if it's the idea of the Confederacy or the men who are working for the Confederacy. It's more personal. They want their land back, maybe kick a few butts while getting it, and go back to how things were before the war.

"Is there any chance that'll happen?"

"Guess we'll find out," Ensign Clark suggested. "You gotta place to stay?"

"I know some people."

Harry walked down Front Street to Sidney's office, opened the door, and walked in.

Sidney shouted, "Hey, Harry! What are you doing here?"

"It's rather complicated.

"So, what's the story?"

"I got drafted by the Confederacy but Beauregard kicked me out of Tampa. I went down the river, got picked up by the Union, and they brought me here. Have you heard anything from Tampa?"

"Not much," Sidney replied. "They're on the other side. McRae got back from Washington and Diego's trying to sneak him into Tampa on a fishing smack. I don't know if he made it but probably did."

257

"I thought the blockade got McRae."

"Did for awhile," Sidney said. "They took him to Washington and Lincoln let him go."

"How'd he manage that?"

"No idea," Sidney answered. "So what are you going to do?"

"Maybe the Army's got something. They want someone to help train some refugees or something."

"Hold out for all you can get," Sidney suggested. "The war's winding down and not gonna last much longer. Get what you can while you can get it. That's always been my motto."

"I wanta get back to Tampa."

Sidney said, "What for, you can make something here. You can't make anything back there."

"My wife and daughter are there," Harry insisted. "I gotta get them out."

"McRae will take care of them," Sidney insisted. "He's probably back there. Besides, there won't be any real rebels in Tampa anyway. Jeff Davis is sending them north to fight Grant and Sherman."

"What are you talking about?"

"The rebels are taking a big licking in the Tennessee Valley and Jeff Davis is screaming for reinforcements. Hear they've pulled most of Beauregard's boys and left him with a few old men and cripples. Beauregard won't be doing anything to anyone anyway. Relax and enjoy yourself."

Harry let Sidney talk, waited around, and followed Sidney over to the next door tavern for dinner. The food was good and Sidney let him sleep in the office.

The meeting with General Woodbury and Admiral Farley the next day was short and to the point. General Woodbury said, "Admiral Farley tells me you've had some combat experience."

"Dallam's Store and I went on boat patrols during the Bowlegs War."

"I've gone through the records they brought down from Brooke," General Woodbury replied, "Appears you were a supply sergeant in the Seminole War and a militia lieutenant during the Bowlegs War. You've had considerable military experience."

"I've had some."

"No need for modesty," General Woodbury insisted. "You're the man we're looking for. We need a Florida man to take charge of a ranger company on Useppa Island. Are you interested?"

Being once again considered a Florida resident, Harry said, "I am."

"Good, I'll start you as a replacement lieutenant and shift you over to your own company as soon as we get it organized."

Harry, once a New Yorker, now a Floridian, became a lieutenant in the 47th Pennsylvania Volunteer Regiment. It made sense, in a way.

CHAPTER FORTY ONE

Blockade Runners and Cow Catchers

Tampa Town
November 1862 through September 1863

Captain McRea and Willy Fairchild, his engineer, made their way back to Tampa on a Spanish fishing smack. They managed to sneak through the blockade and emerged from a hiding place in the hold of the vessel to walk up the long pier leading to Tampa Town's desolate state of affairs. Commerce had vanished.

Nothing was happening on the pier. Willy followed Captain McRea into the hotel taproom. It was empty. Captain McRea rapped on the bar and Isobel shouted from the kitchen, "Hold your horses, I'll be there in a minute."

"Damn it woman," Captain McRae shouted. "Get out here."

Isobel dropped what she was doing to come out and take a look at her husband. She said, "You're a mess. Where've you been?"

"Long story," Captain McRae muttered. He slid up to the bar. "I'll tell you about it sometime."

"Expect you will," Isobel replied. "What happened to the steamboat?"

"Yankees got it. Guess they're using it."

"That figures." She asked Willy. "So, how are you fellows going to make a living?"

"Don't know," Willy replied. "Figure the captain will come up with something."

"Hope so, I'm about down to my last case of rum and Sarah's closed the store. Bemrose ran off her husband. She's spending most of her time taking care of the kid."

Captain McRae asked, "How's the kid coming?"

"About as expected, growing up and getting into trouble." Isobel glanced around the empty taproom. "Don't know what we're going to do. Aint got much left to sell but nobody's got any money anyway. Took a bunch of cotton in trade, got it stashed in the warehouse, but don't know what I'm going to do with it. You gotta get it out of here before it starts rotting and get in some merchandise. That's what you gotta do."

Willy said, "Gotta have a boat."

"You've got 'em," Isobel replied, "just need a few real men with gumption enough to take 'em out."

Captain McRae grumbled, "What are you talking about."

"*Scottish Princess*," Isobel replied. "Simon just ran her up the Hillsborough and tied her up, just sitting there. Bemrose put a few guards on her, but she could be making runs. Go after dark, take some of my cotton to Havana, sell it, and bring back some merchandise, enough to tide us over until after the war."

"Could try it," Captain McRea conceded.

"Probably could," Willy replied.

"Then start doing it," Isobel asserted. "You'll have to cut a deal with Bemrose to get his guards off the boat."

Captain McRae said, "I'll talk with him."

"Be careful what you say and go along with what he wants," Isobel advised. "I don't want any trouble from him."

"I'll do that." Captain McRae got down to business the next day and walked up to the fort. A veteran with one leg was standing guard.

The veteran said, "If you wanta see Bemrose, he's at the stable with Brinton."

Colonel Bemrose and Brinton Hooker were checking out a mare. Brinton, now a major in the Home Guard, and Colonel Bemrose looked up as Captain McRae approached. Colonel Bemrose said, "Heard the Yankees got ya."

"They did but let me go."

Brinton asked, "What you doing back here?"

"I'm getting back into business."

"Doing what," Brinton demanded.

"Twisting a few Yankee tails," Captain McRae replied. "I'm taking cotton to Havana and bringing back supplies."

Colonel Bemrose suggested, "After dark, I presume."

"Precisely," Captain McRae replied. "I need my boat."

"I've got her under guard but open to negotiation. You swore an oath to help us but haven't done much, as far as I can see."

Brinton said, "Was gonna hang you, but you got off."

"About these negotiations," Captain McRae asked. "What you got in mind?"

"Supplies," Colonel Bemrose suggested. "Brinton needs rum and I could use a few Cuban cigars and some gunpowder in about that order. I'll let you use your boat if you get me my stuff."

"Anything else," Captain McRae asked.

Brinton asked, "How do we know he's coming back? He never came back last time."

Colonel Bemrose said, "That's because Yankees got him, but you're bringing up a good point. He might try to cut a deal with those Yankees once he gets out of the bay."

"So how we gonna keep track of him?"

"You'll do that," Colonel Bemrose suggested. "I'll send you along."

"Don't know if I want to do that."

Colonel Bemrose insisted, "You're doing it. That's an order." Then Colonel Bemrose asked Captain McRae, "Got any problems with that?"

"Nope," Captain McRae answered, "no problem."

The *Scottish Princess* was moored to cypress trees about fourteen miles up the Hillsborough River. Two guards sat on the bank and another one sat on deck. The guards waved them through and Willy went down to check out the engine room. Willy came back a few minutes later. "It'll take me awhile to get her cleaned up, but we can do it."

Captain McRea said, "That'll do. We'll paint her black, load her with cotton, and wait for a night without a moon. Then we'll make our run."

Everything decided, Captain McRae left Willy with the boat, went back to Tampa Town, and started rounding up some crew members. Carey came up with a couple of bullwhackers. They loaded the boat with cotton and waited for a dark night.

Jake asked, "How about cows? Any chance you could take a few?"

"Not this time," Captain McRae replied. "We're taking cotton and bringing back cargo.

Jake said, "Guess, I'll start selling cows to the Confederates. They aint paying much and you gotta drive them to Baldwin, but it's better than starving."

Captain McRae and Willy waited until a dark night without a moon. Then Willy got up steam, and they eased the blockade runner out of Tampa Bay. Once they reached the open sea, Captain McRae ran up the Union Jack, and they steamed to Havana.

Captain McRae got a good price for the cotton and purchased a boatload of rum, cigars, gunpowder, and manufactured products. They made a rapid return run and ran *The Scottish Princess* up the Hillsborough where they unloaded the cargo. Brinton was glad to be back, Beauregard got his payoff, and Isobel was pleased by the change in circumstances. She restocked her liquor supply and Sarah opened the store.

Jake Sutherlin rounded up his remaining cowcatchers and went back to catching cows. They drove a couple of hundred head north to the railhead at Baldwin and sold the cows to the Confederate Commissary Commission. The commission paid three dollars a head in cotton money. It wasn't much but better than nothing.

The Commissary Commission wanted more cows. Union victories along the Mississippi had cut off the supply of western beef. Florida had become the Confederacy's only source of beef, and they needed more.

Jake said, "I'll do what I can, but I've gotta have help."

263

The Commissary Commission responded by asking General Bragg, the commander of the Army of the Tennessee, to release some experienced cattlemen to come back to Florida and help round up cows. General Bragg didn't respond until Richmond intervened and ordered General Bragg to release eighty men.

Captain John Pearson, C.S.A., was sent south to take charge of the operation. The local cattlemen in central and southern Florida who had been exempted from the draft were rounded up as conscripts or reserves and ordered to help out in the cattle drives. These men were designated as the 1st Battalion of Florida Cavalry. They called themselves the Cow Cavalry.

When not otherwise engaged on cattle drives, the Cow Cavalry was ordered to round up Confederate deserters and fight off Union Navy incursions into the rivers and along the coastlines of Central and South Florida. When the Union gunboat, *USS Sagamore,* steamed into Tampa Bay and demanded the surrender of the city. Captain Pearson conferred with Colonel Bemrose before declining the request.

The gunboat captain responded by giving the women and children three hours to leave Tampa before shelling the city. After waiting for three or four hours, the gunboat fired three perfunctory shots at the city before withdrawing at dusk.

The *Sagamore* came back the next day with the *USS Ethan Dunigan.* The warships exchanged gunfire with the fortifications along the shore for four hours before the ships finally withdrew and sailed away. There were no reported casualties and no apparent damage to either the ships or the city.

As the ships departed, Colonel Bemrose called his boys together in front of the Tampa Bay City Hotel. He shouted, "Sumabitch, boys! We did it! We kicked their butts."

The few slaves left in Tampa drifted away to find shelter and refuge on Egmont Key. The navy blockading squadron guaranteed their safety and provided them with rations and assistance. Some joined the navy.

The war continued and the Confederacy needed more manpower. Captain Pearson ordered his cow cavalry to round up all eligible men who might be avoiding the draft. There were reports of desperate men being seized in the woods and dragged off to serve in the army. One unconfirmed report told of an old man being strung up and hanged, not quite to death, to make him give up his sons.

The bombardment and rumors added to the resentment, anger, and confusion. Beauregard placed Tampa under martial law. McRae's Merchandise Market was open but nobody had any money or anything left to trade. The weekly stage still ran up the demarcation road to Gainesville but the trip was dusty, dangerous, long and uncomfortable.

It took two weeks to get a letter to Tallahassee and another two weeks to get a response. Richmond was farther away and no longer accessible. Captain McRae maintained an intermittent contact with Havana as he made solitary dashes through the blockade. He went out infrequently and came back a few nights later.

Some wondered how he managed to avoid the blockade. Nobody knew that Captain McRae made it a point to visit the Jacaranda office while in Havana. Diego was there and Diego gave him information on Union ship movements and assignments. Otherwise, Diego was busy running supply ships for the French, maintaining a fleet of fishing smacks, and keeping in touch with Sidney.

The United States Navy knew about the blockade runner but was limited by international law. They couldn't seize the *Scottish Princess* while it was tied in Havana or sink it in Spanish waters. They needed to catch the boat while it was at sea or locate it in American waters. Thus far, they had been unable to do either.

The Union Navy rankled at the impudence and arrogance of the rebel captain who continued violating the blockade. Admiral Farley decided to do something.

CHAPTER FORTY TWO

Useppa Island Rangers

Key West and Useppa Island
September 1863 through January 1864

Admiral Farley faced two perplexing problems. Feeding the refugee community on the barrier islands was getting expensive and he needed to do something about the *Scottish Princess*. The blockade runner was being spotted in the Havana harbor on a regular basis, but he couldn't go after the vessel in Spanish waters because it might provoke a war with Spain or England or maybe both.

He decided to use the islanders to destroy the blockade runner. That way he would be getting a return on his expenditures, get rid of the blockade runner, and spare his own men the peril of embarking on a dangerous mission in enemy territory. The refugees were familiar with the terrain. They knew their way around and no one cared about them. They were cheap, convenient, and expendable

The refugees, several hundred by now, were living in shacks, cabins, and hovels clustered around the old Useppa Island customs house. A lot of these men, probably most, harbored grudges against the rebel home guard, conscription agents, and tax collectors who had disrupted their lives and driven them off their land. The refugees would fight but needed to be organized and trained.

Admiral Farley invited General Woodbury to his office to discuss the project. Admiral Farley greeted General Woodbury, sat him down, and served a mug of warm coffee with a slice of pound cake. Once that was done, Admiral Farley told General Woodbury, "We've gotta take out a blockade runner."

"What you got in mind?"

266

"A Tampa Bay steamboat's been running the blockade. There's a story behind the boat, but needless to say, we've got to do something about it. We can't take her out in Cuban waters and we haven't been able to catch her at sea, so we'll need to send in a shore party. It's the only way we'll get her."

"Sounds a little risky, got anybody in mind?"

"Useppa Island refugees, but we've gotta get them organized and give them some training."

"Got anybody in mind?"

"Your Peace River fellow," Admiral Farley suggested.

"That was the idea. What's he doing?"

"Signing up Key West volunteers, I'm mixing them with my Pennsylvania boys."

"Why bother," Admiral Farley replied. "They don't know anything about Pennsylvania. They'll never fit in."

"Probably not, but I had to do something to get them some training. Figured we'd use them as a base for your ranger company. It'll keep a Florida face on the project."

"Good idea," Admiral Farley replied. "These Florida bushwhackers seem to be a rather independent bunch. They'll get along better with their own kind. What about Lane? Is he ready to go?"

"Ask," General Woodbury suggested. "He's outside."

Admiral Farley stepped to the door and called out to Commander Simms, "Send Lane in." Harry appeared in the doorway and waited to be recognized. Admiral Farley said, "Come on in, lieutenant. We gotta talk."

Harry entered the room. "You wanted to see me."

"Sure do, hear you've been recruiting a few local boys."

"Yes, sir," Harry replied. "I signed up a dozen or so. They believe it's their war and want in on the action."

"Glad to hear that," Admiral Farley replied. "We've got an opportunity for you." General Woodbury didn't say anything.

Being a bit cautious, Harry asked, "What is it?"

"We're thinking about launching a few raids along the coast and would like you to head them up."

Harry asked, "Where?"

"It's around the Tampa Bay area."

Harry asked, "Will this be a raid in force?"

"Definitely," Admiral Farley replied. "You'll need to hold the area while you take out a blockade runner."

"I've only got a dozen men. I'll need more."

"We've got them for you. There's a bunch on Useppa Island. You'll need to take your boys out and get them organized."

Recalling his conversation with Ensign Clark, Harry said, "You're talking about refugees."

"Florida residents," General Woodbury insisted. "All of them, you'll be able combine your Key West boys with the Useppa Island boys to form a company of genuine Florida Rangers. All from the area and they know their way around."

Admiral Farley added, "We'll provide naval support."

Harry said, "I'll need at least sixty."

"They're there," Admiral Farley said. "We're feeding four hundred."

General Woodbury asked, "Interested?"

"Sure am," Harry replied, "I want to get my wife and child out of Tampa."

Admiral Farley suggested, "Might take awhile but we'll help."

Harry said, "I'll get my boys together."

General Woodbury added, "You're getting a promotion."

"To what," Harry asked.

"Field promotion to captain," General Woodbury replied. "You'll be commanding a company. You gotta sign them up and swear them in. We'll provide the uniforms, arms, and ammunition."

Harry clipped on captain's bars, gathered up his dozen warriors, and they boarded the USS *Gem of the Sea* for a ride to Useppa Island. Most of the barrier islands were mangrove covered sand spits, but Useppa Island was different. Low Indian mounds, made from thousands of years of shells, rose above the thickets.

The *Gem of the Sea* anchored in deep water. Harry and his dozen men rowed ashore. The island was only about a mile long and a half a mile wide but several hundred refugees were on the island. The residents gathered at the rickety dock to welcome Harry and his troops. Dozens gathered around as a tall fellow stepped forward. It was Reuben Rigby. "Being the unelected, unofficial mayor of this forgotten relic of paradise let me tell you that I'm damn glad you're here."

"Hey, Rube," Harry blurted. "What are you doing here?"

"I'll be damned!" Rube walloped Harry's arm. "We got a swamp rat."

There were cheers. Rube noted, "You gotta be just about the oldest captain in the whole Yankee army. How'd you do it, and how come it take you so long to get here?"

Harry said, "Thought you were gonna be a farmer."

"Hell, tried it. Cleared a little land and planted a few crops but didn't get anything for the effort. Pigs and bugs ate what the rain didn't wash away. Then Beauregard sent his boys out and dragged me off to be in the rebel army. Beauregard was on my back all the time and put me to work digging ditches. Don't do negra work, so I skedaddled and came down here."

Harry said, "You're a deserter."

"Nope, no way," Rube insisted. "You can't desert from something if you never joined up. There's a big difference between joining and getting' grabbed."

"How about joining us? I'm putting a ranger company together and need a few good men."

"I'll want my stripes."

"You'll get 'em," Harry promised. "Bring in twenty men and you'll be a sergeant."

"In the morning," Rube replied. "We're celebratin' tonight."

Harry moved into the custom house and put his men to work clearing it out. Rube stopped later that evening to take Harry and his troops to a festive gathering. A bonfire burned on the crest of a mound, and someone shoved a cup into

Harry's hand. Others were playing a fiddle and a banjo, but Harry didn't recognize the tune.

Harry took a slug of liquid and gasped when it hit his throat. It was straight rum. Harry coughed and sputtered. Rube laughed. "We get it from the navy but aint got nothing to cut it. We drink it as it comes."

Harry gasped. "It'll do."

They laughed and partied. Useppa Island wasn't half bad.

Rube showed up the next morning with thirty men. Rube got his sergeant's stripes, and they filled out the company. The navy brought uniforms, muskets, side-arms, and ammunition.

CHAPTER FORTY THREE

The Mission

Hillsborough River
February 1864

Harry drilled his rangers, preparing them for action. Commander Simms came out on the *Gem of the Sea*, met with Harry and Rube, and gave them their assignment. They were going after the *Scottish Princess*.

Harry said, "Thought she was being used for coastal runs."

Commander Simms insisted, "Rebels aren't making coastal runs. They've painted the boat and using it to run the blockade, taking cotton to Havana, and bringing back arms and ammunition. We've got to stop it."

"What's the plan?"

"Get ready," Commander Simms ordered. "We'll find out where they're keeping her and you'll have to go in after dark and burn her."

"We can do that," Harry replied.

The USS *Tahoma* was standing picket duty off Tampa Bay a couple of weeks later when they picked up two runaway slaves coming down the Hillsborough River, riding a raft to freedom. The contraband claimed the *Scottish Princess* was being kept in a cove about twelve miles up the river.

The contraband said, "They're covering her with brush but she's there."

The information launched the raid. The gunboats *USS Tahoma* and *USS Adela* steamed into Tampa Bay one afternoon and blasted Tampa Town. Cannon on the beach returned the fire. The gunboats then steamed a short distance offshore where they continued firing into the city. They

271

continued the barrage until dusk and then fired an occasional shot in the general direction of the town.

The *USS Gem of the Sea* steamed into the bay after nightfall and anchored off the headland of the Hillsborough River where they dispatched several small boats loaded with Marines and Florida Rangers. The marines rowed ashore and waited in the boats while they dispatched the rangers.

Harry and Rube led the way as they were familiar with the terrain. They pushed through dense mangrove thickets, avoided houses and roads as they dashed through pine forests, and dashed across open fields. It took about five hours to cover fourteen miles before they came upon the shadowy hulks of the *Scottish Princess* and *Highland Princess* tied to cypress trees along the river. Both were partially covered with brush. Harry and his men boarded the *Scottish Princess* while Rube rushed the *Highland Princess*.

Harry jumped aboard, ran across the deck, and yanked the wheelhouse door open. He startled Willy Fairchild who was dozing on a bench. Willy opened his eyes, looked up, and recognized Harry. Willy sat up. "Wondered where you been."

Harry asked Willy, "Anybody else here?"

"Me and Charlie, he's in the engine room."

Willy glanced at the men wearing Yankee uniforms. "What's going on?"

Harry asked, "Any more guards?"

"We're it, me and Charlie," Willy mumbled, "nobody else."

"We checked it out," a ranger shouted. "There's just the two. The other one took off."

"That's Charlie?" Willy insisted. "Where is he? What time is it? Nobody answered. Willy asked, "What's going on?"

The ranger doused the wheelhouse with coal oil. "Burning the boat."

Willy reached for his hat. "Well, dammit! Let me off."

"Hold it!" Harry shouted. "You're going with us."

"Sounds pretty good to me," Willy grumbled as he put his hat on his head. "Been playing hide and seek on this tub fer about long enough. Maybe you can get me a better job."

"Maybe," Harry answered as they dashed from the wheelhouse, made their way across the deck, around bales of cotton, and scrambled ashore. The *Highland Princess* was burning. Flames exploded along the deck of the *Scottish Princess*.

The deed was done.

CHAPTER FORTY FOUR

Confederate Commissary Commission

Southwest Florida
February through June 1864

Captain McRae was livid. The Yankee gunboats had wrecked his hotel, demolished his warehouse, and ruined his store. Yankee raiders had burned his boats. Willy was gone. Tampa was a mess and Fort Brooke was a shambles. Colonel Bemrose tried to patch up the fort as best he could but couldn't do much with what he had.

Colonel Westcott came over from Fort Meade to check out the situation. Westcott stood on the parade ground with Colonel Bemrose to survey the damage. Colonel Westcott said, "Not much you can do with this place. Old fortifications don't amount to a hill of beans when it comes to modern artillery. Better pull your boys back from the bay and put up some earthworks."

Colonel Bemrose kicked dirt. "Guess so." Then he looked up to spot an old adversary crossing the parade ground. Captain McRea marched up, ignoring Colonel Bemrose, he spoke to Colonel Westcott. "Good morning, Colonel. I want to do something."

"Done more than enough harm already," Colonel Bemrose sputtered, "your boats brought the Yankees."

"You were supposed to guarding the boats," Colonel McRae snapped. "Where were your men?"

"And you are?" Colonel Westcott asked.

"The sumabitch who brought the Yankees," Colonel Bemrose insisted. "That's why they came."

Colonel Westcott ignored Beauregard. He spoke to Captain McRea. "So you're the fellow who was hauling supplies. Jake Sutherlin told me about you."

"You know Jake."

"Sure do, he's been bringing in cows we're shipping north. He's a good man but we're having trouble keeping up with the demand."

"Told you I want to do something," Captain McRae insisted. "The Yankees came in here for no good reason, blew up my buildings, and burned my boats. This thing is getting damned personal."

"Such are the exigencies of warfare," Colonel Westcott suggested. "Perhaps you can help Colonel Bemrose reposition his guards."

"No way," Colonel Bemrose protested. "I don't want him interfering in my operation."

"And I don't want to be part of anything run by this left over loser from the old wars," Captain McRae stormed. "I want to do something that counts."

Colonel Westcott suggested, "Help with the cows."

"Doing what?"

"Moving them," Colonel Westcott explained. "We've gotta get them to Baldwin. Jake's run a couple of drives but we gotta get more there and get them there more quickly. I need someone to handle logistics, organize the operation."

Captain McRae said, "I can do that."

"So long as you're not doing it around here," Colonel Bemrose blustered. "Don't need you or your trouble."

"You're the cause of the trouble," Captain McRae told Colonel Bemrose. "You've set yourself up here like a baboon lording it over a monkey cage!"

"Sumabitch, I can still hang you," Bemrose growled. "Who knows what to hell you've been up to, you and your shenanigans."

Colonel Westcott told Captain McRae, "I'll take you up on your offer."

"What about me?" Colonel Bemrose blustered. "What am I supposed to do?"

Colonel Westcott said, "I told you. Pull your guards back from the bay and put up some earthworks. The Yankees will be back." Colonel Westcott took a horse from the stable for Captain McRae. They left Fort Brooke leaving Colonel Bemrose standing on the parade ground. Bring unaccustomed to being on a horse, Captain McRae endured a dreadful ride to Fort Meade.

Fort Meade provided a welcome respite from the war as it wasn't subject to the harassment and bombardment being inflicted by the Union Navy along the coast. The Confederate Cow Cavalry controlled the community. Merchants, confederate agents, and cattlemen thronged the streets of the little city. Women shopped in markets, and children played in the lots and alleys.

The Confederate Commissary Depot stood on high ground a mile or so back from the Peace River. The depot housed the Commissary Commission and 1st Battalion Florida Cavalry, the cow cavalry. The Commissary Commission was supplying most of the rations and supplies flowing to the Confederate Army engaged in desperate struggles along the northern and western fronts.

Captain McRae dismounted from the horse and followed Colonel Westcott up the porch and into Westcott's office. Captain McRae asked, "So, what's the picture?"

"We feed the army," Colonel Westcott replied. "We've got a couple of hundred thousand fighting in Virginia and another couple hundred thousand men in Georgia. We're feeding Bragg's army and sending stuff to Virginia. We've got to get a more beef to the railhead and get it there more quickly."

"What's the problem?"

"We're short of manpower and need to better organize what we've got. Getting an occasional herd to Baldwin doesn't do the job. We need to get at least two drives a week."

"You'll need more routes," Captain McRae insisted.

"Why?"

"Gotta have sufficient fodder and water for each herd," Captain McRae explained. "Water won't be much of a problem during the rainy season but it'll be a problem during most of the year. You'll need fodder. That's another problem. We'll need to lay out alternate routes and stagger them."

"Sounds like you're the man. Let's take care of the paperwork"

"What paperwork?"

"Your commission, you'll need rank to do your job."

"What rank?

"Major of volunteers, get a uniform."

Captain McRae became Major McRae, Confederate Commissary Commission volunteer. A couple of weeks later Major McRae took leave to gather up his wife, daughter, and granddaughter in Tampa and bring them to Fort Meade.

Sarah was shocked when she saw her father wearing the gray uniform of the Confederacy. She cried, "What are you doing!"

"Doing something," Major McRea asserted. "I'm not waiting around for the Yankees to come back and blowup everything. Enough is enough!"

Sarah said, "But the Confederates drove Harry away."

"That was Bemrose," Major McRea insisted. "Confederacy didn't have anything to do with it. Bemrose is a leftover from the past. The Confederacy doesn't know what to do with him either. I'm keeping the cow business alive until we get through the war, and then I'm going back to doing what I was doing. In the meantime, I'm getting paid a salary and you're getting a safe place to live."

"About half right," Isobel insisted. "I've never been to Fort Meade. Guess I'll try it. Don't have much left here."

"Fine for you," Sarah sobbed. "Harry won't know where to find me."

"Don't know anything about Harry," Isobel insisted. "We haven't heard from him since he ran out the door. I'm not leaving you here by yourself, so you're coming with us!"

"Come along," Major McRae insisted. "The war won't last forever. We'll be out of harm's way in Fort Meade until it's over. Then we'll look for Harry."

"He'll take care of himself," Isobel insisted. "Let's get out of here before the Yankees come back."

Major McRea gathered up his family and took them to Fort Meade. Isobel, Sarah, and Emma moved into the officer's quarters. Colonel Westcott called his officers together to introduce Major McRae, their new battalion commander.

Captain Jake Sutherlin, one of the company captains, was a little surprised to discover that Captain McRae had come ashore but Jake was flexible.

Colonel Westcott explained, "Major McRea will be organizing and dispatching our drives. We haven't been getting a lot of help so we're gonna have to make do with what we got. We've got a couple of assignments. The commissary commission wants more cows and the Tallahassee boys are telling us to defend our borders. The Yankees blew up Tampa last week, destroyed Fort Brooke, and burned our blockade runners."

Captain Sutherlin asked, "What do you want us to do?"

"Do what we have to do," Colonel Westcott replied. It was quiet. "In the meantime, Major McRae's heading up our logistics. He'll be organizing drives and assigning security details. Two companies will be out pushing cows and our third company will respond to hotspots along the coast. Bemrose is covering Tampa Bay with his Home Guard. We've got Charlotte Harbor."

There was grumbling in the ranks. Security duty didn't appeal to cow catchers. Even so, Captain Sutherlin asked, "When do we start?"

"About now," Major McRea insisted. "Yankees landed a raiding party at the mouth of the Myakka but Jake run 'em off." There were some nods. Major McRea asked Jake, "How'd it go?"

"Lost a man and two were wounded."

"That happens," Major McRea replied. "What else?"

"Somethin' else," Captain Sutherlin added.

"What's that?"

"You're not gonna believe this," Captain Sutherlin replied. "Rube, my old foreman, was leading the Yankees. He was all got up in a Yankee uniform and everything. I knew it was Rube. Had him in my sights but didn't pull the trigger."

It was getting complicated. The Yankees struck a couple of weeks later on the Caloosahatche. They blocked the mouth of the river with the *USS Honduras* before sending a landing party ashore to seize to burn a schooner. The detachment caught up with the invaders as they came down the river and traded shots with them until the gunboat came to the rescue.

The detachment was forced to withdraw. Captain Rutherford rushed back to Fort Meade to report, "I knew at least half those fellows. Aint fair! The Yankees got locals boys doing their damned dirty work."

CHAPTER FORTY FIVE

Republican Convention

Key West to Baltimore
March through June 1864

The Union Navy dropped Willy off on Front Street on Key West. They didn't give him a job and nobody wanted him around. Willy made his way to the Jacaranda Import/Export Company office. Perhaps they'd help him find a job.

Sidney was seated at his desk reading a dispatch from Caleb when Willy walked in. The dispatch was perplexing. It requested Sidney's presence in Washington and Baltimore but that wasn't the problem. The dispatch asked him to bring another Florida resident with him, one who wouldn't ask questions, do as he was told, and keep his mouth shut.

Sidney knew several Florida residents but very few of them fit that description. Then Willy appeared. "I need a job."

Sidney dropped the dispatch. "You have a job. McRae gave you a job. What are you doing here?"

"Not anymore." Willy shuffled inside and sat down. "Yankees came and burned the boat, hauled me here, and dropped me off."

"Damn," Sidney muttered. "What happened to McRea?"

"Don't know," Willy replied. "He wasn't there."

Sidney had an idea. He picked up the dispatch, took another look at it, and asked Willy, "You a Florida resident?"

"Guess so," Willy replied. "Been here long enough but aint got a job."

"I'm giving you a job," Sidney replied. "We're going to Baltimore."

Willy asked, "What for?"

"Don't know."

"What do I have to do?"

"Two things," Sidney insisted. "Keep your mouth shut and don't ask questions.

"That's all," Willy asked.

"That's it."

"Sounds pretty easy," Willy conceded. "Figure I can do that."

They rode to Washington on the dispatch boat. Willy spent most of his time in the engine room with the engineering crew. They talked about steam engines, shafts, and pistons. Otherwise, Willy kept his mouth shut.

Master Evans made the arrangements when they got to Washington. He ushered them through the navy yard and took them to a carriage outside the gate. Willy wanted to look at the iron works but Sidney said, "Come on, let's go."

Willy kept his mouth shut and went along. Caleb was waiting in the carriage. Caleb said, "Glad you made it." He asked Sidney, "Who's this fellow?"

"Other Florida resident," Sidney answered. "I brought him along like your dispatch said."

Caleb looked at Willy. "Guess he'll do. What does he do?"

"Engineer," Willy replied.

"What kind?"

Willy said, "Steamboat."

Caleb told Sidney, "He'll do. We'll dress him up and pass him off as a Florida industrialist. He told Willy, "Just keep your mouth shut and don't say anything."

Willy nodded. Sidney asked, "What's this about?"

Caleb said, "The Republicans are holding a convention in Baltimore to nominate President Lincoln for another term. We've got to have representation from all the states to make it look good, so you're Florida."

Sidney brightened up considerably as this had the makings of a financial windfall. He said, "Sounds good, but we'll need a few dollars to pull this off."

"Couple a thousand," Caleb said, "That's it. Don't ask for more and make it look good."

"Should do it," Sidney suggested. "But there's the matter of appearances."

Caleb asked, "What appearances?"

"Willy," Sidney said. "We've got to make him look good."

Willy kept his mouth shut and looked out the window. Caleb took a good look at Willy before saying, "I believe you've got a point."

They took Willy shopping. Sidney picked out three suits, four shirts, and colorful cravats for Willy. Caleb paid for them and they went shopping for leather boots. Willy went along, did as he was told, tried on the clothing, and left the stores looking like a Florida industrialist might look if there was such a thing. Willy kept his mouth shut.

Caleb put them up at the Willard and took them to Baltimore the next day. Caleb ushered them through the rules committee and they were credentialed as the Florida delegates. Sidney was certified as Sidney Benson, the proprietor of the Jacaranda Import/Export Company, a major commercial enterprise, and Willy was certified as William Fairchild, owner and proprietor of Fairchild Engineering, a state of the art company specializing in steam locomotion. The Florida delegation was seated next to the Delaware delegation.

The convention continued for two days. Willy wore his suits, listened to the speeches, and kept his mouth shut. Lincoln was nominated at the end of the second day in a frenzy of excitement and confusion. Delegates shouted, embraced, threw their hats, jumped on the benches, danced in the aisles, waved flags, and yelled. Willy kept his mouth shut. He preferred steam engines.

Then they went back to Washington for a meeting in Secretary Seward's office. Secretary Seward and Thurlow Weed were waiting when they arrived. Seward said, "That went well, but we've got a problem with the election."

Sidney asked, "What's that?

282

Secretary Seward explained, "There should be thirty-five states, counting West Virginia, participating in the election. Eleven states have opted out as they are in rebellion.

Sidney said, "None of them would have voted for Lincoln. This oughta help."

Secretary Seward said, "That's not our problem. The Democrats are running McClellan. He's popular and will probably carry eight or nine states. That'll leave us with about fourteen or fifteen states but we gotta have at least eighteen to win."

Sidney asked, "How come?"

Secretary Seward explained, "The Constitution requires a majority, one more than half of the thirty-five states, to win.

"I see."

Thurlow Weed added, "There's the Electoral College. If McClellan picks up New York and the other six large states, he could end up with more electoral votes than Lincoln but still not have enough states to satisfy the majority requirement."

"So just leave out states in rebellion and count the states that are left," Sidney suggested. "The rebel states have already left."

"Not officially," Secretary Seward warned. "We've never acknowledged their right to secede or withdraw from the perpetual union. Doing so would mean that we've accepted their status as a separate nation. We've never done it and we're not going to do it. We brought you here to represent Florida at the convention. Other men from the South represented other southern states."

Sidney asked, "What for?"

"Protocol and necessity," Secretary Seward argued. "Our rationale for this war is that we're putting down an illegal rebellion orchestrated and carried out by a few illicit individuals. The Union is a perpetual union and must remain so. We're enforcing the status quo."

"I guess," Sidney replied.

"But there's still the matter of meeting the constitutional quorum for the election," Secretary Seward continued. "We need a couple of more states to ensure the outcome of this election."

Sidney asked, "What's that got to do with us?"

"Why you're here," Thurlow Weed replied. "We want you to call a convention on Key West, repeal Florida's ordinance of succession, and request admission to the Union as South Florida, the thirty-sixth state."

"It's the West Virginia solution," Secretary Seward explained. "We did it with Virginia and can work for Florida."

"How are we going to split the state?"

"Already done it," Secretary Seward argued. "We've held Key West and the Keys throughout the war and got an army in Jacksonville. General Woodbury has a Florida ranger company operating on the coast of Southwest Florida and we're establishing a permanent base at Fort Myers."

"Pretty simple," Thurlow Weed insisted. "Once Woodbury's secured Fort Myers, we'll take out the Confederate base at Fort Meade. Then we'll link up our Jacksonville and Fort Myers troops somewhere in central Florida, establish a boundary along the Peace and St Johns rivers and we've got South Florida."

Secretary Seward said, "Go back to Key West, call a convention, twenty or thirty residents, repeal the secession ordinance, and request admission. That's how it's done."

"That's it?" Sidney asked.

Thurlow said, "We're working on another option along with this one. We got a few boys in the Nevada desert writing a state constitution. If they get it done in time, we'll be able to admit Nevada and South Florida before the election."

Sidney listened and thought about the matter for a moment before suggesting. "It'll cost some money."

"Don't worry about it," Caleb insisted. "Just do it."

Willy didn't say anything.

Sidney and Willy rode the next dispatch boat back to Key West. They arrived in the harbor a couple of weeks later and walked up Front Street to the office. Diego was in Sidney's chair. He asked, "Where've you been?"

"Washington and Baltimore," Sidney replied. Willy didn't say anything.

Diego asked Willy, "How was the trip?"

"Don't really know," Willy replied. "Some fellow fed us and got me a bunch of fancy duds. Don't know if I'll wear them again, but Sidney gave me twenty-five dollars for my time and trouble. That was pretty good, but I still gotta find a job."

CHAPTER FORTY SIX

Second Florida Cavalry

Southwest Florida
July through September 1864

The Useppa Island Rangers capitalized on their success by conducting more raids, seizing three coastal schooners, and burning a barge loaded with cotton. More refugees made their way to the island and some joined the rangers. All was going well when Commander Simms stopped over to pay a visit. Commander Simms sat down with Harry and reviewed the operation before announcing, "We're going ashore."

Harry asked, "Where?"

"Fort Myers, the fort's been abandoned since the Bowlegs War. A fellow tried running a pineapple plantation there for a year or so but high-tailed it as soon as the war started. The fort oughta be in pretty good shape."

"What do we do with it?"

"Hold it," Commander Simms insisted. "I'll send up a couple of Pennsylvania companies to reinforce you after you move in. You've got to take the fort to show that Florida boys are reclaiming Florida soil. Let me assure you, this is a matter of strategic significance!"

The rangers boarded the *Gem of the Sea* for the short ride over to the mouth of the Caloosahatchee. Then Harry transferred his rangers to small boats and they rowed up the river. The rangers stormed ashore in the middle of the night. There wasn't anyone at the old fort except three Confederate deserters in the hospital building. One gave up and joined the Union.

The *Stars and Stripes* were flying over the fort when General Woodbury arrived with two companies of Pennsylvania volunteers. The soldiers cleaned out the

286

barracks, posted guards, and got down to business. Harry had over three hundred men under his command but securing the region on foot would be a problem. They needed horses. General Woodbury sent three boatloads of horses.

The rangers took to the horses with enthusiasm as the men had been farmers and frontiersmen. They had grown up with horses, knew how to mange them, and were skilled riders. The Useppa Rangers became the Second Florida Cavalry (Union).

Harry told Rube to secure the area. The cavalrymen rode up the Caloosahatchee River as far as Fort Thompson, an old stockade left from the Indian war, where they exchanged a few shots with a handful of Confederate pickets. Rube's boys drove off the pickets and chased them up the river toward Fort Denaud.

They engaged a small Confederate force along the way. A private was wounded before the Confederates backed off. Then Rube led his men up the road to Fort Denaud, rode into the stockade, and claimed it for the Union. The Second Florida Cavalry (Union) held all three Caloosahatchee posts.

General Woodbury followed through by sending the Second USCT to Fort Myers. This was a colored regiment from Maryland and Virginia. Captain Seacroft, a white officer from Massachusetts, and his two white lieutenants arrived at the landing with over two hundred black men wearing blue uniforms.

Harry's men, for the most part, didn't think much of slavery but they weren't that enthralled with the idea of living and working with colored men. This was an awkward matter at best, so Harry worked out some arrangements with Captain Seacroft before the colored troops came ashore.

They decided that the white cavalrymen would conduct the fort's raids and offensive operations. Black infantrymen would be restricted to support and garrison duty. Living arrangements were more complicated. Black troops were relegated to the hospital building on the far side of the parade ground. Separate mess facilities were provided.

Once this was worked out, Captain Seacroft unloaded his men. A tall black sergeant led the first squad ashore. Something about his manner reminded Harry of Floyd. It was Floyd. Harry forgot about his concern over appropriate race relations by dashing out, shouting, "Hey, Floyd! What are you doing here?"

"Coming ashore," Floyd replied with a twinkle in his eye. He snapped off a salute, saying, "Doing what I gotta do."

"How'd you get in the army?"

"Navy wouldn't let me fight so I tried the army."

Harry returned Floyd's salute. Harry, feeling somewhat awkward by his own behavior, managed a quiet but subdued reply, "Glad you're here."

Floyd tossed off a quick answer, "Guess I'm glad." Then Floyd led his squad up the bank and into the fort.

Activities accelerated with the arrival of the reinforcements. Rube embarked on another expedition, engaged a Confederate force somewhat larger than his own and came home with fourteen horses and thirty-four volunteers. Commander Simms came with another set of orders.

Commander Simms said, "Hold and secure the territory between here and the Peace River. While you're at it, take out the Fort Meade Confederate positions."

"Do I have enough men?"

"More than enough, the Confederacy has pulled their regulars from the region and sent them north to block our Jacksonville advance. There's just a skeleton force of cow cavalry at Meade and a few old men and veterans in the Tampa Home Guard. We'll run a diversion into Tampa Bay, take out the town, and neutralize the Home Guard. Once we do that, make your move on Meade."

Jumping at the opportunity to get to Tampa to rescue his wife and daughter, Harry said, "I'd like to go on the Tampa operation."

"We can use the help."

Harry left Captain Seacroft at Fort Myers as he boarded the *Gem of the Sea* with a company of rangers. They rendezvoused with the *Honduras* off Longboat Key that afternoon and steamed into Tampa Bay the next morning.

The *Honduras* landed sixty marines at Gadsden Point as the *Gem of the* Sea sent Harry and his rangers ashore on the point north of the Alafia River. The troops double-timed toward Tampa with fixed bayonets. They gathered up a few fleeing slaves and converged on the partially rebuilt hotel. Harry dashed across the porch followed by Rube. They pushed their way through a flimsy barricade and into the taproom.

Mayor Dunigan and Brinton Hooker were cowering in the wreckage of the taproom. Harry shouted, "Where's Isobel?"

"At Meade," Brinton blubbered. "McRae took her."

"And Sarah," Harry added.

"Took her too," Mayor Dunigan stammered. "Why are you here?"

"Came to get my wife and kid," Harry growled.

"They aint here," Mayor Dunigan insisted. "Why are you wearing that freak outfit? Beauregard was right! You're a Yankee. You got no business barging in like this."

"There's a war on," Rube shouted. "Where's Bemrose?"

"Fort Meade," Brinton gasped. "All of them, they're all at Fort Meade. They left us. We aint got nothing. Let us be."

A few of the more resolute rebels tried to man an old cannon perched on an embankment. A brief skirmish with the marines left one dead and several wounded. Then the gunboats opened fire on what was left of Fort Brooke. The few remaining male inhabitants of the town were gathered up, marched to the hotel, and held in custody.

A quick search disclosed almost six thousand dollars, a few unclaimed letters in the post office, several rounds of ammunition, and a couple of muskets. The troops gathered up all the slaves they could find and transported them to the *Gem of the Sea*. Quiet prevailed by evening with the *Stars and Stripes* flying over Tampa. Guards were posted and rangers who had friends and acquaintances in town took the time to look them up. It was a visitation of sorts.

Harry, being distressed that his wife and child were not there, was ready to leave. Having decided that Tampa had no strategic military value, the troops boarded their naval vessels the next day, abandoned Tampa, and went back to Fort Myers.

A week later three white officers, a hundred white cavalrymen from the Second Florida cavalry, and a hundred black infantry men from the Second USCT set out for Fort Meade to relieve the "distressed Union families" residing on the headwaters of the Peace River. The Union troops marched up the south bank of the Caloosahatche, crossed at the ford at Fort Thompson, and set off up the Fort Meade-Fort Thompson Road toward Fort Meade.

They ran into their first picket about six miles from the fort. The picket called out, "Who are you fellows."

Rube shouted, "Second Florida Cavalry!"

"You gotta be Yankees?" the picket yelled as he lifted his shotgun and sighted down the barrel. "I aint never seen a genywine Yankee before. Come on up here where I can get a good look at you."

"Seeing a bunch now," Rube shouted as twelve cavalrymen rode up and surrounded the picket."

"You aint no Yankee," the picket grumbled as he looked at Rube and lowered his shotgun. "You were Jake's foreman."

"So I was," Rube admitted. "You got yourself on the wrong end of this war my friend."

"Don't know about that but I spects I can't do much about it now," the picket admitted as he handed over his shotgun.

Rube took the shotgun as he asked, "How many men up ahead."

"More than you're gonna want," the picket warned. "Jake's got his cow catchers and Beauregard brought his Tampa boys down."

"Any regulars," Rube asked.

"Now that's just something fer me to know and you to find out," the picket replied.

"We'll be doing that," Rube assured the prisoner.

Captain Harry rode up with twenty-five men. They took the picket into custody and continued on their way. Lieutenant Rube and his raiders encountered fifteen or twenty irregulars a couple of miles up ahead. Shots were exchanged, and the irregulars scattered.

Rube and his boys watched them ride off before continuing toward the Fort Meade Commissary Depot on the far side of the Peace River. Someone fired a shot from the hotel as Rube's boys splashed across the river and rode into town. Rube's boys took cover and returned fire. Shots were exchanged before one of the boys set the building on fire. More shots were exchanged before a distraught man waved a white flag out the front door.

Rube yelled, "Hold it right there. Now, come out with your hands over your head."

Three old men and an old woman hobbled out. One of the old fellows tossed his musket aside, grumbling, "You boys got no business burning the building. I'd have fought you off but it's too smoky. Besides, you got too many."

Rube asked, "Any more in there."

"We're it," the woman answered.

Rube picked up the musket and examined it. Rube asked, "Where'd you get this?"

"Mine! Give it back," the old man demanded.

Rube said, "I think we'll keep it to keep you out of trouble. Where are the boys who are supposed to be doing the job?"

The woman muttered, "Told you. We're it! They skedaddled."

"Where's your army," Rube asked.

"Aint got none," the woman answered. "Bemrose and his boys were here but they hustled back to Tampa. McRae's catching cows."

Rube accepted the explanation. They had a clean shot at the depot. The boys gathered up the prisoners and continued on their way as flames broke through the roof of the hotel. The fire spread as Captain Harry led his troops to the depot.

They rode across an empty parade ground before they noticed a lady standing on the front porch of a cottage. It was Isobel, and she wasn't in a good mood. She grumbled, "About time you showed up, Harry Lane, but you didn't need to bring that rabble with you."

Harry dismounted. "I tried to find you in Tampa, but they told me you left."

Isobel said, "Hear you pretty much destroyed everything."

"Had our objectives," Harry replied.

Isobel looked at the smoke billowing over Fort Meade. "Burning, shooting, and looting, I guess," Isobel insisted. "Look's like you're getting pretty good at it."

"Trying to end the war," Harry pleaded. "We didn't start it!"

"Somebody did," Isobel replied. "Sure as hell wasn't me!"

Harry said, "I came for Sarah and Emma."

"They're inside. I can't have any of your ruffians scaring my granddaughter. Take them with you but I'm not going. I'm staying here."

"That's your choice." Harry strolled by Isobel. He crossed the porch and entered the cottage.

Sarah and Emma were waiting.

CHAPTER FORTY SEVEN

Diplomacy and Deception

Washington City
October through November, 1864

The Democrats nominated General George B. McClelland. His platform pledged loyalty and fidelity to the Constitution and Union while deploring the destruction and denial of constitutional rights occurring during the war. The Democrats left Chicago sniffing the scent of victory.

But the war changed. General Sherman broke out of the mountains of Tennessee and started toward Atlanta. General Sheridan defeated the Confederates at Winchester and chased them out of the Shenandoah Valley. General Grant encircled General Lee's army at Petersburg. Battles were to be fought but the tide of war had turned to favor the Union.

Even so, the political wars intensified as the election approached. The Democrats shouted fraud and accused the Republicans of deception. The Republicans retaliated by seizing thousands of dry-goods boxes filled with fraudulent ballots prepared for McClellan. Vermont and Maine voted in September. Lincoln carried both states. Lincoln carried Ohio and Indiana when they voted in October. Pennsylvania voted a week later, but the outcome remained undecided. That wasn't good news.

President Lincoln, Secretary Seward, and Caleb Conklin gathered in the War Department telegraph office late one afternoon waiting for news regarding the Pennsylvania election. President Lincoln picked up a message blank. Then he pulled out the stub of the wooden pencil that he carried in his pocket and scratched out a couple of columns on the paper.

The president listed the states he might lose in the first column. These were Pennsylvania and probably New York, New Jersey, Delaware, Maryland, Missouri, Kentucky, and Illinois. They added up to 114 votes. He expected to carry all of New England, Michigan, Wisconsin, Minnesota, Iowa, Oregon, California, Kansas, Indiana, and West Virginia. That gave him 114 votes.

President Lincoln wadded up the blank and tossed it at the waste bucket. "She's gonna be a little like the old schoolmarm on her wedding night."

"How's that," Secretary Seward asked.

"A little tight," President Lincoln chuckled. "Damn tight!"

Secretary Seward ignored the comment as he insisted, "But we haven't played our ace.

"Clubs or spades," President Lincoln asked.

Secretary Seward asked, "What's the difference?"

"Ace of clubs takes a trick," President Lincoln replied. "Ace of spades trumps the other cards. It takes the game.

"Spades," Caleb asserted. "You can admit Nevada with a stroke of your pen. It'll give us three more electoral votes, break the tie, and wrap up the game."

"Only if I get their constitution," President Lincoln reminded Caleb. "I can't do much without a constitution."

"Working on it," Caleb claimed.

"Expect you are," President Lincoln replied. He asked, "By the way, are there any people living out there in that desert?"

"Maybe forty thousand or so," Secretary Seward assured the president.

"Sure about that?" President Lincoln demanded.

"Never been there," Secretary Seward replied. "I'm going on what I was told. He added, "Why are you asking?"

President Lincoln asked, "Just wondering if anybody out there knows how to write a constitution."

"Governor Nye's taking care of it," Secretary Seward assured the president. "He's a good Republican."

"I expect," President Lincoln replied. "You recommended him for the job."

"So I did," Secretary Seward admitted.

"You'll get the votes," Caleb assured the president.

"Maybe so," President Lincoln noted. Then the president asked Caleb, "What happened to the Florida scheme? I haven't heard much about that."

"Not much," Caleb admitted, "Nevada will do it."

"Check it out," President Lincoln advised Caleb. "We're going to need the votes."

"I'll get on it," Caleb mumbled as he left the War Department telegraph office and scurried back to the state department to get access to his own telegraph line. Caleb sat down and clicked a message to his Carson City asset. The response came back about an hour later. Bridget promised to get a draft copy of the new state constitution from Governor Nye and telegraph it to the War Department, word by word, and passage by passage.

Bridget was the right asset, in the right place, at the right time. She suggested her friend Jim Nye, the Police Chief of New York City, might be a good candidate for the territorial governor's job in Nevada. Jim dealt with the secessionist element upon his arrival and championed the drive for statehood. Of course Bridget had a lot to do with it. She had gone along with Governor Nye, set up the Carson City Club on her arrival, and was pushing railroad interests.

The Nevada State Constitution contained over sixteen thousand words. Bridget's telegram was the longest ever sent. The telegram was relayed through Chicago and Philadelphia and sent on to the War Department telegraph office at a cost of $4,303.27. The machine clattered for hours as the operators scribbled down the text of the constitution. Then Caleb rushed the text to President Lincoln and President Lincoln signed a formal proclamation on the last day of October admitting Nevada as the 36th state. Nevada provided three electoral votes for President Lincoln.

The election was no longer a matter of concern as President Lincoln ended up carrying all of the states except Kentucky, Delaware, and New Jersey. His 212 electoral votes more than offset McClellan's paltry return and more then met the constitutional requirement needed for the election. Thousands of soldiers and citizens swarmed through the streets of Washington City on November 10th and converged on the Executive Mansion. President Lincoln greeted them from a window over the portico and read a short statement.

With the election behind him, President Lincoln asked Secretary of War Stanton and Secretary of State Seward to come over to his office at the Executive Mansion to work out plans for the coming term. The war was ending and the Union would prevail.

President Lincoln, Secretary of State Seward, Secretary of State Stanton, General Halleck, and Caleb met in the president's study. President Lincoln started the meeting by saying, "It appears we've got our jobs for four more years so let's make the most of it."

"Tossing around a few ideas," Secretary Stanton assured President Lincoln. "We're coming out of the war with the biggest army and most powerful navy in the world. If we play our cards right, we'll be able to use this power to establish our rightful sovereignty over our geographical area of influence."

"Which is?" President Lincoln asked.

"Western hemisphere," Secretary Seward insisted. "I've been negotiating with Russia and Denmark. We can pick up Russia's Alaska Territory for a reasonable sum and Denmark will sell us Greenland and the Virgin Islands. The purchase of Alaska and Greenland will strengthen our northern position and limit England's access. The Virgin Islands will provide us with a strategic operating base in the Caribbean."

"There are a few other matters that need to be resolved," Secretary Stanton insisted. "Spain has moved on Hispaniola and France has set up a puppet regime in Mexico."

President Lincoln asked, "What are we doing about Mexico?"

"Supporting Juarez," Secretary Seward replied. "Juarez has launched a resistance movement. We're loaning him money at six percent to fund the operation but he needs more support."

"What kind?' President Lincoln asked.

"Manpower," General Halleck insisted. "He needs troops."

"How are we managing that?"

"Carefully, we're moving a couple of regiments to the Mexican border and augmenting them with Confederate volunteers."

"How are you doing this?"

"I've put General Schofield on a leave of absence from the army to go to Texas and raise a Legion of Honor, a quasi-independent military force."

"Interesting name," President Lincoln suggested. "What's a Legion of Honor?"

General Halleck insisted, "We needed a separate military entity. The Legion of Honor will ostensibly be a bunch of Union and Confederate veterans hired by Juarez. He's not making an issue about funding. Besides, a lot of rebel prisoners will sign up for a Mexico junket if they don't have to join the Union army or wear a Union uniform."

"Expect so," President Lincoln replied. "What are they wearing?"

"Variant of our West Point uniform," General Halleck explained. "We're using the gray blouse with white trousers. It's a throwback to Scott's Brigade. We'll be shifting three infantry divisions, an armed cavalry division, and nine artillery batteries to Schofield's command. He'll be augmenting the force with three infantry divisions drawn from former Confederate ranks.

The president nodded. "And how are we paying for this?"

"Simple, really," Caleb insisted. "O'Donnell's working out funding arrangements. We're shifting funds to a New York account through our Key West contacts, and O'Donnell will be making draws on that account."

"Roundabout," the president noted.

"Not really," Caleb insisted. "O'Donnell's lending the money to Juarez at six percent. When Juarez defaults, the Legion of Honor will hold Mexican territory as collateral."

"But you'll need more than you're sending," President Lincoln insisted. "We'll need a credible backup."

General Halleck said, "Got it. I'm sending Sheridan to New Orleans with forty thousand and we're moving General Steele's division to the Rio Grande. General Woodbury's taking his boys up to secure Tallahassee. Once he does that, I'll hold his division in reserve to cover out Mexican operation. We'll have over a hundred thousand in the area and be ready to move if Schofield needs backup."

"Sounds like you got it thought out pretty good but we've gotta keep it quiet," President Lincoln insisted. "No sense getting congress aggravated until it's over. Besides, we don't want any trouble from the Spanish, French, and English while we're working this out."

"We're keeping on top of that," Secretary Seward assured the president, "Caleb's got everything covered.

"Do what you got to do but keep it quiet," President Lincoln insisted. "Anything else we need to talk about?"

"Not really," Secretary Stanton insisted.

"Well," the president replied, "Let me think on it for awhile. I don't want to rush off half-cocked like a rooster chasing a duck."

Secretary Seward threw up his hands but didn't say anything. Secretary Stanton rubbed his head. The meeting broke up and Caleb walked along with Secretary Seward on their way back to the State Department. Secretary Seward asked, "How is Woodbury doing in South Florida?"

Caleb asked "Why?"

"Stanton's counting on him for reinforcements? How's he doing with the Tallahassee caper?"

"Hasn't launched it yet," Caleb replied. "Securing the area south of the Peace River Boundary, I believe."

"Well, he'd better pull that off before we start chasing the duck that the president was talking about."

"Probably," Caleb replied with a smile.

CHAPTER FORTY EIGHT

Siege of Fort Myers

The home grown Union Army romping across South Florida was becoming a problem for the Confederacy. The Union troops had been launching periodic raids along the coast for some time. Now, they had permanent bases along the Caloosahatchee, burned Fort Meade, and for the most part, controlled the territory south of the Peace River. This was bad enough, but Rube and his cow catchers were catching cows and shipping them to Key West. Four thousand cows were shipped to the Union in a four month period.

The Union was paying thirty dollars a cow, Union money, and the Confederacy was paying three dollars a cow, Confederate money. This was a powerful inducement for south Florida residents to shift over to a Union point of view. As the situation was becoming intolerable, Jake talked with Major McRae about the problem, and McRae told Colonel Westcott. Colonel Westcott talked with the boys in Tallahassee, and they told him to take care of the problem. Colonel Westcott came back to Fort Meade, met with Major McRea, and told him, "Take care of it."

"How am I going to do that?"

Colonel Westcott said, "Give up cow catching for awhile, take your boys down to Fort Myers, and drive them out. That'll take care of the problem."

"I've only got about two hundred boys and the Union's got twice as many at Fort Myers."

"About half are negras," Colonel Westcott insisted. "Negras can't fight. You ought to be able to take care of a few colored boys."

300

"It'll take a bunch of men to keep 'em under guard," Major McRea grumbled. "I'll need more men."

Colonel Westcott said, "Beauregard's in Tampa. Get him and his boys to help out. They'll take care of the negras."

"That all you got," Major McRae grumbled.

"That's it. Take it or leave it."

"How many men does Beauregard have?"

Colonel Westcott said, "Maybe seventy or eighty. Some are wounded veterans, but they'll know how to fight."

"Gives me about three hundred, I'll take the men but do I have to take Bemrose?"

Colonel Westcott said, "He'll want to go. What's wrong with Beauregard?"

"Where do you want me to start," Major McRea replied. "He's a fool to start with. We don't get along and he outranks me."

"His rank is a historical anomaly," Colonel Westcott argued. "It doesn't mean anything."

"Does to Bemrose," Major McRea insisted. "I know him. He'll use it!"

"Run separate commands under my authority," Colonel Westcott suggested. "That'll work."

The meeting ended and Major McRea walked back to his cottage. He told Isobel, "We're taking Fort Myers."

She sputtered, "You're doing what!"

"Taking out Fort Myers," he insisted.

"No way," Isobel scolded. "Our daughter and granddaughter are there. You'd better watch what you're doing!"

This complicated things. Then Colonel Bemrose showed up at Fort Meade with his Home Guard. They were a bedraggled mob of old veterans, wounded survivors of northern campaigns, and swamp rats who had managed to avoid conscription.

Bemrose insisted on exercising the prerogatives of rank. He started out by asking Colonel Westcott, "What's your date of rank?"

301

"April 12, 1862," Colonel Westcott replied.

"Mine dates from February 12, 1835," Bemrose boasted. "That makes me the ranking officer."

"I have a regular Confederate army commission signed by Jeff Davis," Colonel Westcott argued. "Commissioned army officers outrank militia commissions of an equal or lesser rank. It's official."

"Never heard of such a thing," Colonel Bemrose blustered. "But I'll go along with it for the time being."

"Thank you, it'll work better."

But things didn't work that well. First of all, the Fort Myers campaign delayed the cattle flow. The men were short of arms and ammunition and had to transport everyone and everything down the old Fort Meade-Fort Thompson Road to Fort Myers. Bemrose couldn't walk that far and wasn't able to ride a horse but insisted on a conveyance suitable for his rank.

Colonel Westcott got an old ammunition wagon, fixed it up a little, and hitched it to a couple of mules. Bemrose figured it would do. Colonel Westcott, Major McRae, and McRae's cow cavalry rode down the road. Beauregard's boys walked.

It took a week to reach the Union outpost at Fort Thompson. Colonel Westcott and Major McRae led about thirty cow cavalry men into the post one morning as the sun was coming up. The pickets were captured by the time they figured out what was going on. Then the Confederate boys rousted out the duty sergeant and seventeen men holding the fort. The outpost was taken without casualties.

One of the private soldiers stationed at Fort Thompson happened to be collecting wood when the Confederate forces took the fort. The soldier dropped what he was doing and dashed down the Caloosahatche to warn Fort Myers. This gave the Union garrison warning of the pending attack. Then the Confederate attack on Fort Myers had to be delayed while Colonel Westcott and his cow cavalry waited for Beauregard and his Home Guard.

Beauregard and his troops straggled in over the course of two days. Then Colonel Westcott and his troops spent another day working out the plans for the siege. Once the plans were formulated, Colonel Westcott and Major McRae led the way down the trail. They came upon three Union soldiers about eight miles from the fort and captured them without incident. Then Colonel Westcott and Major McRae waited for Beauregard. Beauregard and the Home Guard arrived over the course of the next few hours. As it was getting late, Colonel Westcott decided to hold off on the attack until the next day.

Colonel Westcott held a quick meeting with Major McRae and Colonel Bemrose to explain the strategy of the attack. Colonel Westcott insisted, "We don't have enough men or ammunition for a lengthy assault so we're going to have to go in there in a big way. We've got to convince them that they're surrounded by a superior force."

Beauregard asked, "How we going to do that?"

Colonel Westcott told Beauregard, "Move your men in from the east. Work your way through the stables and outbuildings along the river. We'll fan the cow cavalry out in front of the fort and along the other side. Look alive when you get there but hold your fire until I give the word. Anybody got any questions?"

Beauregard asked, "How you giving the word?"

Colonel Westcott said, "I'll tell you when we get there."

Beauregard shrugged his shoulders. Major McRae remembered his wife's admonition so he suggested, "Let's try bluffing. They don't know how many men we got. We just got to show enough to make them think we got a lot."

Colonel Westcott said, "Might work."

Major McRae continued, "Once we get everyone in place, we can send somebody up to the fort under a flag of truce and demand their surrender. If they surrender, that's good. If not, we'll try it your way."

Colonel Westcott said, "Good idea. Let's do it."

Beauregard asked, "Who's doing the talking?"

Major McRae said, "I know some of those boys. I'll do it."

"To hell too," Beauregard grumbled. "You were in business with a bunch of them. How can I trust you?"

"We'll both go," Major McRae suggested.

"I've got to be there," Colonel Westcott insisted. "I give the word when this thing goes down."

"All right, we'll all go," Major McRea concluded.

The Confederate forces encircled the fort. As the Union boys knew they were coming, the fort was buttoned up. Beauregard sent his Home Guard into the outbuildings, around the pigsties, and behind the stables. Major McRae fanned his men out around the fort. They looked impressive. Colonel Westcott tied a white banner around a stick and the three officers walked to the fort.

A black sergeant shouted, "What do you want."

"Talk with someone in charge," Colonel Westcott shouted back.

"I'll get someone," the sergeant replied.

A few minutes later the gate opened and Captain Harry walked out followed by Captain Seacroft. Harry nodded at his father-in-law. Then he asked Colonel Westcott, "What do you want?"

Colonel Westcott said, "I've got your fort surrounded. I'm willing to spare you needless bloodshed by providing you with an opportunity to give up the fort."

Harry gazed at his father-in-law and then Beauregard. He told Major McRae, "I see you've taken up with an interesting traveling companion."

Major McRea said, "Not by choice."

Beauregard snapped, "You heard the offer. What are you going to do?"

Harry told Beauregard, "We're not surrendering the post. I suggest you make the most of this opportunity to get your people back to your own side of the Peace River Boundary."

"Sumabitch," Beauregard blurted. "You're mouthy."

"I'm consistent," Harry insisted. Then he told Colonel Westcott, "I'm giving you gentlemen a chance to pack up and get out of here. I suggest you make the most of your opportunity."

Captain Seacroft said, "You gotta get moving!"

Major McRae didn't say anything. He signed on to catch cows. This army thing was getting to be a bit serious. Colonel Westcott said, "As you've given us little choice, we'll proceed with the attack."

Colonel Westcott snapped off a quick salute, turned on his heel, and walked back to his waiting troops. Beauregard and Major McRae tagged behind.

When they got back behind their lines, Beauregard said, "That didn't go so good. What do we do now?"

Colonel Westcott said, "Prepare your positions. We'll go in at daybreak."

The Confederate troops settled into position around the fort and waited for daybreak. It started raining. Then black Union troops dashed out of the fort in the middle of the night armed with knives and bayonets. They rushed between the outbuildings and around the stables and fell upon the Tampa Bay Home Guards. The confrontation was quick and effective.

There were a few standoffs but most of Beauregard's boys split, leaving the area, and fanning out in all directions. Beauregard, being caught off guard by the unexpected attack, plunged into the mud and muck of the nearest pigsty and waited. Sergeant Floyd arrived on the scene as the sun was coming up. He found a group of his boys grouped around a pigsty and asked them, "What's going on?"

A corporal said, "There's an old rebel officer hiding out in there."

"Is he a big guy with a limp?"

"Sure enough, that's him."

Floyd walked to the pigsty and called out, "Hey, Beauregard! Is that you?"

The voice came back, "Sumabitch! Is that you, Floyd?"

"Sure enough Mr. Beauregard. It's me. Come on out."

Beauregard crawled out of the pigsty, stood up, wiped himself off as best he could, and limped out. Floyd took a whiff before suggesting, "I'd surely appreciate it if you walked on the downwind side. I'll take you back to the fort."

Major McRae pulled his men back as Beauregard's boys scattered. Colonel Westcott decided that enough was enough. He took his cavalry home. The Union Cavalry pursued them for awhile but gave up the chase. Once the cow cavalry was back in Fort Meade, they went back to doing what they were supposed to be doing.

The Union control of Fort Myers and South Florida being secure, Commander Simms proceeded with his plan. He told Harry, "I'm pulling you out of Myers."

Harry asked, "What for?"

"Going after Tallahassee," Commander Simms explained.

"How do we do that?"

"The *Gem of the Sea* will pick you up and run you to Cedar Key. You'll pick up a couple of companies up there, Florida troops, and then go up the St. Marks River to Port Leon to secure our left flank for the attack. Everything's been worked out. Got any questions?"

Harry asked, "How about running my wife and daughter to Key West?"

"No problem," Commander Simms replied. "I'll take them with me."

Over sixteen ships and a thousand troops gathered on Cedar Key for the attack on Tallahassee. A dense fog covered the rendezvous for four days and when the fog lifted, they were on they're way. But then the troubles occurred. The ships went aground in the St. Marks River and the troops were marooned on the stranded ships. The men who were ashore tried to launch an invasion across a natural bridge but were picked off by Confederate sharpshooters. The navy finally floated the ships free and they made their way back to Cedar Key.

General Lee surrendered a few days later, but the war sputtered on. Then events fell one upon another. President Lincoln was assassinated. Benjamin Judah, the acting Confederate Secretary of War and Secretary of State, fled to

Cuba through Tampa and on to England. Then the *USS Matchless*, a Union gunboat, brought Harry and his Second Florida Cavalry back to Tampa Town to occupy the city.

Tampa was in bad shape. Houses were destroyed, the old fort was a shambles, and weeds grew in the streets. Most of the people were gone. A few who came out to greet relatives and former friends as the Second Florida Cavalry (Union) took possession of the city.

Harry rode up the ridge, turned, and sat on his horse. Rube rode up beside him and stopped. "War's over."

"Guess it is," Harry replied.

"What do we do now?"

"Pick up the pieces," Harry suggested, "and get on with our lives."